The Corporation of the Future

Although largely unseen, the industrial revolution taking place before us is picking up steam – dramatically. Dissolution of traditional global trading partnerships, the affect of COVID-19 on supply chains and the formation of new trading blocks, such as China's Belt and Road Initiative, are creating turmoil and rapid change in the international business domain. Continual advances in technology, health treatments, political and societal change are underpinning these transformations. It is unclear just how this revolution will unfold or what the role of the corporation will be in the long run. This book helps us navigate through these challenging times by identifying areas where opportunities will develop.

Written by highly qualified experts from a diverse range of backgrounds, the book takes a novel backcast view to present more critical arguments. The book has been set in the not-so-distant future, reflecting on the changes that have led to a new type of corporation and the conditions that have led to it. Each chapter presents a complimentary view about the nature of and context for the 2040 Future Corporation.

The backcasting perspective will provide a very effective discipline for readers to analyse contemporary trends while presenting an integrated and balanced future perspective.

Stuart Orr is the Head of School, School of Business, at the Melbourne Institute of Technology in Australia.

Paul Hunter is the founder of the Strategic Management Institute and the management consulting firm Paul Hunter Strategy and Leadership.

The Corporation of the Future

Edited by Stuart Orr and Paul Hunter

Routledge
Taylor & Francis Group
LONDON AND NEW YORK

First published 2023
by Routledge
4 Park Square, Milton Park, Abingdon, Oxon OX14 4RN

and by Routledge
605 Third Avenue, New York, NY 10158

Routledge is an imprint of the Taylor & Francis Group, an informa business

British Library Cataloguing-in-Publication Data
A catalogue record for this book is available from the British Library

Library of Congress Cataloging-in-Publication Data
Names: Orr, Stuart, editor.
Title: The corporation of the future/edited by Stuart Orr and Paul Hunter.
Description: Abingdon, Oxon; New York, NY: Routledge, 2023. |
Series: Routledge advances in management and business studies |
Includes bibliographical references and index. |
Identifiers: LCCN 2022025273 (print) | LCCN 2022025274 (ebook) |
ISBN 9781032025087 (hbk) | ISBN 9781032025094 (pbk) |
ISBN 9781003183679 (ebk)
Subjects: LCSH: International business enterprises. | Corporations.
Classification: LCC HD62.4 .C6677 2023 (print) | LCC HD62.4 (ebook) |
DDC 658/.049–dc23/eng/20220907
LC record available at https://lccn.loc.gov/2022025273
LC ebook record available at https://lccn.loc.gov/2022025274

ISBN: 9781032025087 (hbk)
ISBN: 9781032025094 (pbk)
ISBN: 9781003183679 (ebk)

DOI: 10.4324/9781003183679

Typeset in Galliard
by Deanta Global Publishing Services, Chennai, India

Contents

Figures

Tables

Acknowledgement

I would like to thank those who took part in the interview process prior to the pandemic.

Contributors

Robert Cagnoli (BEng Ind Monash, MBA (AGSM)) developed a management consulting career in EY, PWC, Kearney, CVA and his own advisory firm, advising clients on strategic issues for financial institutions and other regulated industries (telecommunications and defence). Robert has supported companies restructuring and the M&A cycle across Asia and Europe. Major clients included Mitsubishi Bank, CBA, NAB, BNP, Fortis, Rolls Royce, General Motors and Telstra, among others. Robert also held the role of General Manager Strategy and Efficiency for NBN Co. and more recently has been the CEO of an E-mobility business and is launching a health and wellness business for over 50s.

Mike Donnelly (BA, MSc, PhD) is Honorary Professor at Heriot-Watt University in Edinburgh, Scotland, the Victorian Institute of Technology in Melbourne, and Queen Margaret University, Edinburgh. He was Dean of Faculty in business schools in the UK and in Australia over a 35-year academic career. Mike acted as Principal Special Adviser to the First Minister of Scotland and advised the Home Secretary in the reform of the UK Home Office. Mike served as a local government elected member and as a consultant with the Scottish Local Authorities Management Centre. A lifelong member of the UK Labour Party, Mike now enjoys writing, reading and knitting in retirement.

Paul Hunter (Professional Nudger) is a researcher, author, concept developer and implementer of futuristic and dynamic ways of thinking, formulating and implementing strategy; in the context of organisational transformation and renewal, a format that thrives on finding answers to wicked strategic problems. As an adviser to CEOs and other C-Suite executives, Paul deploys tools drawn from third-wave strategy, an approach described in his books (*Corporate Strategy (Remastered) I and II*). Paul is Founder of the Strategic Management Institute and the consulting firm Paul Hunter Strategy and Leadership. He has presented in many national and international conferences and as well as running executive education programmes in strategy and leadership.

Tim MacTaggart is a forward-thinking entrepreneur, business leader and student of disruptive innovation. He has been involved in a number of industries over the past 20 years including cleantech where he has worked on concentrating PV, flow batteries and flywheel energy storage systems. Tim has been the inaugural QUT bluebox Entrepreneur in Residence, founder of the start-up Smart Sensor Technologies and is currently on the Executive Team of ASX listed battery developed Redflow Ltd. He has an engineering degree, an MBA and a professional doctorate from Deakin University.

Stuart Orr has published a large number of refereed journal articles, as well as ten research books and research book chapters. He is regularly interviewed on radio and television and in international magazines and media such as Forbes and Bloomberg. Stuart is a Professor of Management and the Head of School, School of Business, at the Melbourne Institute of Technology. He was previously a Professor of Management at Deakin University, having also worked at Monash, RMIT and Melbourne universities. He has worked in industry (engineering) and consulting (management) and has set up and operated two successful businesses. Stuart has been president of one of Australia's largest NGOs and a board member of several peak global academic associations including the Decisions Sciences Institute.

Claire Tomlins (PhD, MBA, FRSA, FHEA) is an author and educator with business experience in the public and private sector. As a management consultant, with her own business, she has worked on operational and strategic projects in the energy sector, manufacturing and IT. When digital transformation was progressing she decided to undertake PhD research into the how businesses would appear and operate online (CSM, 2010). She has presented papers at international academic conferences, conducted workshops and is an International Business Visiting Lecturer at Hertfordshire Business School. Her book *What's Your Business? Corporate design Strategy Concepts and Processes* (Routledge, 2014, 2019) concentrates on the application of creativity at the intersection of corporate and design strategy as digital innovations progress.

Greg Trainor (DBA, MBA, and B/Business Studies) has over 35 years of experience in the energy sector internationally, having held leadership roles in the areas of strategy, logistics, software development and consulting through organisations such as GE, Accenture, Texas Utilities and Engie. He has occupied multiple senior roles in GE involving extensive engagement and collaboration with energy utilities and government energy departments and institutions across many countries. His earlier Doctor of Business Administration, Research through RMIT in Melbourne, Australia, resulted in a major thesis on the "Utility of the Future". He has been part of Faculty delivering MBA programmes at Melbourne Business School, RMIT and La Trobe Business School in Australia. Greg is currently General Manager, Advisory and Technology Services, at DB Results – a multidisciplinary consulting company.

1 Introduction

Stuart Orr

Overview

This chapter explains why we need a research-based book on the Future Corporation. It explains the characteristics that the Future Corporation is likely to possess. The chapter also explains the backcasting process which is used throughout this book to illustrate the journey that separates contemporary business in the Future Corporation. The background to the development of this book, the numerous sources of information upon which each of the chapters is based, which provides the foundation for the perspective on the Future Corporation presented in each chapter, and the analysis approach adopted in each chapter are also explained.

Each of the principal chapters in this research-informed book represents a separate project intended to identify features of the Future Corporation from a specific perspective, including the nature of disruption and its connection to discontinuities in industries, the technology aspect of the Future Corporation, a manager's eye view of life in the Future Corporation, interactions between government, regulations and the Future Corporation, the organisational configuration of the Future Corporation, the industry-level dynamics experienced by the Future Corporation, new actors appearing in the Future Corporation and a concluding chapter which ties all of the perspectives together.

This chapter will dissect the fundamental problem affecting our current understanding of what the Future Corporation will entail, why it is important, how we have approached answering this question in this book and a summary of each of the chapters.

Conceptualising the Future Corporation

Understanding the nature and function of the Future Corporation is an important contributor to effective strategic management in all industries (Grant et al., 2020). As the dot-com boom experience and more recently, Covid-19 demonstrated, an inability to understand how the organisation will function in the future can lead to a significantly increased likelihood of business failure. Most future forecasting is based on historical trends or single event hypotheses (such

DOI: 10.4324/9781003183679-1

as those used in scenario planning). Industries operate as systems, however, involving a large variety of interactions with suppliers, customers, regulations and competitors. As a result, an accurate understanding of the Future Corporation can only be achieved through a systematic analysis of the conditions in which it will operate. Providing this conceptualisation using a significant evidence base is the objective of this book. This section will consider the problem for strategic management that a limited understanding of the Future Corporation provides, how this issue can be solved and the benefits that will result.

The problem

When the changes to industry, market and global conditions are relatively minor, prediction of the future nature of organisations is relatively simple – current trends can be extrapolated to predict future conditions, actions and results. The future, however, is rarely characterised by minor changes. In the past 20 years, major disruptions have resulted from the dot-com boom, the global financial crisis, the Asian financial crisis and, most recently, Covid-19. On top of this, there are factors such as trade wars, including the current China-US trade war, terrorism and technological developments in commercial and recreational space travel. It would be impossible to predict, for example, that an online book distributor in the 1990s would develop and operate commercial spacecraft just over 20 years later. The disruptions that significantly affect industries sometimes dissipate, leaving the industry, markets and organisations in it relatively unaffected (Grant et al., 2020). On other occasions, however, these disruptions will be significant enough to create discontinuities, after which the industry, market, supply chains and global conditions are permanently changed. The foresight offered by adaptation practices, including responses to disruptive innovations, does not prepare organisations for major discontinuities in their industries and environments. The capacity for business to change in synchronisation with world developments such as these requires the capability of predicting the likely disruptions and casting a perspective of the corporation that will result.

As the Lewin (1947) change model explains, organisations frequently respond to significant developments in their environment through punctuated equilibrium – slipping behind the normal rate of change in their environment, responding with a major surge to bring them back into line with key industry conditions and then slowly slipping behind again as the changes are cemented in the organisation and its operations are frozen for a time. The cycle is then repeated, as shown in Figure 1.1. This approach is inefficient, both in terms of being maladapted to the environment for most of the time and in needing to implement drastic and often inefficient rapid change when the organisation slips too far behind.

These approaches are even less effective when the external environment changes dramatically. Covid-19 indicates how unprepared major organisations and structures such as international supply chains were to adapt to change at that level. Dissolution of traditional global trading partnerships, such as the trade war between China and the United States, the exit of the UK from the EU and the

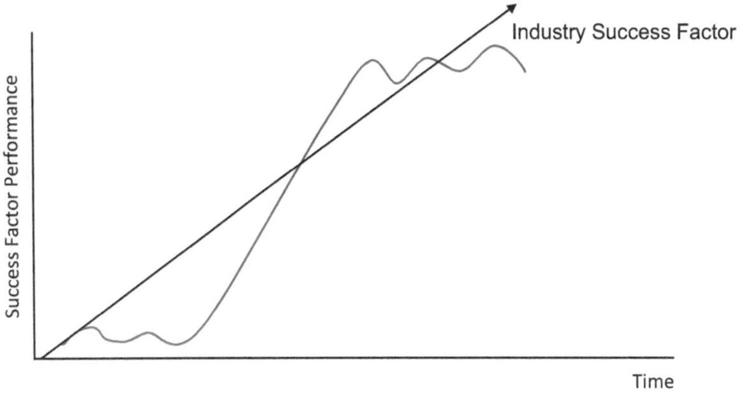

Figure 1.1 Punctuated equilibrium.

formation of new trading blocs such as China's Belt and Road initiatives, are creating turmoil and rapid change in the international business domain. Continual advances in technology and health treatments and political and societal change are underpinning these transformations.

The backcasting approach to mapping the future

Creating an adaptive organisational structure, focused on the understanding of the future nature of the corporation, will enable the organisation to develop and manage capabilities and characteristics in tune with changes in the external environment. Forecasting the future requires more than current trend extrapolation or a single event hypothesis-based analysis, such as scenario analysis, as scenarios depict a single future context rather than future organisational structures, technologies and systems (Wright et al., 2019). To provide the appropriate perspective, a substantial evidence-based enquiry is required, along with an analytical approach that can adapt to the different aspects of the conditions being identified. This book uses evidence from a variety of expert sources in conjunction with the reporting technique called backcasting, which presents the path to the future as a historical event (Quist & Vergragt, 2006). The book defines the Future Corporation at the target date of 2040, as well as explaining the methodology which can be used for developing perspectives of the Future Corporation at different times.

Benefits of the backcasting approach

Quist and Vergragt (2006) explain that creating valid and defensible views of existing industries and business systems in a future context through backcasting requires input from a variety of different actors including government, companies and knowledgeable authorities to create a sufficiently representative evidence base. The chapters in this book combine findings drawn from several focused systematic literature reviews, two conferences, workshops, two independent surveys, interviews with business executives and a Delphi study to create a sufficiently broad and inclusive evidence base with which to develop an integrated conceptualisation of the journey that leads from contemporary organisations to the Future Corporation of 2040. This broad evidence base enables the concept of the Future Corporation described in this book to be represented through the perspectives of industry systems, technology, industry, workplace environment and job type features, along with the forms of government and regulation that combine to mould the format of the Future Corporation. This broad evidence-based perspective provides the basis for a detailed interpretation of data, the opportunity to evidence causality through multiple perspectives and the ability to avoid bounded rationality effects that could limit the explanatory power of this project. Analysis with this level of validity and defensibility is required to support strong conclusions about future events (Shaver, 2021).

Figure 1.2 represents the backcasting process used to develop the chapters in this book, based on a description of the backcasting process described by Staley (2002). This process involves critical argument and matching identifiable features with well-understood patterns (for example, the well-understood "S" curve of technology lifecycles), which are the stock in trade for historical descriptions of past events. This process avoids non-objective and impassioned views of the future. Instead, future conditions are evaluated as the product of interactions of enabling factors which are identifiable from the present, along with the effect of natural boundary conditions that will constrain their behaviours. The process of evaluating the relative "strength" of the different systems and evaluating the relative merit of counterfactual arguments leads to an objective interpretation of the future.

Scope of this book

As Staley (2002) suggests, writing about future events using a historical perspective allows the development of heuristic narratives and a more effective way of

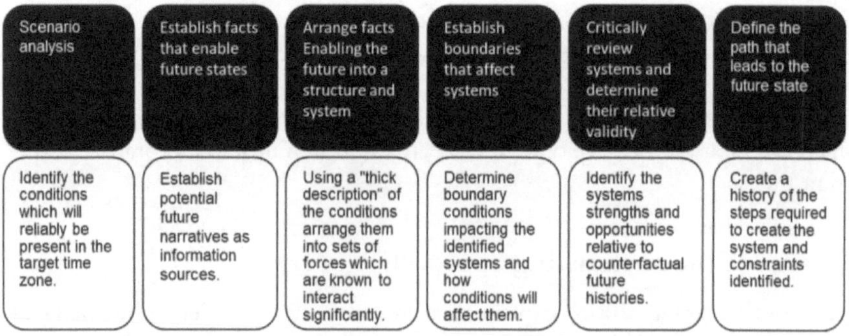

Figure 1.2 Backcasting process diagram.

explaining the impact of these disruptions. The book has been set 20 years in the future. It discusses the changes that have led to the nature of corporations in 2040 and the conditions that have created those changes. Each chapter presents a complimentary view about the nature of and context for the 2040 Future Corporation.

In this text, corporations are defined as entities engaged in commercial activities, either owned by private, institutional or government owners, interacting with society to generate value for customers and stakeholders. These entities are considered to operate within business systems which comprise the industry, economies within which they operate and the government and social regulations with which they must comply. As a result, corporations are not considered to be standalone organisations, rather, they are considered to be in a constant state of interaction with competitors and other institutional bodies which influence, limit and facilitate their operations and development.

Method

To develop the concepts presented in this book, the team of authors (academics and practitioners from different countries and different areas of business) engaged in a four-year, two-stage research process. The first stage involved a dialogue process conducted through two dedicated conferences and a two-year workshop-based conversation to identify the key features of the Future Corporation. In the second stage, the key observations from the first stage were used to develop a series of research projects to further examine these issues. This book presents the key findings from both stages. In the first stage of this work, researchers were surprised to discover how limited the understanding of the 2040 corporation was – beyond unconnected and often conflicting viewpoints about individual technologies which are floating around the literature. During the second stage, the individual research projects produced a much more cogent and interesting picture – which is captured in the subsequent chapters. The backcasting perspective was used because it is the most objective and effective method for identifying and presenting an integrated, defensible and balanced future perspective.

To support this analysis, the key dimensions against which the Future Corporation should be defined were identified. This was done to ensure consistency in the analyses conducted for the chapters. The definition of the corporation was based on the following perspectives:

- Drucker's (1946) concept of the corporation as an economic, human and social agency.
- Orr in Grant et al.'s (2020) description of the organisational purpose of the corporation as who the organisation exists to serve and how they should be served.
- Barney's (1991) resource-based view of the corporation as comprising capabilities to be leveraged for competitive advantage.

- John and Senbet's (1998) view of corporate governance as the mechanisms through which stakeholders control corporations to protect their interests.
- Bustos and Hernández-Lara's (2016) ownership perspective of corporate strategy as being driven by ownership concentration, the typology of owners and the interactions between them.

These concepts are represented in Figure 1.3, showing their interactions and the system nature of corporations. The longevity of some of these foundation perspectives indicates that these features can be expected to be characteristics of the Future Corporation as well.

Summary of workshop and conference findings

The first stage workshop and conference led to a range of findings. These findings were startling, not for the unexpected perspectives that they presented, but instead for the tightly bounded rationality displayed by the participants. In particular, the Future Corporation appeared to be viewed as an extension of existing corporations with primarily technical and some social extensions based on

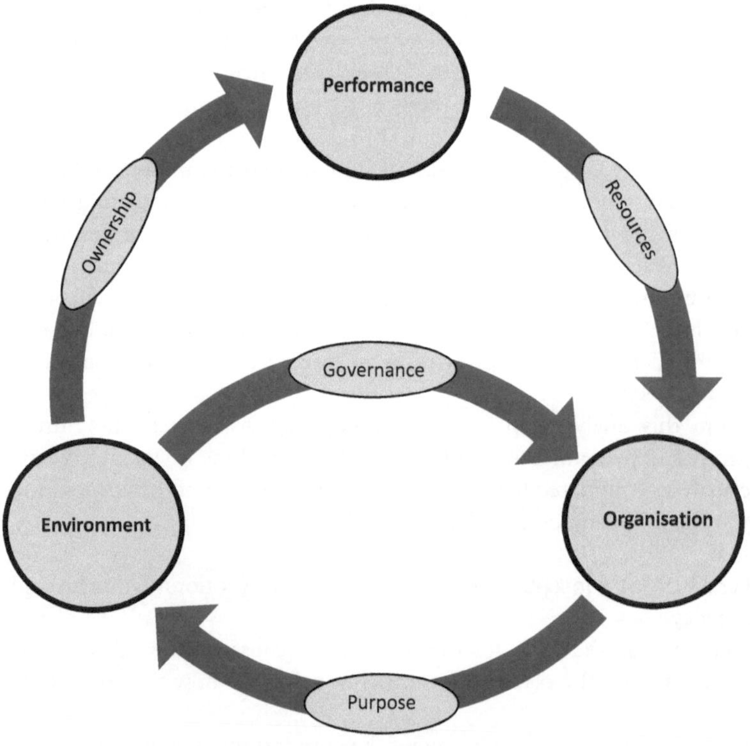

Figure 1.3 Key dimensions of the Future Corporation examined in this study.

current trends. Integration between corporations and elements of their environment such as stakeholders, government or unanticipated events (such as Covid-19) was not expected to change the nature or systems of the Future Corporation much. Interaction and system perspectives were limited in their scope of effect on the corporation, which confirms the need for an approach such as backcasting to develop a more holistic perspective of how the Future Corporation might evolve.

The key factors identified in these dialogues included:

- Technology developments
- Greater stakeholder focus
- Some evolution in the role of government
- Improvements in information management
- More automation
- More streamlined organisational structures facilitated by technology

Overview of chapters

Chapter 2 (Disruptions that lead to new types of corporations: A process view) is authored by Professor Stuart Orr and Dr Paul Hunter. It is a systematic literature review of the contemporary literature on disruption and describes how disruption leads to new types of corporations and new businesses formed out of existing corporations from a process perspective. It explains the types of disruptions that corporations can experience and identifies the difference between temporary disruptions that allow organisations to return to their prior state (or a similar state) and disruptions that lead to discontinuities in industries, markets and value chains. The chapter will also examine the disruption of operations and industries from a system perspective, identifying the important system characteristics present in disruptive change. In particular, this chapter will reflect on the sociotechnical aspects of industry disruption and introduce an assessment framework for identifying where discontinuities have occurred. This chapter presents an overview of concepts resulting from the workshops and conferences conducted in the first stage of the research in combination with business systems and sociotechnical theory.

Chapter 3 (Strategic foundations of the Future Corporation) is authored by Dr Paul Hunter and presents a description of the strategic development of the organisation. The chapter follows the strategic development of the corporation and the parallel development of strategic management theory. This chapter describes, with reference to the key authors of strategic management and general management theories, the consequences of the systemic nature of organisations identified in Chapter 2. This chapter uses case data from well-known organisations such as Meta, Corning and Apple, as well as theoretical concepts such as socionology to explain how technological factors such as the internet and network effects have changed the nature of the corporation. This is then used as the scenario base for backcasting from which a description of the foundation features of the Future Corporation and the transformation required to achieve them are produced.

Chapter 4 (Technology evolution in the Future Corporation) is authored by Dr Paul Hunter and Professor Stuart Orr. It presents the results of a thematic analysis of the technology-focused data collected from the conferences and workshops. Three analysts, coding from recordings of the conferences and workshops in parallel, identify the principal themes relating to technology which define characteristics of the future organisation and coded to the specific observations under each. The three sets of coded data were then compared, and the differences were discussed until agreement on the individual coding was achieved and the results were finalised. This analysis was then used to form the foundation of backcasting of the effect of technology trends on the Future Corporation. The chapter introduces the type of technology-generated disruptions that are possible and presents four possible Future Corporations based on four technology development trend outcomes. The most likely outcome is then described and the reasons for that selection are presented using a critical path perspective. A full backcast perspective is then developed and explained which demonstrates how this Future Corporation results from technology development.

Chapter 5 (Internal purpose in the Future Corporation) was written by Dr Claire Tomlins and presents an organisational design view of the purpose of the Future Corporation. The chapter focuses on how work is defined and constructed in the Future Corporation, how these corporations interact with their environment and the subsequent structure and purpose developed by these corporations in response to the environment. It is based on an open-ended survey of senior executives and a follow-up round of interviews. This data was then mapped onto an analysis framework which was developed from the systematic review of the literature, conducted in the design stage of the project. This framework included key dimensions of sociological, political geography, environmental, economic, exploration, computing, cyber security, intelligence data, aid legal and security. A content analysis of the information collected was then conducted on the mapped data to produce the findings presented in this chapter. The findings are then used to construct a backcast explanation of how these dimensions of the Future Corporation came into being.

Chapter 6 (UK local and national government in 2040) was prepared by Professor Mike Donnelly. It considers how government and legislation drive the formation of the Future Corporation. The chapter is based on a Delphi panel study of senior government actors and advisers. In line with normal Delphi studies, the participants remained anonymous to one another and communicated directly with the facilitator. Their views were analysed and summarised and returned to the panel members for further comment. This process was repeated until consensus was achieved on the identified issues. The chapter describes the rounds of interviews and the outcomes and presents descriptions of each of the issues identified by the panel and the descriptions of those issues upon which the panel reached consensus. The chapter uses these descriptions to define the complexity and function of governments anticipated in 2040. It also uses them to explain the purposes of government in that era and how these purposes will affect the nature of the Future Corporation. The chapter concludes by considering how Future Corporations will interact with the government and provides a backcast view of how these interactions produced the Future Corporation of 2040.

Chapter 7 (The Future Corporation as a utility) was prepared by Dr Greg Trainor. The findings in this chapter were based on a survey and interviews of senior executives conducted by the author in his role as a senior executive with GE. The data from the surveys and interviews was thematically analysed to identify a range of themes which explain the customer expectations of utility services in the future and how this will lead to different organisational configurations in the Future Corporation. The data coded under these themes were used to create a backcast view of the path that led to the service features of the Future Corporation.

Chapter 8 (Backcasting of the electricity industry from 2040) was prepared by Dr Tim Mactaggart. It provides an industry-level perspective on the development of the Future Corporation. The chapter was based on a systematic review of the literature relating to the technical and infrastructure development in the electric power supply industry, viewed through a sociotechnical framework. The sociotechnical framework recognises that systems comprise a technical component, which includes rules and technologies and a social component which includes people skills and their interactions. This perspective was used to identify the dominant trends applying to the energy generation sector and a backcast argument was developed based on these trends to describe and explain the path through which the Future Corporation in an industry such as the electrical supply industry would develop.

Chapter 9 (Entrepreneurship in the Future Corporation) was prepared by Robert Cagnoli and describes an important potential aspect of the workforce in Future Corporations, the Seniorpreneur. The findings in this chapter are based on a combined review of the literature, in combination with an analysis of economic and social demographic data to construct an argument for the development of a new workplace role. This chapter uses backcasting to describe the changes in the workplace that are experienced in the Future Corporation and how this new role influences the characteristics of Future Corporations.

Chapter 10 (Conclusion) was prepared by Professor Stuart Orr. This chapter summarises and contrasts the different perspectives on the Future Corporation that were presented in each of the preceding chapters. It applies an activity theory framework to combine these perspectives into a cogent description and backcast the process that led to the Future Corporation. Activity theory has its origins in an activity-based theoretical development in Russian psychology literature, with particular contributions from Engeström (1987) and Leont'ev (1978). This framework enables the division of labour, instruments and rules which lead to the objective (in this case the Future Corporation) being identified. The division of labour instruments and rules are then presented as a backcast and history of the process that leads to the Future Corporation. The chapter concludes with a consideration of what this means for the direction of strategy developments in contemporary corporations.

Conclusion

This book presents a deeply considered view of the Future Corporation in 2040 based on a grounded approach comprising deep and sustained concept development projects (stage one) and subsequent individual research projects to explore the key issues identified (stage two). The key features discussed include the possibility of disruptions leading to discontinuities in industries and value chains, the system nature of such disruptions, the important role of technology in creating the opportunities for disruption, the motivating effect of government and legislation affects, markets and service drivers which create discontinuity out of disruption, the ability of industries to be transformed by discontinuity generating disruptions and the subsequent effect of such discontinuities on workforces.

The research and practical concepts presented in this book should be of significant benefit to organisations wishing to chart the turbulent waters ahead and create sustainability in their organisations and management approaches that will lead to (1) maintaining the ability to be relevant and connected to the external environment as it evolves and (2) identifying opportunities for new growth and building new business entities in the future.

References

Barney, J. (1991). Firm resources and sustained competitive advantage. *Journal of Management*, *17*(1), 99–120. doi:10.1177/014920639101700108

Drucker, P. F. (1946). *Concept of the Corporation*. New York: John Day Co.

Engeström, Y. (1987). *Learning by Expanding: An Activity-theoretical Approach to Developmental Research*. Helsinki: Orienta-Konsultit Oy. Retrieved December 23, 2015.

Gonzales-Bustos, J. P., & Hernández-Lara, A. B. (2016). Corporate governance and innovation: A systematic literature review. *Corporate Ownership and Control*, *13*(3), 33–45. doi:10.22495/cocv13i3p3

Orr, S. (2020). Strategy: Concepts and Perspectives. In R. Grant, P, Murray, S. Orr, B. Butler, & P. Bezemer (Eds.), *Strategic Management*. Brisbane: Wiley.

Grant, R., Murray, P, Orr, S, Butler, B, & Bezemer, P. (2020). *Strategic Management*. Brisbane: Wiley.

John, K., & Senbet, L. W. (1998). Corporate governance and board effectiveness1This paper was an invited paper on the occasion of the JBF 20th anniversary.1. *Journal of Banking & Finance*, *22*(4), 371–403. doi:10.1016/S0378-4266(98)00005-3

Leont'ev, A. (1978). *Activity, Consciousness, and Personality*. Englewood Cliffs: Prentice-Hall.

Lewin, K. (1947). *Frontiers in Group Dynamics: Channels of Group Life: Social Planning and Action Research. II*. London: Tavistock Publications.

Quist, J., & Vergragt, P. (2006). Past and future of backcasting: The shift to stakeholder participation and a proposal for a methodological framework. *Futures*, *38*(9), 1027–1045. doi:10.1016/j.futures.2006.02.010

Shaver, J. M. (2021). Evolution of quantitative research methods and strategic management. In I. M. Duhaime, M. A. Hitt, & M. A. Lyles (Eds.), *Strategic Management: State of the Field and Its Future*. New York: Oxford University Press.
Staley, D. J. (2002). A history of the future. *History & Theory*, *41*(4), 72–89.
Wright, G., Cairns, G., O'Brien, F. A., & Goodwin, P. (2019). Scenario analysis to support decision making in addressing wicked problems: Pitfalls and potential. *European Journal of Operational Research*, *278*(1), 3–19. doi:10.1016/j.ejor.2018.08.035

2 Disruptions that lead to new types of corporations

A process view

Stuart Orr and Paul Hunter

Introduction

Schumpeter advised innovative companies to increase their competitiveness by creating a "perennial gale of creative destruction" (Schumpeter, 1934). Since then, only a few of the bravest companies have taken this advice. Even fewer have exercised the perennial option. The supermarket industry provides one such example (Smith, 2014). Already game changers, technologically advanced, lower-cost and disruption-focused global supermarket chains such as Aldi and Lidl have been very successful in breaking into the supermarket industry in many countries (Giammona, 2017). Even they, however, have been upstaged by another entrant focused on disruption – Amazon Fresh. In a remarkable reversal of play, online giant Amazon is investing in physical retail stores as a means to deliver additional growth in sales. Although in its infancy, the retail chain is called Amazon Fresh; it is a physical grocery store that was launched in 2020, three years after its acquisition of the US-based supermarket Whole Foods. Empowered by its existing and highly efficient supply chain capability, Amazon Fresh currently has 30 stores operating in North America. The first UK store was opened in Ealing, London – there are now 17 stores operating across London. Amazon, according to its website (Amazon, 2022), has ambitious plans to expand on many continents, and in many cities around the world. In establishing Amazon Fresh, the company has been able to take the concept of cost competitiveness to a whole new level. Its supermarket offering, as described on its website, is a new grocery store that offers a seamless grocery shopping experience, for both in-store and online shoppers (Amazon, 2022).

To obtain and maintain a competitive advantage in the supermarket space, everyday low prices and free home delivery to its customers are a given. From there however, traditional supermarkets are left somewhat behind. Using Amazon Dash Cart as a centralised platform for its in-store navigation and payment system, this AI-powered shopping trolly allows customers to exit the store without pausing at the checkout. Amazon's Dash Cart uses a combination of computer vision algorithms and sensors to identify items put into the cart, which enables the customer to complete the purchase process (Amazon, 2022).

As a key enabler of the shopping experience, the cart allows customers to use Alexa virtual assistant technology to quickly find items in the store via

DOI: 10.4324/9781003183679-2

pre-programmed shopping lists. Alexa also allows customers to easily find and check off acquired items. As a final swipe at more moribund competitors, customers can obtain a 5% discount when they use their Amazon loyalty cards on payment.

This new business model is complementary to Amazon's pre-existing e-commerce capability, which has a superior span of control over its competitors. Amazon's system is a recognised retail industry disruptor that has found success through its scale and ability to tailor its supply chain outputs to individual requirements. Amazon's founder, Jeff Bezos, claims that he has created a corporation that differentiates itself via customer centricity, long-term thinking and invention (Gallo, 2021). The combination of the scale of their supply chain and their ability to customise orders down to the individual customer preference level has been used to continually disrupt the retail industry. They have extended this disruption to other industries by capturing and adding more services such as movie rental and cloud storage – and now Amazon Fresh.

Disruption is becoming an increasingly common component of the business environment. As Birkinshaw et al. (2016) and others such as Freeman et al. (2007) note, it is important to understand how Future Corporations respond to disruption and use it to develop new opportunities – as in the case of Amazon Fresh. Using a systems perspective to deconstruct the process of disruption, this chapter describes how managers can intentionally disrupt their environment to create the opportunity for inimitable forms of competitiveness. We contribute to this literature by describing a new process for building competitiveness in a disrupted environment.

A systems view of disruption

Although disruption and the different types of tactical responses made by corporations to disruption are well recognised, our understanding of the mechanisms behind the system effects and strategic responses to disruption is surprisingly limited (Burt, 2007). The change to an industry's business system, which is generated when disruption occurs under uncertain and urgent conditions, makes it very challenging to develop appropriate and timely strategies using existing organisational systems (Day and Schoemaker, 2016). Once the industry business system has changed, the organisational systems developed for that business system will no longer be as effective. Different types of disruptions also have different effects on the corporations in that business system. For example, disruptions that only reform the market will tend to provide more advantages for corporations already operating in the market; however, disruptions that redefine industry boundaries and norms will favour new entrants (Day et al., 2003).

The type of response corporations make to disruption is critical as well. A global survey of 2000 senior executives' responses to digitally driven disruption found that they either imitated other companies' responses or adopted bold strategies to literally transform their corporations entirely (Bughin, 2017). Transforming was found to lead to a significantly positive financial outcome. Responding by imitation resulted in reduced profitability because the change to the industry system caused by the disruption reduced the effectiveness of the responses that had worked in the past. In addition, making an isomorphic response to disruptions increases the corporation's reliance on other, more inventive partners to step up to change. This leads to a knock-on effect of reducing the isomorphous Future Corporations' ability to adapt. Another study of responses to disruptions in the computer equipment industry also found that transformation in response to disruption provides a greater return than adaptation (Rosenbloom and Christensen, 1994). Transforming the corporation in response to a disruption in the industry is still a gamble, however. Disruptions due to technology, for example, can cause major structural changes in the industry due to the redistribution of knowledge, changes in scale, changes in adjacent industries and industry membership changes (Ehrnberg and Jacobsson, 1993). This can make it difficult to identify how to appropriately transform the corporation. In addition, the tendency of management systems to return the corporation to its previous state can limit the extent of the transformation which is possible (Zaida et al., 1999).

The processes which create a disruption can be most easily explained using a systems perspective (Johnson-Cramer et al., 2007). The systems perspective is particularly helpful for understanding the process through which a disruption becomes a discontinuity and creates the potential for a fundamental change in the industry. The process is most easily understood by viewing both the industry and the corporation as systems. For example, the patterns and behaviours of the US energy regulators when their business system was disrupted by the emergence of renewable energy become clear when the system is viewed as a network rather than a group of disparate service providers. The energy network at play in this instance is made up of regulators, distribution networks, energy generators and energy retailers (Grübler, 1991). It is also important to appreciate that disruptions are not expectedly or unexpectedly imposed on markets or corporations by random events. As Elon Musk and Tesla (Stringham et al., 2015), and previously Mangram (2012), have demonstrated, they can also be intentionally constructed. Corporations such as Tesla interpret the structure and dynamic characteristics of their industry's business system and identify opportunities to introduce disruptions that lead to favourable future conditions for the corporation. This approach extends the strategy development process to include the process of analysing the system that drives the market and initiating disruptions that create the context in which a competitive advantage can be built for the corporation (Sanchez, 1997). This chapter presents some of the mechanisms of such a strategy.

Response orientations to disruption

A corporation naturally possesses a capacity to adapt (Bostik, 2017) to change, but many corporations can also spontaneously initiate disruptive change as well. Despite this, most corporations limit their capacity for change to adaptation alone, choosing to adapt reactively or proactively (Engau et al., 2011). Disruption-generating corporations, such as Amazon and Tesla, however, compete by actively invoking change. These corporations shape their future by literally inventing it. Instead of being provoked into change by an external or internal stimulus, these corporations invoke change through a deliberate disruption of existing external environmental systems.

Even if a corporation chooses to invoke change through a deliberate disruption, its underlying management and control systems will likely attempt to maintain their previous state (as that is their purpose). This state of inertia can be observed in corporations such as Nokia and Blackberry who invoked changes in their industry by introducing smartphone features but were unable to adapt quickly enough to the new smartphone technology developments to maintain their position in the new external environment that they had created (Harford, 2018). These companies lost market share to more adaptive corporations, even though those corporations did not invoke the change in the first place.

Corporations that recognise that their capacity to change is limited, but also appreciate the desirability of disrupting the external environment, may choose to invoke small levels of disruption, to which they can easily respond. This may manifest as a major marketing campaign or possibly a push into a new and developing international market with existing products and services. While the level of disruption in the external environmental system (such as the new international market) might be quite observable, the requirement for change from the disrupting corporation would be relatively low. Unfortunately, it would also only require a modest change for competitors (i.e. entering an international market following the lead competitor), meaning that this approach may not lead to a sustained competitive advantage. The Chinese e-commerce, retail and Internet conglomerate, Alibaba, is a good example of a corporation in this position. Alibaba adapted the Amazon business model to the Chinese environment before Amazon had time to establish its presence in that country. Developments in this market have shown that Alibaba is also at risk of successful imitation by competitors such as Baidu and Tencent (Lashinsky, 2018). Another good example is the introduction of the graphical computer user interface – originally introduced by Xerox and quickly adopted by Apple and then Microsoft, one year later. Xerox failed to develop the computer production capability quickly enough to take advantage of the disruption that it had created, while neither Apple nor Microsoft were able to convert this particular disruption into a sustained competitive advantage as these companies had not initiated the disruption.

Corporations that manage to combine both a significant disruption to the external environment and the commencement ability to change to take advantage of that disruption will generally display high levels of innovation and creativity as well as strong levels of financial performance. Richard Branson has attempted to create a discontinuity in the airline industry by introducing retail space flight with his company Virgin Galactic. Virgin has also shown the organisational change capability to add spacecraft manufacture to operations that were primarily focused on service provision (Sheetz, 2020). Consistent with the type of innovative and creative change that these types of corporations display when adapting to the disruptions they introduce, Virgin's new aircraft combines both current aircraft and aerospace designs and represents a significant innovation in the industry. Virgin is now attempting to use this approach to gain a significant share of the new industry it has produced through this disruption, creating a sustained competitive advantage over other industry heavy hitters SpaceX and Blue Origin. The combined earth and space travel agency would then create a whole new business system and introduce a new set of rules and systems.

The combined ability to create significant disruption and change significantly in response to the disruption in order to gain a sustainable competitive advantage introduces a new dimension of industry disruption, with the intention to disrupt in order to create a discontinuity. It is the discontinuity that permanently resets the external environmental system, into a new format, and one in which the company which invokes the disruption can gain a sustainable competitive advantage. A small disruption which does not lead to a discontinuity is likely to result in a return of the external environmental system to its original conditions and not create a sustainable competitive advantage for the company invoking the disruption.

Virgin is now facing the challenge of ensuring that the disruption does successfully generate a discontinuity. In order to ensure a permanent discontinuity, Virgin may need to extend the current technology and process-based disruption to the rest of the aerospace industry system. Introducing the Virgin Galactic aircraft technology into the commercial airline industry would create the ability to provide higher-speed commercial flights to traditional destinations which the rest of the industry is unable to offer. The past success of Concorde (in which British Aerospace and Aérospatiale created customer dedication for 30 years), even though it was less disruptive and more of an incremental technology development, suggests that this operational adaptation could lead to a permanent discontinuity in the industry.

Schumpeter explained his concept of deliberate disruption (Schumpeter, 1934), which he believed leads to a sustainable competitive advantage as being the "process of industrial mutation that continuously revolutionises the economic structure from within, incessantly destroying the old one, incessantly creating a new one" (Schumpeter, 1942). Thus, it can be seen that strategic mutation describes the process of creating a disruption in the external environment and responding in a way that enables the corporation to move outside the boundaries of its existing environmental systems (Dekkers, 2005).

Tesla disrupted the market by introducing viable and highly attractive electric cars that created demand from traditional and upmarket car buyers. It prepared itself for the market demand that it created by being ready to mass produce these vehicles as the demand emerged (Morris, 2020). Unlike the other automotive companies, it did not adapt existing products (petrol vehicles) to the new opportunity – it developed a new battery capability and a vehicle that suited the new market demand that it had created through its disruption. This provided Tesla with a competitive advantage in the market that it had created. Tesla's disruption is still spreading out to other areas, such as the energy grid industry, where again Tesla is already transforming and supplying market opportunities as a key driver of growth.

Environmental system responses viewed as a typology

The possible response orientations to disruption can be viewed through the dimensions of the level of the disruption that is invoked and the capacity to implement change as a response (strategic mutation). These four categories are shown in Figure 2.1 and had the following effects on the corporation's competitive advantage.

Quadrant 1: Inertia. For companies located in this quadrant, surprise is not the norm. The lack of change creates a false perception of security, and this type of corporation is poorly positioned to anticipate change. Nor are they well prepared to deal with it when things do change. This complacency is a threat to the viability of the business. Lego is a good example of this type of corporation; its core competency is precision engineering, but they continue to compete through high-volume and low-cost manufacturing, using a design "push" system that has not changed for 40 years (Gronholt-Pedersen et al., 2017). They are constrained by a "mass production" strategy that has led them to focus on operational effectiveness ahead of customer demand. Struggling to change their ties to this tradition, Lego is now addressing the challenge that customers present as they expect a greater say in the design, features and functionality of their products.

Quadrant 2: Agile adaptation. A corporation in this quadrant is normally prepared to respond in advance of an anticipated innovative idea being launched or respond at the time of the unanticipated innovation becoming apparent. This corporation will be cautious about taking risks with its core business and doesn't create disruption itself. It will be aware, however, that one day it may have to move away from its core business if no more disruptive innovations are introduced into its external environmental system for it to exploit. Trump, for example, sought

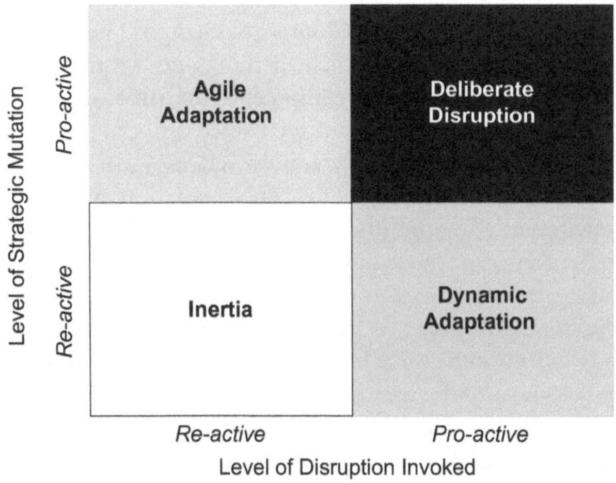

Figure 2.1 Environmental system response matrix.

to drive the whole of US industry to upgrade its capabilities in response to the disruptions introduced by its trade war with China (Boylan et al., 2021).

Whenever there is a significant disruption, competitors will find it difficult to respond. An example is China's major aircraft manufacturer, Comac, which in 2018 launched the production of an aircraft similar to US-based Boeing's highly popular 737. Comac was able to achieve a significant cost advantage over Boeing by blending imported and domestic components (Johnson, 2015). The introduction of this new aircraft, however, has not created a disruption for the global aerospace manufacturing industry, even though Boeing's sales in China will be reduced in the future.

Tesla has demonstrated a similar approach by introducing electronic systems, such as autonomous driving capabilities, which other competitors, have also introduced. Another Tesla innovation is the substitution of petrol and diesel engines with electric engines in a sports car. Neither the electric technology, nor the concept of an electric vehicle, are new, however; so this does not represent a disruption which is likely to lead to an industry discontinuity. It certainly hurried the major automotive manufacturers into larger-scale electric car production, however, they had already begun this change before Tesla started producing vehicles.

The slow speed of fundamental change in the automotive industry enabled Tesla to adapt and exploit the latest electronic technologies, but Tesla has not created a sufficiently strong disruption to create a discontinuity and change the nature of the automotive industry system. By comparison, many national electricity industries around the globe have reluctantly, but fully, integrated renewable energy sources and significantly changed their systems and businesses from operating a concentrated energy system to operating a distributed energy generation, with private providers.

Quadrant 3: Dynamic adaptation. Corporations in this quadrant seek to explore innovations that deliver new opportunities and new business ventures. These corporations, however, are not aggressive adopters of change. They "play it safe" and only commit to the extent from which, if things go wrong, they can retreat or quickly correct the issue. Medical equipment companies, such as ResMed, are good examples of this type of corporation. These corporations produce disruptive innovations and create new markets; however, they are slow to respond to other disruptions in their industry. They only enter into industry systems and take up opportunities after the disruption has settled. Companies following this strategy can be likened to those pursuing a "Second Mover" competitive advantage. By waiting to see how the market evolves, second movers can sometimes become the dominant player as they benefit from observing the learning curve of competitors without the same level of risk. Whereas first movers intend to dominate the market most of the time and for all time, as Microsoft has with its Windows product, for example, second movers have been known to overtake the leaders in the end (Suarez and Lanzolla, 2005). No company knows this better than Nokia, for example, who were leaders in the smartphone marketplace until Apple came along, as discussed previously.

Quadrant 4: Deliberate disruption. Corporations in this quadrant consciously build a proactive capacity for both adaptation and innovation. This leads to a relatively uncommon ability to generate disruptions that lead to discontinuities and engage in strategic motivation so as to benefit from the discontinuity. Jeff Bezos, still CEO of Amazon during the launch of Amazon Fresh, demonstrated a strategic mutation ability with a sharp focus on doing things differently. As CEO, Bezos was focused on exploring opportunities where innovation enabled disruptions and relied on a systems thinking approach, six sigma and deep analytics to drive the required adaptation (Six Sigma Daily, 2021). As a result, Amazon moves quickly into new markets and is engaged in industries as diverse as fair-trade certified coffee and film production. It can be argued that Amazon is in a perpetual state of strategic mutation.

A sociotechnical systems view of industry disruption

The capability for strategic mutation that Bezos achieved in Amazon is not common. The time compression associated with responding to a disruption/discontinuity event leaves little time for organisational learning (Birkinshaw et al., 2016; Day & Schoemaker, 2016). Interestingly, however, strategic mutation capabilities are usually developed by the adaptation to the environmental disturbances that corporations normally experience. Uber demonstrates this capability. This corporation constantly explores opportunities to extend its delivery service using new technologies, such as drones (Bandoim, 2018). Incorporating existing technologies or processes into existing processes is unlikely to disrupt an industry sufficiently to create a discontinuity. Were Uber to combine this technology with new processes, such as the use of driverless cars, it might create a discontinuity in its industry. Uber does display the ability to engage in strategic mutation and, having created discontinuity, it would be likely to achieve a competitive advantage.

The natural world offers an alternative and simple explanation for the process of strategic mutation. The evolution of a species in nature commences with the mutation of an individual that increases its competitiveness/survival rate and leads to the reproduction of more individuals with similar characteristics. As Figure 2.2 shows, mutation starts with a stimulus. While this stimulus may come from a random external source, such as exposure to unusual conditions, it can also be the result of intentional activity, such as moving into a new environment which requires adaptation. Of course, not all mutations are successful in producing a more competitive organism, and the experimental approach to organisational development has shown that failure is more likely than success. As part of their strategic mutation process, Amazon experiences a very large number of failures, as does Google (Green, 2019).

The New York milk producer Elmhurst Dairy attempted to disrupt its external environmental conditions (in its industry) by introducing products that changed the expectations of the industry's customers. In 2017, Elmhurst Dairy introduced plant-based milk products including almond, rice, oat, walnut, hazelnut, cashew and peanut milk. While this was innovative, it did not create a strategic

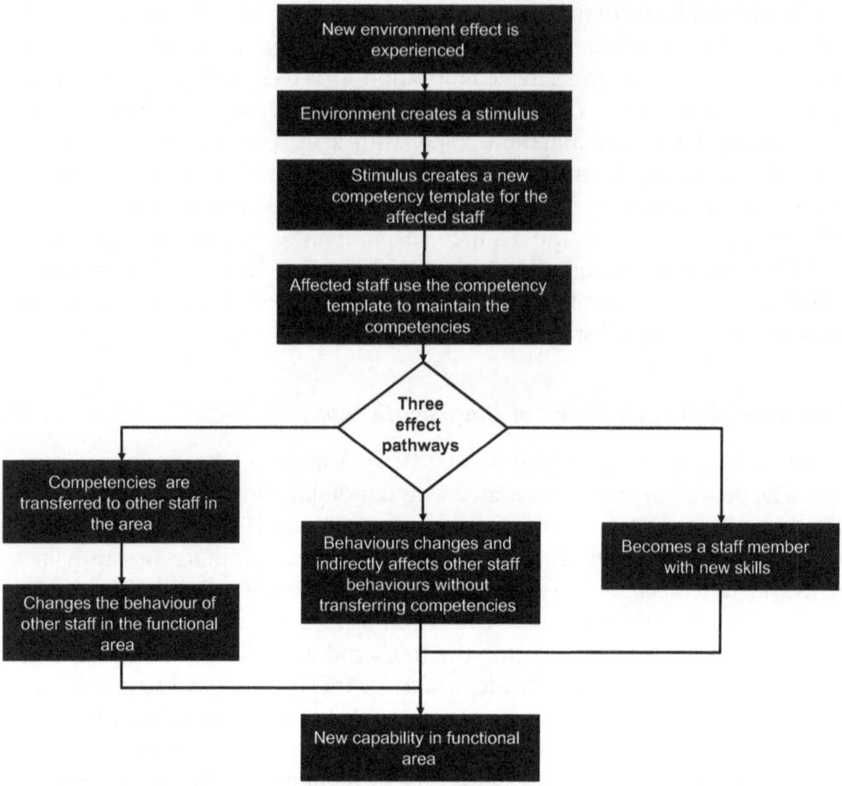

Figure 2.2 Green shoot-induced mutation process.

mutation and did not disrupt the industry sufficiently to create a discontinuity in Elmhurst's favour (Fox, 2017). Elmhurst mutated its production process just enough to enable it to survive in the new external environment (plant milk market) that it created. It missed the opportunity to create a more fundamentally different production process (or delivery process, packaging process, etc) that would have given it a competitive advantage, which may not have been possible in its traditional markets. For example, most cow and alternative milk products are 97% water. While customers prefer that the producer does not remove the water from cow milk (i.e. produce powdered milk), they may be much more accepting of buying concentrated nut-based milk if there is a cost advantage. Alternatively, it could have replicated the success of microbreweries and set up small dairies in suburban locations producing fresh nut milk from pre-processed nut materials.

Corporations that have achieved increased competitiveness through strategic mutation become dominant, just as more competitive individuals become dominant in their species. Thus, strategic mutation leading to increased competitiveness is a process involving stimulus and change, with some changes producing a more competitive corporation (Chesbrough and Appleyard, 2007). Natural processes also provide an important lesson about the process of mutation for increased competitiveness. Mutation in the natural world rarely changes the entire organism. It normally affects one functional area of the organism and increases competitiveness by changing the capability of that single functional area. By comparison, most business development processes are intended to introduce a small change across the entire corporation, for example, business process management for efficiency initiatives. The natural world tends to be very focused on efficiency and achieving competitiveness by making a significant change to one functional area to produce competitiveness more efficiently than making a small change across the entire system.

Within the corporation, the natural approach mutation would be analogous to the development and entirely new process in an existing department. For example, strategic mutation could involve the marketing division of a traditional corporation, such as a railway, spontaneously acquiring the capability to consistently produce trending messages on social media. The external environmental system change that could create such mutation would result from an event, such as a change in ownership of the corporation from government to private owners. The change would not directly affect the function of the rest of the corporation, only the behaviours of the marketing department. For example, when Zeta Interactive, an AI marketing company started by former Apple CEO John Scully, acquired eBay's customer relationship marketing division, it added a dramatic capability to Zeta and increased its competitiveness overnight (Hof, 2015). Such a change requires fewer resources than a corporation-wide change and yet still makes the corporation more competitive.

Figure 2.2 shows that there are three pathways through which a mutation can affect the functional area of a corporation. The left-hand side pathway is a contagion process through which the competency is adopted by other staff members who then change their behaviours. In the centre pathway, the staff possessing the competency influence the behaviour of other staff without the competency being transferred. For example, an accounting department may only require one staff member to develop a competency in international company tax in order to support the internationalisation of the company. The right-hand side pathway involves adding a new behaviour to the functional area without affecting the behaviours of other staff in the functional area. In this instance, staff in the functional area become more specialised and perform individualised tasks reflecting their competencies.

Achieving the conditions necessary for strategic mutation

Just as a biological process leaves markers in the circulatory system of the organism, the development of disruptive capability leaves markers in the operations of the corporation. These markers are unique because they reflect the critical characteristics of the mutation. They form the basis of a test for the presence of a strategic mutation and are represented by the acronym "OPEN". All four of the elements of OPEN are necessary for strategic mutation, which will generate and sustain a new and valuable competency in a new environment system.

Open business system: Elements of an open business system are owned by both the corporation and by other corporations in the business system and function as part of both the corporation and environment. A manufacturing process which includes some outsourced activities is a simple example of an open system. More complex open systems also include elements with interdependencies, dynamic characteristics and pathway choices. A corporation must be capable of both operating within open systems and interacting with the environment in order for the mutation stimulus from the environment to affect one of its systems. The biological world provides evidence for the importance of this. Organisms with a very strong ability to repel the stimulus of viruses, such as sharks, mutate infrequently and evolve very slowly. They would not be competitive in a rapidly changing environment. A biological organism must also have mechanisms that can accept modification.

Permanent adaptation: Permanent adaptation is a key characteristic and is required to sustain the acquired ability. Business systems naturally try to return to their original state. In order for a mutation to have an effect, the corporation's systems must accept permanent change. Typically, bureaucracies are resistant to change and will therefore attempt to suppress the mutation before it affects the systems. In the biological world, internal immune systems constantly monitor, identify and destroy mutations. Some of these mutations slip through, however, and introduce new characteristics to the organism, which can lead to increased competitiveness (or weakness). Once a mutation has changed the behaviour of a function in the corporation, the corporation must be able to adapt to the new characteristics of that function. An inability to adapt to and utilise the new characteristic will interfere with the increased competitiveness.

Emerging strategies, policies and culture: The new competencies resulting from the mutation must lead to the formation of new dedicated strategies. The development of new strategies, policies and culture in the corporation is evidence that the mutation has increased the competitiveness of the corporation. If no competitive advantage is created, the mutation is ignored and there is no effect on the competitiveness of the corporation. The new strategies, policies and cultures formed to utilise the mutation will also reflect the new conditions in the changed external environment system. The new environmental system provides the opportunities for competition through these new strategies. These new strategies, policies and culture must therefore reflect the new opportunities available in the altered environmental system which create a comparative advantage. In the biological world, the acquisition of competitive competencies will lead to behavioural changes. A mutation producing a greater capacity for thought, for example, would encourage the organism to adopt the strategy of planning prior to action, while a mutation increasing strength would lead to the strategy of direct confrontation.

New system competencies: New strategies based on competitiveness increasing mutations will require the development of new complementary competencies. They must also be relevant to the new external environment system so that the advantage created by the mutation can be effectively applied. The application of competencies developed for the old external environmental system is a mimetic behaviour which is likely to mask the advantage of the strategic mutation. In the biological world, these new competencies are the modified genes of the organism. Changes in competencies reflect changes in strategy and policy and a new path for the evolution of the corporation (Sammut-Bonnici and Wensley, 2002).

Conclusion

Disruption as a business strategy is intrinsically attractive to any corporation which views its industry and itself as a system. The required long-term systems thinking orientation is not common among today's corporations, however, but is likely to be a more prevalent feature of Future Corporations. The introduction of rare and inimitable capabilities such as these requires leadership with a deeply informed and diverse understanding of what these characteristics mean, how they are developed and how they are maintained (Franklin, 2001). This type of capability development cannot be outsourced and a lack of understanding or commitment to this capability will limit its development. Authentic leadership is the best approach for building these capabilities. Building the conditions necessary for familiarity with disruption, the ability to respond under urgent conditions, high levels of organisational energy and innovative behaviours involves introducing characteristics to the corporation which are rare and unfamiliar (Plummer, 2019).

Corporations are generally familiar with taking action; however, the actions required for disruption and strategic mutation are untaken when conditions are at their most uncertain. Corporations are inherently conservative, relying on systems and experience for decision-making. Actions taken to disrupt and mutate usually have no precedent. Therefore, taking action under these conditions requires faith, responsiveness and a stakeholder perspective (Duzel and Guitart-Masip, 2013). These are the characteristics which leadership must demonstrate if the strategy is to be successful.

Corporations such as Facebook, Apple, Uber and Google have understood these needs and their leaders demonstrate many of these characteristics. Consideration of the economic costs associated with disrupting industries also needs to form part of their leadership. While it may be argued that disruption leads to long-term increases in competitiveness and therefore greater economic efficiency, there is little doubt that the economic costs of disruption in the short term are significant to an industry system (Lund et al., 2020). Use of strategic disruption to create discontinuities to facilitate strategic mutation within the corporation, therefore, also needs to be viewed with economic responsibility.

References

Amazon. Amazon Dash Cart, Make Your Quick Trip Even Quicker. https://www.amazon.com/b?node=21289116011. Accessed 18/01/2022.

Amazon. Introducing the First Fresh Grocery Store. https://www.aboutamazon.com/news/retail/introducing-the-first-amazon-fresh-grocery-store. Accessed 18/01/2022.

Bandoim, L. Uber Plans to Launch Food-Delivery Drones. *Forbes*, Oct 23, 2018 https://www.forbes.com/sites/lanabandoim/2018/10/23/uber-plans-to-launch-food-delivery-drones/?sh=224c4006e147. Accessed 03/02/2022.

Birkinshaw, J., Zimmermann, A., & Raisch, S. How do Big Firms Adapt to Discontinuous Change? Bridging the Dynamic Capabilities and Ambidexterity Perspectives. *California Management Review*, 59(4), 2016, 36–58.

Bostik, M. Building Resilience from Disruption. *Harvard Business Review Analytic Services* (Report), 28th Sep, https://hbr.org/sponsored/2017/09/building-resilience-from-disruption, downloded May 1, 2018.

Boylan, B. M., McBeath, J., & Wang, B. US–China Relations: Nationalism, the Trade War, and COVID-19. *Fudan J. Hum. Soc. Sci.* 14, 2021, 23–40. https://doi.org/10.1007/s40647-020-00302-6

Bughin J, & Van Zeebroeck N. The Best Response to Digital Disruption: Companies that Adopt Bold Strategies in the Face of Industry Digitization Improve Their Odds of Coming out Winners. *MIT Sloan Management Review*, 58(4), 2017, 80–86.

Burt, G. Why Are We Surprised at Surprises? Integrating Disruption Theory and System Analysis with the Scenario Methodology to Help Identify Disruptions and Discontinuities. *Technological Forecasting & Social Change*, 74(6), 2007, 731.

Chesbrough, H. W., & Appleyard, M. M. Open Innovation and Strategy. *California Management Review*, 50(1), 2007, 57–76.

Day, G. S., & Schoemaker, P. J. Adapting to Fast-Changing Markets and Technologies. *California Management Review*, 58(4), 2016, 59.

Day, G. S., Fein, A. J., & Ruppersberger, G. Shakeouts in Digital Markets: Lessons from b2b Exchanges. *California Management Review*, 45(2), 2003, 131–150.

Dekkers. *(R)Evolution: Organizations and the Dynamics of the Environment.* Springer Science & Business Media, New York, 2005.

Duzel, E., & Guitart-Masip, M. Not So Uncertain At Last: Locus Coeruleus and Decision Making. *Neuron*, 79(1), 2013 Jul 10, 9–11.

Ehrnberg, E., & Jacobsson, S. Technological Discontinuity and Competitive Strategy: Revival through FMS for the European Machine Tool Industry? *Technological Forecasting and Social Change*, 44(1), 1993, 27–48.

Engau, C., Hoffmann, V. H., & Busch, T.. Airlines' Flexibility in Facing Regulatory Uncertainty: To Anticipate or Adapt? *California Management Review*, 54(1), 2011, 107 –125.

Fox, K. Why This New York Dairy Ditched Cows After 92 Years And Started Making Nut Milks. *Forbes*, Oct 17, 2017 https://www.forbes.com/sites/katrinafox/2017/10/17/why-this-new-york-dairy-ditched-cows-after-92-years-and-starting-making-nut-milks/?sh=35fb3d8cff82. Accessed 03/02/2022.

Franklin, P. Guest Editorial: From Routine Recipes to Deep Strategic Thinking: Strategy Making as an Intellectual Challenge, Strategic Change, Briefings in Entrepreneurial Finance. *Wiley on Line*, 10(7), 31 October 2001. https://onlinelibrary.wiley.com/doi/10.1002/jsc.561. Accessed 03/02/2022.

Freeman, J., & Engel, J. S. Models of Innovation: Start-Ups and Mature Corporations. *California Management Review*, 50(1), 2007, 94–119.

Gallo, C. How Jeff Bezos Consistently Communicates Four Core Values that Made Amazon a Success. *Forbes*, 11 Feb, 2021. https://www.forbes.com/sites/carminegallo/2021/02/11/how-jeff-bezos-consistently-communicates-four-core-values-that-made-amazon-a-success/?sh=5128b9386e24. Accessed 05/03/2022.

Giammona, C. Aldi and Lidl Take Supermarket Battle to the U.S. *Bloomberg*, 12 Jun, 2017, https://www.bloomberg.com/news/articles/2017-06-12/european-grocery-rivalry-expands-to-u-s-as-aldi-lidl-bulk-up. Accessed 03/02/2018.

Green, D., Jeff Bezos Has Said that Amazon Has Had Failures Worth Billions of Dollars: Here Are Some of the Biggest Ones. *Business Insider Australia*, Mar. 13, 2019, https://www.businessinsider.com.au/amazon-products-services-failed-discontinued-2019-3?r=US&IR=T. Accessed 03/02/2022.

Gronholt-Pedersen, J. and Thomsen, J. A. Lego to Cut 1,400 Staff as Decade-long Sales Boom Ends. *Reuters*, Sep5, 2017, https://www.reuters.com/article/us-lego-results/lego-to-cut-1400-staff-as-decade-long-sales-boom-ends-idUSKCN1BG0WK. Accessed 15/01/2018.

Grübler A. Diffusion: Long-term Patterns and Discontinuities. *Technological Forecasting and Social Change*, 39(1), 1991, 159–180.

Harford, T. Why Big Companies Squander Good Ideas. *Financial Times*, London, September 6 2018. https://www.ft.com/content/3c1ab748-b09b-11e8-8d14-6f049d06439c?emailId=5b9298b1918d4a0004b98d0f&segmentId=2e4343f6-b08f-9184-785d-0a53b99d57bf. Accessed 02/02/2022.

Hof, R., Eyeing Expansion, Zeta Interactive Buys eBay's CRM Division. *Forbes*, Nov 2, 2015 https://www.forbes.com/sites/roberthof/2015/11/02/eyeing-expansion-zeta-interactive-buys-ebays-crm-division/?sh=25003b4e2d8a. Accessed 03/02/2022.

Hunter, P. *Strategic Revitalisation: A Strategic Business Model of Innovation and Growth*, Doctor of Business Administration Thesis, Graduate School of Business and Law, RMIT University, Melbourne, Australia, 2000.

Johnson, P. Competition for Boeing As COMAC's C919 is the New Kid on the Block. *Forbes*, Dec 17, 2015. https://www.forbes.com/sites/pierrjohnson/2015/12/17/competition-for-boeing-as-comacs-c919-is-the-new-kid-on-the-block/?sh=51ff800a176c

Johnson-Cramer M., Parise S., & Cross R. Managing Change through Networks and Values. *California Management Review*, 49(3), 2007, 85–109.

Lashinsky, A., Alibaba v. Tencent: The Battle for Supremacy in China. *Fortune*, June 21, 2018. https://fortune.com/longform/alibaba-tencent-china-internet/. Accessed 02/02/2022.

Lund, S., Manyika, J., Woetzel, J., Barriball, E., Krishnan, M. Alicke, K., Birshan, M., George, K., Smit, S., Swan, D, and HutzlerRisk, K. Resilience, and Rebalancing in Global Value Chains. *McKinsey Global Institute*, August 6, 2020, https://www.mckinsey.com/business-functions/operations/our-insights/risk-resilience-and-rebalancing-in-global-value-chains. Accessed 03/02/2022.

Mangram, M. E., The globalization of Tesla Motors: A Strategic Marketing Plan Analysis. *Journal of Strategic Marketing*, *20*(4), 2012, 289–312.

Morris, J. How Did Tesla Become the Most Valuable Car Company in the World? *Forbes*, Jun 14, 2020, https://www.forbes.com/sites/jamesmorris/2020/06/14/how-did-tesla-become-the-most-valuable-car-company-in-the-world/?sh=177945c8f473. Accessed 03/02/2022.

Plummer, M., A Short Guide to Building Your Team's Critical Thinking Skills. *Harvard Business Review*, October 11, 2019, https://hbr.org/2019/10/a-short-guide-to-building-your-teams-critical-thinking-skills. Accessed 03/02/2022.

Rosenbloom, R., & Christensen, C. Technological Discontinuties, Organizational Capabilities, and Strategic Commitments. *Industrial and Corporate Change*, 3(3), 1994, 655–685.

Sammut-Bonnici, R., & Wensley, R., Darwinism, Probability and Complexity: Market-Based Organizational Transformation and Change Explained through the Theories of Evolution. *International Journal of Management Reviews*, 4(3), 2002, 291–315.

Sanchez R. Strategic Management at the Point of Inflection: Systems, Complexity and Competence Theory. *Long Range Planning*, 30(6), 1997, 939–946.

Schumpeter, J. A. *An Inquiry into Profits, Capital, Credit, Interest, and the Business Cycle*. Cambridge, MA, Harvard University Press, 1934.

Schumpeter, J. A. *Capitalism, Socialism and Democracy*. London: Routledge, 1994 [1942], pp. 82–83. ISBN 978-0-415-10762-4. Retrieved 23 November 2011.

Sheetz, M. Virgin Galactic Says Each Spaceport It Launches from is a $1 Billion Annual Revenue Opportunity. *CNBC*, Nov 6 2020. https://www.cnbc.com/2020/11/06/virgin-galactic-each-spaceport-is-1-billion-annual-revenue-opportunity.html. Accessed 03/02/2022.

Six Sigma Daily. Working Backwards: Amazon Uses Lean Six Sigma to Improve Customer Satisfaction. March 22, 2021. https://www.sixsigmadaily.com/working-backwards-amazon-lean-six-sigma-customer-satisfaction/

Smith, D. Brutal Competition Batters Supermarkets the World Over. *The Guardian*, 5th Oct 2014.

Stringham, E. P., Miller, J. K., & Clark, J. Overcoming Barriers to Entry in an Established Industry: Tesla Motors. *California Management Review*, 57(4), 2015, 85–103.

Suarez, F., & Lanzolla, G. The Half-truth of First-mover Advantage. *Harvard Business Review*, (April 2005). https://hbr.org/2005/04/the-half-truth-of-first-mover-advantage

Zaida, L., Priesmeyer, H., Richard, A., & Mark, P. Nonlinear systems theory: A more dynamic approach to international strategic management. *Managerial Finance*, 25(2), 1999, 16–29.

3 Strategic foundations of the Future Corporation

Paul Hunter

Introduction

The mid-1960s lay witness to the time when the roots of modern management theory were established. Notable among scholars contributing to the foundation of strategy and organisational structuring was Alfred Chandler (1962) whose book *Strategy and Structure* described practices related to these topics in post-war, multidivisional (M-Form) corporations. Fundamental to his work was the identification of the nature of the M-Form, one characterised by a phenomenon of structure follows strategy and systems follow structure. Another was Richard Cyert who collaborated with James March to co-author a book that reflected their views on the topic of the behavioural theory of the firm (Cyert and March,1963). A third was Joseph Bower (1970) who extended Chandler's findings through his research concerned with the resource allocation process adopted by M-Form corporations of that period.

From that base, many advances in corporate strategy and structuring practices had emerged by the mid-1980s. So much so that in the late 1980s, Professors Christopher Bartlett and Sumantra Ghoshal (Bartlett and Ghoshal,1993) embarked on a research programme that would lead them to an understanding of the specifics of those developments and, more importantly, what the implications were. Focusing solely on the work of Chandler, Cyert and March and Bower, their findings were published in summary form in the *Strategic Management Journal* (SMJ) titled "Beyond the M-Form: Toward a Managerial Theory of the Firm". In their article, the authors described the extent of change that had occurred in the field of strategy and structure since the mid-1960s. It was, in their view, substantial, to the extent, they suggested, that it was time to create a new "managerial theory of the firm". This new theory would replace Chandler's "top-down", machine-like hard-edged strategy-structure-system hierarchies, superseding them with a form of structuring observed within European conglomerate, Asea Brown Boveri (now known as ABB) which they referred to as a "proliferation and subsequent aggregation of small independent entrepreneurial units, managed from the bottom up".

From the perspective of observers in 2022, it is apparent again that much has changed in the corporate strategy and structuring domain. Investments in

DOI: 10.4324/9781003183679-3

the digital revolution have commenced and new, flexible post-Covid-19 work practices are everyday occurrences. The purpose of this chapter is to revisit the questions asked by Bartlett and Ghoshal. Rather than a study of the past though, the focus of this chapter is on the future. It is a study of the plausible and possible characteristics of corporate level strategy and organisational structures in use by the Future Corporation. The discussion starts in the here and now, with an exploration of the features of the business environment from which the corporation of the future will evolve. This understanding is treated as the starting point of a story of its journey back to today. The strategic management methodology applied to do this is referred to as backcasting.

Following the direction set by Bartlett and Ghoshal, this chapter intends to "identify emerging organisational forms and their logics, rather than a description of the average or the dominant patterns" (Bartlett and Ghoshal,1993). In particular, the contributing research was focused on the identification of organisational forms that demonstrated strategies that relied on organisational structuring methods reflective of a networked and system-based format. The ideal structure is observed in its "organisational forms and their logics" as described by Chandler (1962) and determined to be a predominant characteristic of the Future Corporation. A confirmation of the adoption of a systems-based format as a predominant structuring methodology is expressed by several commentators on this topic. The global consulting firm, Deloitte, for example, observes the continued rise of business ecosystems and their impact on society, the economy and businesses (Deloitte, 2022). In academia, Julian Birkinshaw (2019) suggests that businesses today are deliberately structuring themselves in the form of (eco) systems.

However. the idea is not new according to Deloitte. They refer to *Harvard Business Review* contributor, James Moore (1993), who is an active proponent of systems structuring, suggesting it "should not be viewed as a member of a single industry but as part of a business (eco)system that crosses a variety of industries". This construct is said to achieve value beyond the boundaries of any single, independent business. With these observations in mind, the research method used to establish a depiction of the Future Corporation is based on an adaptation of Bartlett and Ghoshal's research method.

Research method

Fundamental to the research method deployed by Bartlett and Ghoshal was their approach to data collection. It relied on an interpretation of findings from the same perspective as Chandler, which was to extract the point of view of the "busy men responsible for the destiny of the enterprise" (Chandler, 1962). This meant that Bartlett and Ghoshal were required to undertake face-to-face interviews with senior executives as well as a physical review of company records. This form of research Chandler argued was far superior to the overly academic views evolved by social scientists working from theoretical concepts The source of this view Bartlett and Ghoshal note was Weber (1964), who supported an interpretative approach to the evaluation of social behaviour. This, Weber proposed, would allow researchers to better understand the causes of behaviour and the associated effects (Weber, 1964). In other words, Bartlett and Ghoshal sought to obtain insight into contemporary strategy and structuring methods from a perspective of practice as opposed to (social) scientific conjecture.

Ready access to data via the internet and sheer common sense meant that a less invasive approach to data gathering was appropriate. This decision allowed the researchers to rely on a remote, online analysis drawn directly from Fortune 500 corporations or similar. Information was obtained through the probing of credible publications available within the public domain, published papers, journal articles and company websites.

Those selected for scrutiny had to demonstrate a leaning towards a strategy practice that consciously or subconsciously demonstrated a dynamic, systemic approach to strategy, and ideally, an organisational structuring discipline oriented towards an integrated value system. An illustration of that system is shown in Figure 3.1.

An integrated value system has been developed by Paul Hunter (2020); it provides structure to strategy in a form that is readily translated into an organisation structure. Grounded in empirical research, its physical construct is made up of two subsystems. The first is an outside-in, top-down oriented dynamic market system. The second is an inside-out, bottom-up core competence platform. Each is described as follows.

1) **Dynamic market system**. A market-driven, interactive system designed to engage, capture, inform and retain customers found within specific categories, locations, interests and other personal preferences. Its construct is made up of the two dimensions described as follows:

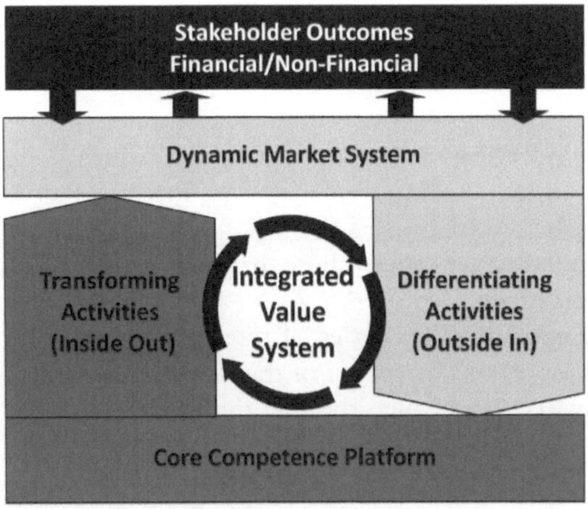

Figure 3.1 An integrated value system.

i. **Sustainable/renewable industry/market position.** Recognised as something a company *has* – its market share, market position, market niche – it is the epitome of the focus of strategy espoused by Michael Porter (1985).

ii. **Differentiating activities.** Representative of things that an organisation *does,* Porter defined the notion of differentiation in his paper What Is Strategy? (Porter, 1996) as the act of "deliberately choosing a different set of activities to deliver a unique mix of value". These activities, he proposed, were *the* fundamental components of strategy.

2) **Core competence platform.** The combination of "inimitable" resources/(core) competencies or unique, tangible (plant and equipment, technology) or intangible (brands) assets possessed by an organisation and transforming activities; those activities required to strengthen a corporation's resource base.

Each is described as follows.

i. **Resource/core competence (inside-out).** Also something the firm has; this component of the integrated value system originates from the concept known as the resource-based view (RBV) of the firm (Penrose, 1959). The definition of resources in this context are as strategic assets (Aaker, 1989). These include competences, brands, knowledge, learning systems, specialist plant and equipment, management information systems and broad-based technology platforms (Wernerfelt, 1984). The RBV concept was developed further by Prahalad and Hamel, who referred to them in a broader context of the core competence of the corporation (Prahalad and Hamel, 1990).

ii. **Transforming activities (inside-out).** Defined as something a firm *does*; the notion of transforming activities is described (Hunter, 2020) as an extension of the scholastic description of "dynamic capabilities" (Teece et al., 1990). Similar to differentiation in the marketplace, transforming activities are those that alter the resource base. There are three types of dynamic capabilities (Ambrosini, Bowman and Collier, 2009), they are:

a. **Incremental transforming activities.** Those capabilities concerned with the continuous improvement of the firm's resource base.
b. **Renewing transforming activities.** Those that refresh, adapt and augment the resource base.
c. **Regenerative transforming activities.** Those that impact the firm's resource base and its current set of transforming activities, that is, those activities that change the way the firm changes its resource base.

A compounding characteristic of those organisations identified for further analysis was a demonstration of a structuring method that favoured a networked, collaborative approach to both the management of an organisation's operations and servicing of markets within which it competes. Such characteristics would or could confirm its potential to become a leader/member of a corporate collaborative system. This construct is defined here as a collaboration of transaction processing entities that deploy platform-based services capable of hosting many large commercial networks. As an integrated network, a corporate collaborative system is capable of delivering greater depth and value in its service offering than those limited to singular products and services delivered on a piecemeal basis. Such a system can be likened to a health system rather than an independent hospital for instance. As a virtual and interconnected network, a health system is made up of precision instruments, medical equipment, insurance, management information systems, research and health services addressing prevention, treatment, cure and rehabilitation. In contrast, a hospital is constrained to that of a centralised physical building prioritised for health treatment with other services treated more like extras than components of an integrated system. In a corporate context, a dynamic corporate collaborative system can be likened to Amazon or Apple rather than a bookshop or even a bookshop chain. Those corporations that met the foregoing criteria are Meta, Alphabet, Amazon, Microsoft, Shell, Phillips Health, DHL, Corning, Sysco, Toyota, Uber and Bitcoin.

Backcasting: the context of the transformation journey

In the conduct of the backcasting journey described next, Bartlett and Ghoshal once again provide guidance. This time in reference to their work published subsequent to their 1993 SMJ journal article and summarised in their book "The Individualized Corporation" (Ghoshal and Bartlett, 1999). In it, the authors identify a structure of organisational transformation they describe as a *process of corporate renewal* (Ghoshal and Bartlett, 1999). Drawing on this content, his own research and a related contribution (Gouillart and Kelly, 1996), Hunter (2000) developed a corporate transformation framework he refers to as a *Cycle of Organisational Transformation and Renewal.* Each of the stages of that framework is illustrated in Figure 3.2. It is deployed here to provide a structure to the backcasting journey described in this chapter.

The four stages are described as follows:

Stage 1: Reframing. As the starting point of the transformation journey, reframing is an essential exercise that encourages free, creative, critical and challenging

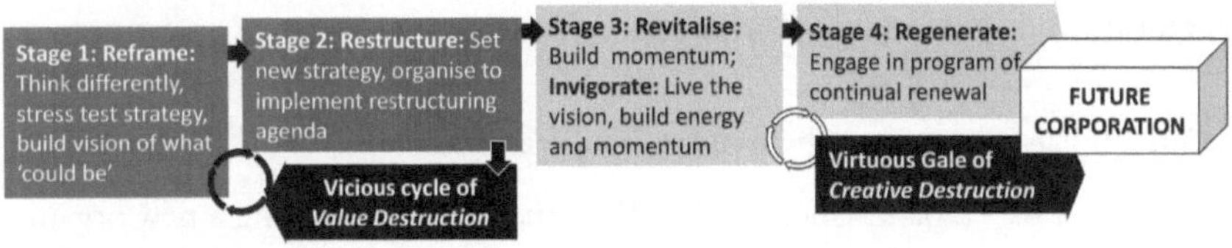

Figure 3.2 Cycle of organisational transformation and renewal.

strategic thinking. Its objective – perhaps challenge – is to break down the dominant logics (Prahald and Bettis, 1986) of teams; particularly those engaged in strategising activities. These logics represent the negative attributes that act as blockers to innovation, free thought and positive strategising activities. They include long-held beliefs, embedded (adverse) cultures, sacred cows and other forms of bias that are detrimental to constructive strategic thinking.

Stage 2: Restructuring. Hunter's (2000) research showed that insufficient imagination or lack of future-oriented, strategic thinking carried a strong likelihood of failure (value destruction). As illustrated in Figure 3.2, those organisations that focus on restructuring alone face a risk that plans for change will end up destroying value rather than creating it. The usual cause of value destruction was an unintended entrapment in a downward spiral of cost reduction, often considered internally to be the only viable source of competitive advantage.

Stage 3: Revitalisation. A process of morale and business building deemed necessary as a result of the enormity of change created as a result of the Stage 2 restructuring. An ability to survive restructuring and revitalisation provides entry to the Stage 4 experience of regeneration.

Stage 4: Regeneration. A programme of continual organisational renewal. This is an organisation demonstrative of Schumpeter's (1934) definition of entrepreneurship whereby entrepreneurs: "create a perennial 'gale of creative destruction". Enabled by optimistic momentum, it is characterised by ongoing growth, positive value creation, effective management of resources and the entrepreneurial drive to pioneer new and innovative opportunities as they arise or are created.

Based on the principle that the generic purpose of backcasting is to provide plausible and causal connections from the future to the here and now, the discussion in this chapter continues with this framework as the roadmap, from the future to today.

The journey described in this chapter starts with, and is based on, a depiction of a corporation residing in Stage 4. No depiction of the future, however, can be established without a fundamental understanding of the reality of today. The starting point for discussion, therefore, is an overview of elements of relevance in the business environment of today. Key to the discussion is the notion of socionology – a description of the blending of a future environment that survives through an ability to integrate the hard power of new, mostly digitalised technology with that of increasing demands for greater engagement, awareness and responses to the soft issues of social and societal welfare. Other dynamics to consider are the rise of technology and a systems perspective of organisational structuring and associated corporate strategy.

Socionology as a platform for strategy implementation

According to Bartlett and Ghoshal (1993), corporations innovating a new organisational form close to the late 1980s were relying on a premise that the importance of capital and scale was being replaced by knowledge and expertise. While the latter has assumed new levels of importance, capital and scale remain extremely important today. Still in the form of economies of scale (high volume, global distribution), but also from the perspective of economies of scope (producing a wider variety of goods or services in tandem – complementarity) and potentially the attractiveness of bespoke (personalisation at scale). Rather than factories and chimneys, the main enabler of scale and scope will be found within the corporation's technological infrastructure and human capability. Although not a manufacturer, Amazon has amassed a technological capability that is typical of this form of operation. Hence its strong growth in the physical delivery of goods and services as well as its presence in the cloud-based data warehousing industry (Amazon Web Services [AWS]), where its revenue now represents 10% of annual sales (Novet, 2021).

Now, in 2022, insight into the future of business is provided from an observation about the future of the internet made by Facebook CEO Mark Zuckerberg. Published by the BBC (BBC, 2021), Zuckerberg was reporting on the pending development of a new internet platform known as Web 3.0, or in his terminology, the metaverse. The report is based on an announcement that Zuckerberg made in October 2021 that he is committed to hiring 10,000 people in Europe to establish the foundations of the metaverse. Demonstrating a degree of caution however, Zuckerberg acknowledges in his post that a Meta construct would not be built quickly and that it would require the cooperation of several parties to do so. (BBC, 2021). To cope with the enormity of the task, he professes his willingness to collaborate with others in its development. Proclaiming an expectation that the true metaverse will take another 10 to 15 years to materialise, he also expressed his desire to get the transformation started quickly. Such was the extent of his commitment to start quickly and endure the journey, he proclaimed in early November 2021 that Facebook would change its name to reflect that ambition, the new name being Meta (Murphy, 2021).

Web 3.0 is the embodiment of a socionological platform in practice in the Future Corporation. It provides the link between the soft sciences of societal behaviour and the hard science of technology. As a technology that stores information in an encrypted digital format of distributed ledgers (a blockchain), this is recognised as the most likely technological host for Web 3.0. Transaction processing and potentially social interaction are enabled via a virtual ledger where each event is reliant on a predetermined contractual arrangement for authentication exercised on a basis of trust between the parties. Using this technology, transaction processing and intercompany movement of goods and services are initiated automatically and processed seamlessly; always protected by encrypted providence (Silver, 2020).

Digitalisation of everything and Web 3.0 are not the only technologies that will be key influencers and drivers of massive change in the future. Other examples of potential/imminent, ground-breaking technology include quantum computing, space travel and nuclear fusion. Until recently, Quantum computing was considered to be a few decades away. Now it is expected to be operational by the mid-2030s. This claim was expressed in November 2021 by a director of the Silicon Quantum Computing (SQC) organisation, Michelle Simmons (Thomson, 2021). She reported that an SQC research partner, Silex Systems, was about to start work on a pilot plant that will produce a highly specialised form of silicon that is a key ingredient in the specialist computer chips SQC needs to put their quantum algorithms into action. The key benefit of the accelerated computing power offered by Quantum according to *Forbes* (Kaafaran, 2021) is that it could provide "an efficient solution for computational problems that may never be solved on a conventional machine". In essence, Quantum provides the means for substantial analytical processing capabilities delivering benefits on a scale that, as yet, is difficult to imagine.

Similarly, now emerging from a very long gestation period, space travel has arrived and along with that, realistic expectations of broad-based commercial activities have been activated. SpaceX, Blue Horizon and Virgin Galactic each completed tourism journeys into space in 2021. It was also the year that NASA awarded SpaceX a US$2.9 billion contract to transport astronauts from lunar orbit to the surface of the moon (Chang, 2021). While space tourism, research and satellite launching are the current services in demand, future plans include the colonisation of the Moon and Mars for mining, remote manufacturing and a role as a launch pad for further exploration of deep space.

In another breakthrough in 2021, a Massachusetts Institute of Technology offshoot, Commonwealth Fusion Systems (CFS), announced that the company had succeeded in building an experimental (nuclear fusion) reactor. Due for completion in 2025, CFS plans to build a fully commercial power plant by the early 2030s (Thornhill, 2021). Needless to say, unlike nuclear fission, the fusion version offers the ecological and financial benefits of free, clean energy that is powerful enough to fuel the sun.

Even with all the technological capabilities available now or forthcoming, a fundamental premise is applied to this chapter that assumes humans will always own it, control it and have a capacity to either extend it or undo it. That is not to say the risk of this not happening is not high or unrecognised. There is no doubt that it is an issue that needs to be addressed urgently. Such an awareness however must be followed by positive, adaptive and inventive action. Julia Powles, Associate Professor of Law and Technology at the University of Western Australia, was reported by the *Financial Times* (Murphy, 2021) to have stressed her belief that regulation will be key to defining the (constraints) and rules for the kind of technology that Web 3.0 represents. Such measures Powles suggests could include the use of permits, licences, fees or taxes. On the other extreme, decision-making is a form of human nature, which, in turn, is rarely enforceable and is subject to bias, inaccuracies, vagueness and distraction (Kahneman et al., 2021). There must be mechanisms in place to ensure those factors of human nature do not find their way into Web 3.0, AI-based decision-making.

Adoption of a systems approach to corporate strategy and structuring

Given the enormity of change that leaders face within this world of extreme volatility and uncertainty, an awareness of the value of organic, system-based leadership styles and organisation structuring has risen dramatically. Similar to the post-Covid-19 changes to work practices, for example, business leaders are now allowing themselves the freedom to adopt far more "open" ways of thinking and leading (EIU, 2020). Early adopters of a fundamental systems approach to thinking and organisational structuring can be observed in many settings. One group consists of proponents of a corporate management model that is referred to as a "living company" (de Gues, 1997). This model draws on the conceptualisation of a corporation that can be related to the biology and ecology of a living system first proposed by Miller (1965). A purer interpretation of a corporation as a living system is one that literally imitates nature. Referred to as biomimicry, this terminology is described by The Institute of Biomimicry as the practice of "emulating natural processes in technological and industrial design". An example is the emerging use of algorithms grounded in insect behavior. These are used to enable autonomous vehicles to communicate and safely interact with each other in real time. Known as swarm behaviour, McFadden (2017) used data analytical techniques (artificial intelligence) to develop simulated algorithms of the way ants navigate around their nests without crashing into each other or impeding the trajectory of fellow ants.

Another example of biomimicry is the application of the structuring of the brain to the design of a corporate collaborative system (described previously). Officially known as cybernetics, an emulation of the brain structure was first applied to management science by Stafford Beer (1972). Referring to it as a viable systems model (VSM), this system is representative of "a model of the organisational structure of any autonomous system capable of producing itself". A description of the elements of a VSM and its application to corporate functions is demonstrated in Figure 3.3. This concept is further adapted and applied to

Five Brain functions	Associated systems of the brain	Corporate functions	Associated elements of corporate strategy
S5: Higher brain functions	Formulation of policy decisions, identity	Ultimate authority, Policy and Strategy, Governance, Purpose	Mission, Vision, Long Term Strategy (Strategic Architecture), Integrated Value System
S4: Mid brain	Connection to the outside world through the senses: plans, projections, forecasts	Forward planning, environmental scanning, stakeholder engagement	Short Term Strategy, Strategy Narrative, Strategy Blueprint
S3: Base brain	Oversees entire complex of muscles/organs, optimises internal environment	Internal regulation, optimisation, synergy	Strategy Implementation: Program of continual strategy renewal
S2: Sympathetic nervous system	Monitors muscles and organs and ensures that their interactions remain stable.	Control: Communication, conflictresolution, stabilisation, training and monitoring	Stakeholder Engagement, Portfolio Management, Organisation Learning, Strategic Alignment
S1: Muscles and organs	Parts of the brain that physically 'do' something; the activities	Operations: Project teams, project management, quality control	Operational efficiency and effectiveness

Figure 3.3 Stafford Beer's construct of the brain assigned to corporate functionality and elements of corporate strategy.

the practice of corporate strategy, the result of which is depicted in the far-right column of Figure 3.3.

Assuming the form of an interactive, web-based network, the construct of a VSM is extrapolated from Beer's interpretation of the structure of a human brain. This construct is further adapted as an organisation structure, as depicted in Figure 3.4.

Within the construct of the VSM illustrated in Figure 3.4, the Meta system can be interpreted as a corporate management system (with no relationship to Zuckerberg's use of the term "meta") – this is the controlling componentry labelled as S5, S4 and S3. The portfolios of corporate collaborative systems can be interpreted to be the operating componentry of the operating systems labelled as S1 and S2. A construct demonstrating these titles appears in Figure 3.5.

An example of a corporate VSM-based system in operation today is Apple. More likely an outcome of savvy leadership as opposed to deliberate design, Apple is a prime example of a corporation that for years has thought differently about its future. It also reflects the presence of a strategic doctrine that reflects the construct of an integrated value system (Figure 3.1). Ultimately, it is demonstrative of a prime level, integration of all of the above, in a form representative of a corporate collaborative value system. The company is famous for its capabilities in design and its approach to strategy and organisation structuring that entices customers to not only stay with them but also invest further as shareholders and as customers.

Apple has been described (Dans, 2021) as an ecosystem made up of several consumer products and gadgets that can interact with each other. As a global corporation however, Apple is much more than that. Apple owns nearly all its functional operations (design, research and development, supply chain, even executive education). One exception is its manufacturing infrastructure. Although outsourced to trusted partners, Apple keeps tight control over their

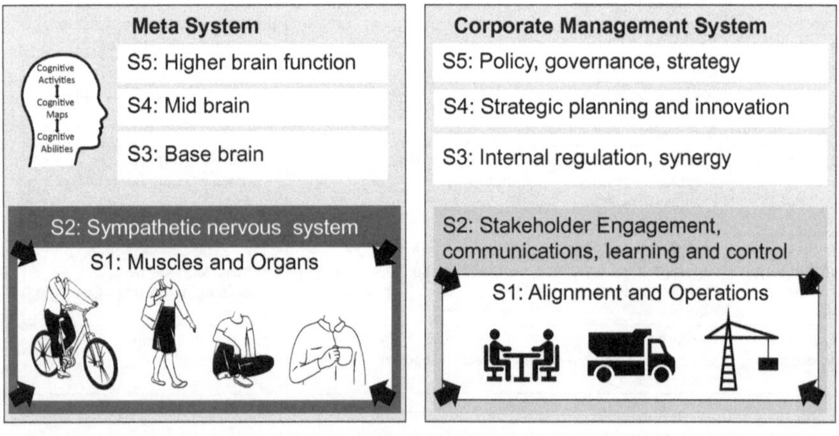

Figure 3.4 Adaptation of Beer's viable systems model of organisational structuring.

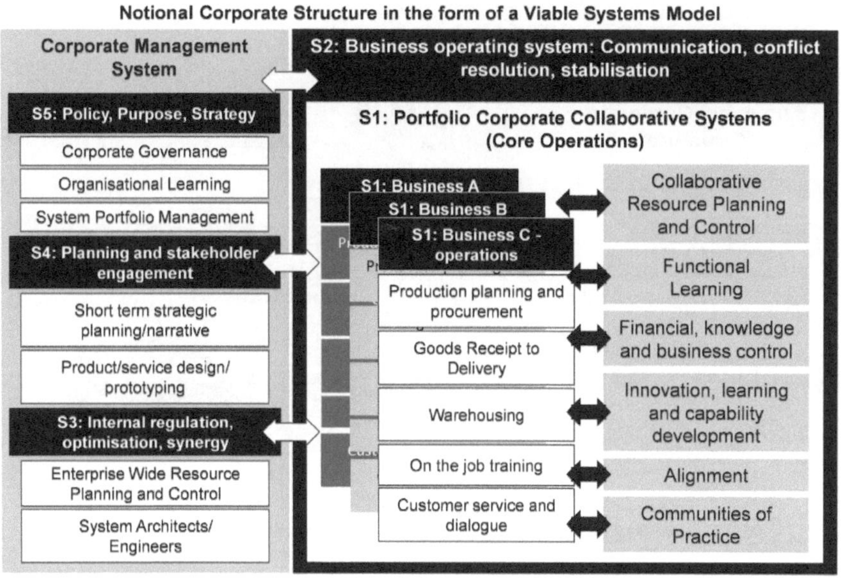

Figure 3.5 Interpretation of Beer's VSM as an organic model of the corporation.

activities, as if they were in fact a part of the Apple company. As explained on its website (Apple, 2020), the purpose of this level of control is to ensure the standard of social behaviours expected by Apple is maintained. According to the *Harvard Business Review* (Podolny and Hansen, 2020), then Apple CEO Steve Jobs in 1997, when seeking to reduce complexity and improve productivity, restructured the entire company under one P&L by combining numerous, disparate functional departments into one functional business entity. The ensuing structure, described as a U-shaped organisation (a functional, as opposed to product-focused, integrated hierarchy), has many benefits (Thompson, 2016). One substantial benefit observed by Dudovskiy, (2021) is its ability to form open collaborations within and across Apple divisions and business units. Clearly, consistent with Chandler's findings, Apple senior executives are very much in control of operations – as a collaboration between members of the network everywhere in the world, from the top down, in similar fashion to that observed by Chandler (1962).

That control emanates from an inside-out, resource-oriented functional hierarchy, the foundation of which is a core competence platform. At the same time, Apple's go to market system (Dans, 2021) can be viewed as a dynamic market system, the top half of the integrated value system proposed by Hunter (Hunter, 2020) and depicted in Figure 3.1. As demonstrated in Figure 3.6, Apple's product/service offering could in fact be interpreted as a fully integrated value system. Lurking in the background too is a depiction of Chandler's M-Form structuring (Bartlett and Ghoshal, 1993). While the construct illustrated in Figure 3.6 does

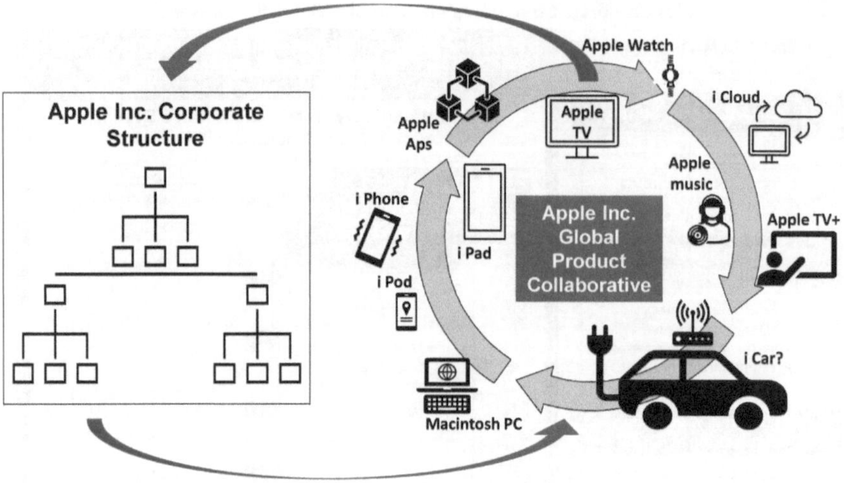

Figure 3.6 Apple as a global, corporate collaborative system.

not necessarily depict such a framework, it could be argued that an M-Form mode of global control is still very much in place. The difference between Bartlett and Ghoshal's interpretation of ABB and Apple, however, is that rather than a collaboration between various groups and divisions of the company, Apple is a systems-based network that operates a portfolio of corporate collaborative systems within one company. Noticeably, both have a corporate control centre which acts as the overall direction setting authority for the corporation.

Commencement of the backcasting journey: a depiction of the Future Corporation

The following is a description of the journey that starts with an envisioned future; a depiction of the Future Corporation in Stage 4. One that is in operation around the decade of the 2040s.

Stage 4 regeneration: A depiction of the Future Corporation as a utopian state of continual renewal

Unlike ABB, the company referred to by Ghoshal and Bartlett (1993) as an aggregation of independent (top-down) entrepreneurial businesses, the Future Corporation is a networked, integrated system. It exists in a similar form to that described in Castells (1996) as one that is continually reinvented and renewed. In other words, it exists as a system residing within a state of continual regeneration; a construct that is sympathetic to the idea of a corporate collaborative system illustrated in a generic format in Figure 3.7.

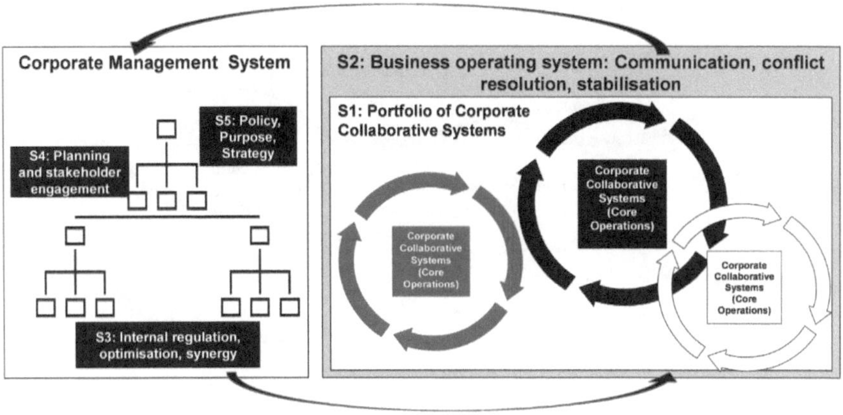

Figure 3.7 Generic corporate collaborative system.

In practice, operational components of the business are split off from the corporate entity and outsourced effectively to form or be a part of the collaborative system as illustrated in Figure 3.7. In this environment, operations are part of a fully automated network and are a primary source of revenue, along with other related corporate collaborative systems. Similarly, forms of ownership are vested in the arms of financers who in turn invest in many forms of corporate collaborative systems – or similar. In the marketplace, Web 3.0 platform-based transactions take place via trust-based, virtual contracts – for all transactions. Similarly, interventions, monitoring and negotiating activities are conducted via virtual and augmented reality – the new interface between humans and super processing computers. At a higher level, managerial decision-making will be conscious of the need to manage within the boundaries of community-based social responsibilities, effective organisational learning, effective corporate strategy and the welfare and personal development of all stakeholders associated with the business entity – and beyond. In the Future Corporation, the sheer volume of information, communication, specialised knowledge and complexity will have to be managed by machines. Responsibility for its management will remain with humans, but AI and associated technologies will be doing all the physical processing.

Apple is only one of three different types of corporate collaborative systems. Each of these three is discussed next with examples from current-day systems described as examples of what is to come.

Group 1: A technologically reliant collaborative. This is a closed collaborative system generally established by a single corporation. As discussed, Apple is representative of a prime member of this group. A prime member is the leading entity, a subprime member is a participant. As illustrated in the case study, Corning Life Sciences, Glass (Silicon and Ceramics) is an emerging prime

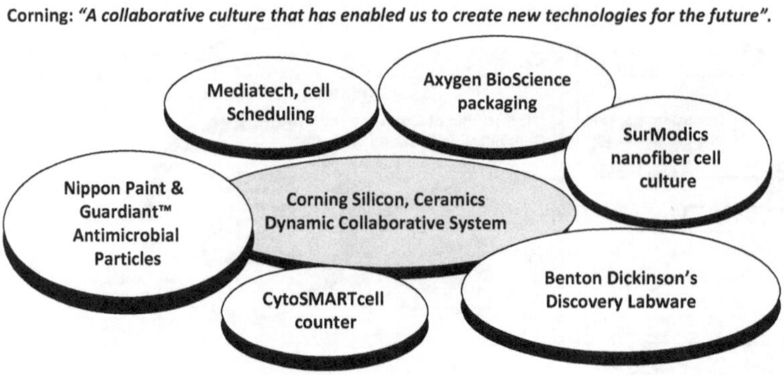

Figure 3.8 Corning Life Sciences, Glass, Silicon and Ceramics business unit is depicted here as an early version of an emerging corporate collaborative system.

member; it currently has several subprime members in its collaborative. An illustration of an emerging corporate collaborative system at this division of Corning is described next and depicted in Figure 3.8.

CASE STUDY: CORNING, AN EMERGING GROUP 1 CORPORATE COLLABORATIVE SYSTEM

Historically known for its Pyrex brand of baking dishes, Corning today describes itself as a world leader in materials science (Corning, 2021). As a supplier to mobility systems, consumer electronics and other high-tech applications, Corning is conscious of its existence as an "upstream" industry participant. It attributes its success to its "sustained investment in research, ... innovation, and close collaboration with customers". Corning demonstrates many characteristics of a primary member of a Group 1 corporate collaborative system. This is evident across its business, one example is its Life Sciences Business Unit, which Corning describes as "a leader in lab products, cell culture solutions, bioprocess vessels, and specialty surfaces". In this capacity, Corning considers it is helping the world by providing more reliable access to medicines. It is achieving this through the use of what they perceive to be revolutionary new glass packaging for the storage and delivery of drugs. As illustrated in Figure 3.8, Corning is doing this in the context of an organically grown corporate collaborative system that has several subprime members that are either partners to Corning or have been acquired by Corning. Ultimately, the Life Sciences, Glass (silicon and ceramics) may emerge as a corporate collaborative system in its own right, similar to Apple, Google and Amazon.

Management of the technology reliant corporate collaborative system

The conduit for the management of the corporation as a corporate collaborative system in this group is the quintessential socionological environment of the Future Corporation. This corporate construct can only be managed and optimised in a social environment that is receptive to the complexity of technology offered by Web 3.0. Other prime members identified from the research group include Alphabet, Microsoft, Shell, Toyota, Phillips Health and DHL.

Most Group 1 companies are consumer-facing businesses, they have little interest in collaborating with others to optimise customer (and stakeholder) value – other than in special circumstances. As high-volume commodity providers, these corporations invest in their own corporate collaborative system to optimise economies of scale and scope. They only include outsiders in their resource set on an as-needed basis, mostly where it makes no sense to own it. Subprime members however may come and go. Examples of subprime members are professional advisers, purveyors of specialist technology and purveyors of specialist, low volume supplies such as rare earths, instruments and contract staff. In making the distinction between a supplier and a collaborative market system member, Apple saw fit to buy the headphone manufacturer Beats (Apple, 2014) rather than design and build their own headphones or invite them to work with them in a collaboration. Group 1 prime members seek to build a customer value proposition which is highly attractive to consumers and thereby less prone to resistance and highly prone to voluntary acceptance. Given the uniqueness of the Apple operating system, for example, it makes a lot more sense for consumers to buy devices that are readily synced with others in the system. Similarly, once a customer has bought into Amazon Prime there are many benefits from buying more from the Amazon family/dynamic market system.

The collaborative systems owned by the above companies have evolved through a process of natural organic growth, complementary acquisition, collaboration or all the above. Apple for example built a corporate collaborative system via organic growth and occasional acquisition. Amazon did the same, although it has become more of an open system by allowing other retailers to rent space and operate sales outlets on its website. These customers are participants in a collaboration but are subject to Amazon's rules and regulations.

As technology evolves so will these already successful corporations adapt and invent. Each of the organisations identified previously is purportedly already looking at Web 3.0 as a future platform for their services, the list of those doing so is growing every day.

Group 2: A predominantly socially oriented format, enabled by high technology. Characterised as an open system that anyone with the right credentials can join, this group is a virtual marketplace where complementarity makes collaborations more sensible. An example of existing collaborative systems typical of this group, but on a smaller scale than major corporations, are cooperatives, traditionally the domain of remote rural farmers. Instead of dairy farmers combining as a cooperative to distribute milk, cream and cheese, for example, a corporate collaborative system will enable them to benefit from a dynamic market system that could be extended to include every stakeholder engaged in the growing, processing, packaging and processing of an entire supply chain/system. Examples of members could be milk suppliers, producers of chocolate, cheese, milk, cakes, biscuits and bread, wholesalers and retailers, resellers and recyclers. There is no reason why producers of jams, tinned fruit and even ocean produce could not join such a collaboration. Corporations identified from the research exhibiting features of the phenomenon or the potential to become a member of this group are Sysco and Uber.

There is a lot that Group 1 corporations can learn from this group of business owners where the value of individuals with skin in the game have a greater involvement and risk than those of suppliers and employees. This ownership naturally evokes different approaches to relationships between each stakeholder. Above and beyond the financial aspects of business, cooperatives often build and share a common code of values and beliefs, and more importantly, a capacity for, and commitment to, sharing them with business partners across the spectrum.

A small cooperative made up of dedicated dairy farmers is portrayed in an Australian Broadcasting Commission (ABC) documentary, *Fightback Farmers: Feeding Australia Together* (ABC, 2022). The story demonstrates how farm-based collaboratives are able to both embrace advanced technology and advance their social "wellness" through the strength of their relationship with other farmers in their network-based, localised communities. Rather than competing with each other, members of the cooperative collaborate through an agreed set of values and purposes. Each of these farmers is oriented towards social ambitions rather than technological (or financial) ones. Recently formed Mountain Milk is an example; their priorities are "the care of our animals, our soils and our waterways". Their objective is to exercise a discipline of transforming activities (demonstrated in Figure 3.1) through a form of organisational learning that equates to "innovate and educate so we can continually improve and strengthen our farms and our community" (ABC, 2022). Given the capacity for social platforms such as Facebook, LinkedIn and Twitter to connect individuals on a global scale, the Future Corporation is well placed to embrace a shared collaboration of like-minded corporate leaders anywhere in the world. Within this cooperative, the farmers appoint representatives from various farms to form a board which makes the "meta"-level corporate management decisions. Everyone then joins in to share experiences in milk production and farm management (a core competence platform) while seeking complementary product and service solutions to build a dynamic market system.

Group 3: A variety of hybrid versions of Group 1 or 2 collaborative systems

In one iteration of this group, a primary member may instigate the emergence of a group of complementary participants that are voluntarily and/or required by others (at the same level) to join in. Those most likely to establish or become members of this corporate collaborative system include professional advisers, small business owners, artists, artisans and musicians. It is a group that will evolve exponentially over time, in the same way that ecosystems evolve in nature.

More recently, digital decentralised autonomous organisations (DAOs) have been formed in a format consistent with this group. An example is Bitcoin, a cryptocurrency based on a blockchain platform. It is described as a form of investor-directed venture capital fund that has no prime member; everyone is equal. A DAO according to Hackle (2021) is defined as “an organisation represented by rules encoded as a transparent computer program, controlled by the organisation members, and not influenced by a central government”. The rules of the game, Hackl advises, are embedded in the platform’s coding in a format which requires limited human intervention. As a fully automated app, its administration requires no human supervision, no bureaucracy and no hierarchical hurdles. Attributes of automation include pre-programmed rules, autonomous functionality and predetermined/consensual rules.

The main value in the formation of a corporate collaborative system is the opportunity to optimise utilisation of knowledge, technology and other scarce resources on a universal scale. It is up to each corporation to decide who and how the collaboration will be administered, funded and “enabled”. Within Groups 1 and 3, each is usually self-administered and funded. Within Group 2 alternatives are (1) a prime host not associated with the collaborative at all, (2) a prime company which is either the founder of the collaborative, the most influential or the biggest and (3) the entity that possesses the greatest control over the financial transactions. That could be the distributed ledger provider. Others that could be interested include the merchandise platform provider – the one that controls all customer data. Alternatively, it could be the one that has a monopoly on production know-how and know-what. Another option is a single corporation that has built its business around the operation and hosting of the metasystem. As discussed previously, the CEO of Meta, Mark Zuckerberg, is a lead player in this ambition.

Stage 3: Revitalisation. Building momentum

Now in the 2030s, this was an era of excitement, enthusiasm and energy generated by design and default. The design component was driven by post-restructuring (Stage 2) recovery programmes that saw displacement, relocations, retraining, replacement and reinvention at the fore. The default outcome was the inevitable but unpredictable and sometimes unintended consequence of change. Now in an era when stale, inefficient businesses are drawing to an end and new challenging and highly efficient businesses have been established, many of which are flourishing, there is at last real hope for optimism. Mostly technology-driven, the ongoing maturation of Web 3.0 and the structuring of corporate collaborative systems is the platform of the day. Just as some corporations were early starters in the transformation journey however, others were happy to, or simply could

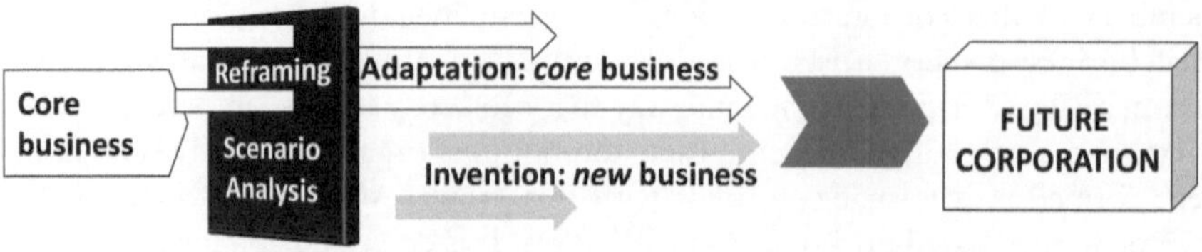

Figure 3.9 An ambidextrous approach to strategically focused organisational transformation.

not, get out of the starting block (Stage 1). For those that were first out, it didn't necessarily mean they were the first into Stage 3. The restructuring journey itself is a long one as illustrated in Figure 3.9. The outcome was not necessarily the establishment of two very different businesses either, but it could be. Those driving change will always need to juggle the two different trajectories shown in the transformation path illustrated in Figure 3.9.

Stage 2: Restructuring. Implementing the new strategic intent

The realisation of the system-based corporate collaborative system was well on the way to replacing industry-focused "Porteresque"-styled organisational structuring in the latter stages of the 2020s. As illustrated in Figure 3.9, arrival at the end of the transformation journey from two streams, but under the management of a single leadership team, is an ambidextrous exercise, and a concept shown through empirical research (Chakravarthy and Lorange, 2007) to be the most effective. The application of this practice provided executive teams with sufficient clarity to nurture "core" business while also engaging in a programme of reinvention. An ambidextrous transformational leadership platform Chakravarthy and Lorange suggest "establishes project teams that are structurally independent units, each having its own processes, structures and cultures, but are integrated into the existing management hierarchy". The extent and scope of transformational complexity vary, its application being dependent on circumstance.

With many corporations in this era still tied to the *hard-edged strategy-structure-system* machine-oriented form of operation dismissed by Bartlett and Ghoshal (1993) as mentioned previously, not everyone was as comfortable as Shell for instance. Having agreed to transform from an oil and coal company to an electricity and other energy company, the transformation journey was expected to be quite straightforward. Having agreed on the strategy internally during the Stage 1 reframing period, Shell executives felt comfortable taking their time in its transformation from one profitable company format to another. It could simply roll with the dynamics of the energy industry, or so it thought. With such latitude available to it, it came as quite a shock when it was ordered by a court of law to speed things up for external environmental reasons (Raval, 2021).

In contrast, the transformation from a lighting company to a health services company was an excruciating journey for Phillips. A new health division was the outcome of a transformation from a struggling company operating in the lighting industry. It saw its entry into an entirely new industry as its saviour (Gillezeau, 2019). As demonstrated previously, Corning demonstrated how a small, but profitable division can be transformed on a progressive basis through continual acquisition and partnering. The Corning approach is a middle-of-the-road process that enabled the corporation to slowly evolve through continual organic and inorganic extensions to the core.

Few transformations are as well planned as German-based engineering and technology company, Robert Bosch GmbH. Having been through an extensive exercise in reframing, it announced in early 2022 that it would prepare for its restructuring with an initial commitment to spending some €2bn on retraining around 400,000 of its staff from the automotive component division of its company. The writing was on the wall – its core automotive business would have to be absorbed into existing businesses or split off into a new business that hadn't yet been invented. If history repeats, the worst-case scenario for mishandled restructuring is the formation of a similar movement formed by those affected by the dramatic change, as shown in the first Industrial Revolution that took place throughout the late 1800s. Known as the Luddites, this was a group of disempowered employees who felt they had no other choice than to physically fight for their survival. The group is renowned for smashing machines and burning down factories that had threatened to or already had replaced their jobs through the introduction of high-volume automated machinery. The authorities of the day are equally renowned for their response, which was to deploy the army who were prone to shoot when rebels resisted or round them up for transportation to Australia – or simply hang them (Brain, 2022). In some ways, evidence of Luddite behaviour has already occurred in recent times. One of many examples is the taxi industry – in 2014, drivers in many cities in the world deliberately caused traffic jams, denied customers their service and generally wreaked havoc when the industry disrupter Uber entered what they saw as a market they owned (Free, 2014).

On the flip side, there were also many winners at a time when corporate transformation plans were well underway and good progress was being made. It was a time when core business was readily optimised as essential commodities continued to be in high demand. In Australia, for example, it became apparent that there would be no producers of the essential "fossil fuel" product – petrol. All current producers had announced plans to close their inefficient and declining oil refining facilities, leaving Australia without any petrol supplier at all. To address this problem, the Australian government had to intervene. It was in effect forced to offer substantial subsidies to the two remaining producers who were then happy to continue operations for a while longer (Reuters, 2021).

From a societal perspective, it was only at this time that politicians and business leaders appreciated the reality of the technological explosion that was seeping through the Covid -19 barriers. It was a time when the Bank of England, for example, along with many other central banks, was seriously considering the use of digital currency – "Britcoin" or similar. It was a time when car manufacturers were committing billions in the electrification and hydrogenation of cars, trucks and buses. Their strategy now involved an ambition to transform into providers of "mobility systems" (Abuelsamid, 2019). Exercising control over the power of AI attracted the attention of the more philosophical leaders of business who were fretting about its downsides. No less an authority than the late Steven Hawking, for example, had already declared AI represented the end of humankind (Cellan-Jones, 2014). Elon Musk, the SpaceX and Tesla founder, held a view on AI that is consistent with Hawking's warning. Musk is reported to have uttered a similar warning that suggests that building AI is similar to building a kill switch for humanity.

This is also an era of design, a time when big bet moves were made. It is an era unlike any of the three revolutions that have gone before, this is the so-called Fourth Industrial Revolution (Schwab, 2016). That is because the focus is as much on the societal, behavioural outcomes from change as it is on the financial outcomes. It needed to be one that was enabled by technology rather than a slave of technology. It demanded a capacity for deep and critical strategic thinking. Unlike previous revolutions, this era was all about agility in thinking, flexibility in resource allocation, adaptiveness to change and deliberate/disruptive invention.

Stage 1: Reframing. Thinking differently about the future

Still in its infancy, Web 3.0 today is more conceptual than real. As demonstrated previously, Apple appears to have adopted or even invented many of the attributes of the Future Corporation, both technological and social. So confident is The Deloitte Centre for Integrated Research (Deloitte Insights, 2020) that web 3.0 is a reality, they predict it will have replaced Web 2.0 (the current platform) by 2030. Referring to it as the "Spatial Web", the fundamental technology is made up of a combination of converged technologies. These include virtual reality, AI, machine learning, 3D printing, geolocation mapping, pervasive computing and the Internet of Things (IoT). When combined, the outcome will incorporate "virtual" access to the internet which will take place via visual and sensing technologies such as virtual and augmented reality, 5G connectivity, digital scanning, voice recognition and touch screens embedded in doors, windows, bench tops, dashboards and more.

Summary and conclusion

The extent of analysis required to establish a clear picture of what is – and then undertake a Stage 1 reframing exercise depicting all aspects of the Future Corporation – is substantial. The exercise for each demonstrated in this chapter provides a strong indication of the extent of work and depth of critical thinking required. SWOT analysis, gap analysis and a five-year, static strategic plan are no longer enough. Rather than short-term plans and a reliance on adaptation, a mode of both adaptation and invention driven by a dynamic, flexible strategy system is now mandatory.

No amount of reframing and no matter how far into the future the depiction projects, a definitive outcome can never be treated as an absolute outcome from strategy – especially in the form of a depiction of the Future Corporation. Rather, the strategising activities undertaken in both the realms of formulation and implementation must be a depiction of the desired future, one that is both aspirational and achievable. That is where backcasting provides value; it provides that link between the reality of today and a plausible depiction of what could be. The resulting story then provides the focus for evaluation, dialogue and reframing, and produces a depth of insight and foresight. In this chapter, one aspect of a possible and plausible Future Corporation was demonstrated and discussed. Grounded in an understanding of current trends and influences on the average corporation of the future, a depiction of a systemic, dynamic entity emerged, one that is grounded in living examples in existence today.

In many ways, the work undertaken by Bartlett and Ghoshal has finally come of age. The detail of how the Future Corporation will be managed will be the subject of new theories and practices. Its administration and governance will be the subject of new legislation. Ideally, each will be sufficiently operable to provide substantive support to the transformation process. Above all, the resolution of the socionological conundrum of finding the balance between people and machine must be the focus of future academic research. Undoubtedly, an absence of human intervention will inevitably be filled by overzealous and ill-informed, biased algorithms. New insight into structuring will be required and new insight into "agile" strategy practices and organisational learning will be essential. The two constants within management theory among the entire transformation process seem to be that Chandler's (1962) M-Form corporate structure will prevail and De Gues's (1997) observation that the speed of learning must now be extended to suggest that not only is it the only source of competitive advantage, it will also be the corporation's primary source of survival.

References

Aaker, D., Managing Assets and Skills: The Key to a Sustainable Competitive Advantage, *California Management Review*, 31 (2), 91–106, 1989.

ABC Documentary, Fight Back Farmers, https://coopfarming.coop/fightback-farmers/. Accessed 12/02/2022.

Abuelsamid, S., Ford's Farley on Building Mobility Technology And Services Amid Auto Industry Disruption, *Forbes*, 21 October 2019, https://www.forbes.com/sites/samabuelsamid/2019/10/21/fords-jim-farley-on-building-mobility-technology-services-and-brands/?sh=76aed8d99a8d. Accessed 27/01/2022.

Ambrosini, V., Bowman, C., and Collier, N. 2009, Dynamic Capabilities: An Exploration of How Firms Renew Their Resource Base, *British Journal of Management* 20 (S1), S9–S24.

Apple Web Site, Apple to Acquire Beats Music & Beats, *Electronics*, 28 May 2014, https://www.apple.com/au/newsroom/2014/05/28Apple-to-Acquire-Beats-Music-Beats-Electronics/. Accessed 27/05/2022.

Apple Web Site, Supplier Responsibility, https://www.apple.com/au/supplier-responsibility/. Accessed 09/02/2022.

Bartlett, C. and Ghoshal, S., Beyond the M-Form: Towards a Managerial Theory of the Firm, *Strategic Management Journal*, 14 (Special Issue), 23–46, 1993.

BBC, Facebook to Hire 10,000 in *EU to Work on Metaverse*, 18 October 2021, https://www.bbc.com/news/world-europe-58949867. Accessed 21/10/2021.

Beer, S. *Brain of the Firm; Allen Lane, The Penguin Press*, Herder and Herder, London, 1972.

Birkinshaw, J., Ecosystem Businesses Are Changing the Rules of Strategy, *Harvard Business Review*, 08 August 2019, https://hbr.org/2019/08/ecosystem-businesses-are-changing-the-rules-of-strategy. Accessed 12/02/2022.

Bower, J. L. Managing the Resource Allocation Process. *Division of Research, Graduate*, School of Business Administration, Harvard University, Boston, 1970.

Brain, J., The Luddites Historic UK, https://www.historic-uk.com/HistoryUK/HistoryofBritain/The-Luddites/. Accessed 15/02/2022.

Castells, M. *The Rise of the Network Society*, Blackwells, Oxford, 1996.

Cellan-Jones, R, Stephen Hawking Warns Artificial Intelligence Could End Mankind, *BBC News*, 02 December 2014, https://www.bbc.com/news/technology-30290540. Accessed 14/02/2022.

Chakravarthy, B. and Lorange, P., *Profit or Growth? Why You Don't Have to Choose, Wharton School Publishing*, Pearson, London, 2007.

Chandler, A. D., *Strategy and Structure*, The MIT Press, Cambridge, MA, 1962.

Chang, K., SpaceX Wins NASA $2.9 Billion Contract to Build Moon Lander, *New York Times*, 16 April 2021, https://www.nytimes.com/2021/04/16/science/spacex-moon-nasa.html. Accessed 11/11/2021.

Corning Website, https://www.corning.com/worldwide/en/about-us/company-profile.html. Accessed 21/09/2021.

Cyert, R. M. and March, J. G. *A Behavioral Theory of the Firm.* Prentice-Hall, Englewood Cliffs, 1963.

Dans, E., Apple's Smart Use of Its Product Ecosystem Just Got Smarter, *Forbes*, 28 April 2021, https://www.forbes.com/sites/enriquedans/2021/04/28/apples-smart-use-of-its-product-ecosystem-just-gotsmarter/?sh=6f7afc9b217f. Accessed 09/02/2022.

de Geus, A. P., *The Living Company*, Harvard Business School Press, Boston, 1997.

Deloitte, Business Ecosystems Come of Age, *Deloitte University Press*, 2015, https://www2.deloitte.com/za/en/pages/strategy-operations/articles/business-ecosystems-come-of-age.html. Accessed 12/02/2022.

Deloitte Insights, The Spatial Web and Web3, *The Deloitte Centre for Integrated Research*, 2020, https://www2.deloitte.com/us/en/insights.html. Accessed 20/02/2022.

Dudovskiy, J., Apple Organizational Structure: A Brief Overview, *Business Research Methodology*, 03 February 2021, https://research-methodology.net/apple-organizational-structure-a-hierarchical-structure-that-may-change-in-near-future/. Accessed 11/02/2022.

Economist Intelligence Unit (EIU), The Asia Pacific CEO Survey: Business Leaders Chart the Road Ahead, *The Economist Intelligence Unit Limited*, 2020, https://

www.westpac.com.au/corporate-banking/westpaciq/ceo-survey/. Accessed 08/02/2022.

Free, M., The Luddites Are At It Again, *Forbes*, 11 June 2014, https://www.forbes.com/sites/mitchfree/2014/06/11/the-luddites-are-at-it-again/?sh=609848ef569b. Accessed 18/02/2022.

Ghoshal, S. and Bartlett, C., 1999, *The Individualised Corporation: A Fundamentally New Approach to Management*, William Heinemann, London.

Gillezeau, N., Why Philips Got out of TVs and into Health, *The Australian Financial Review*, 05 June 2019, https://www.afr.com/work-and-careers/leaders/why-philips-got-out-of-tvs-and-into-health-20190503-p51jok#:~:text=in%20healthcare%20technology.-,%E2%80%9CWe%20looked%20at%20the%20core%20DNA%20of%20the%20company%2C%20and,%2C%20for%20example%2C%20in%20televisions. Accessed 15/12/2021.

Gouillart, F. and Kelly, J., *Transforming the Organization*, McGraw Hill, New York, 1996.

Hackle, C., What Are DAOs And Why You Should Pay Attention, *Forbes*, 1 June 2021. Accessed 10/02/2022.

Hunter, P., *Corporate Strategy (Remastered)*, Routledge, Oxford, 2020.

Hunter, P., *Strategic Revitalisation: A Strategic Business Model of Innovation and Growth*, Doctoral thesis, RMIT University, Melbourne, Australia, 2000.

Kaafaran, A. E, Four Ways Quantum Computing Could Change the World, Forbes Technology Council, *Forbes*, 30 July 2021 https://www.forbes.com/sites/forbestechcouncil/2021/07/30/four-ways-quantum-computing-could-change-the-world/. Accessed 18/10/2021.

Kahneman, D., Sibony, O. and Sunstein, C., *Noise: A Flaw in Human Judgment*. William Collins, Glasgow, Scotland, 2021.

McFadden, C., Swarm Intelligence: How Autonomous Cars Might Need to Learn from Ants, *Interesting Engineering*, 2017, https://interestingengineering.com/swarm-intelligence-how-autonomous-cars-might-need-to-learn-from-ants. Accessed 10/10/2021.

Miller J. Living Systems: Basic Concepts, *Journal of the Society for General Systems Research*, Wiley, New York, 10 (3), 193–237, 1965.

Moore, J., Predators and Prey: A New Ecology of Competition, *Harvard Business Review*, May 1993, https://hbr.org/1993/05/predators-and-prey-a-new-ecology-of-competition. Accessed 17/02/2020.

Murphy, H., Facebook Changes Name to Meta in Corporate Rebranding, *Financial Times*, 29 October 2021, https://www.ft.com/content/b20fd8ea-2dda-45ad-aa15-1ed7a7e5e46f. Accessed 18/11/2021.

Murphy, H., in San Francisco and Murgia, M. in London, Why Facebook has become Meta, *Financial Times*, 30 October 2021, https://www.ft.com/content/29762a96-419f-41b2-9e96-fa7423abb125-. Accessed 21/12/2021.

Novet, J. Amazon's cloud division reports 28% revenue growth; AWS head Andy Jassy to succeed Bezos as Amazon CEO, CNBC, 02 February 2021, https://www.cnbc.com/2021/02/02/aws-earnings-q4-2020.html, Accessed 09/02/2022.

Penrose, E., *The Theory of the Growth of the Firm*, Basil Blackwell, London, 1959.

Podolny, J. and Hansen, M., How Apple Is Organized for Innovation, It's About Experts Leading Experts, by *Harvard Business Review* (November–December 2020), https://hbr.org/2020/11/how-apple-is-organized-for-innovation. Accessed 03/02/2022.

Porter, M., *Competitive Advantage: Creating and Sustaining Superior Performance*, The Free Press, New York,1985.

Porter, M., What is Strategy, *Harvard Business Review*, November–December, 61–78, 1996.

Prahalad, C. K. and Bettis, R. A. The Dominant Logic: A New Linkage Between Diversity and Performance, *Strategic Management Journal*, 7 (6): 485–501, 1986.

Prahalad, C. K. and Hamel, G., The Core Competence of the Corporation, *Harvard Business Review*, 68, No 3, (1990), 79–91.

Raval, A., Shell to Speed Up Energy Transition Plan after Dutch Court Ruling, *Financial Times*, 9 June 2021, https://www.ft.com/content/878cb5cd-9814-4cb2-bbfb-c3f7b8927716. Accessed 22/11/2021.

Reuters, Australian Parliament Approves $1.8 Billion Oil Refinery Subsidies, 23 June 2021, https://www.reuters.com/article/us-australia-refineries-idUSKCN2DZ00U. Accessed 09/02/2022.

Schumpeter, J. A. *An Inquiry into Profits, Capital, Credit, Interest, and the Business Cycle*. Cambridge, MA, Harvard University Press, 1934.

Schwab, K., The Fourth Industrial Revolution: What it Means, How to Respond, *World Economic Forum*, 14 January 2016 https://www.weforum.org/agenda/2016/01/the-fourth-industrial-revolution-what-it-means-and-how-to-respond/. Accessed 12/02/2022.

Silver, C., What is Web 3.0? *Forbes*, 06 January 2020, https://www.forbes.com/sites/forbestechcouncil/2020/01/06/what-is-web-3-0/?sh=3b6d08ea58df. Accessed 18/09/2021.

Teece, D. J., Pisano, G. and Shuen, A., Firm Capabilities, Resources and the Concept of Strategy. *Economic Analysis and Policy Working Paper EAP 38*, University of California, 1990.

Thompson, B., Apple's Organizational Crossroads, *Stratechery*, 19 April 2016, February, https://stratechery.com/2016/apples-organizational-crossroads/#:~:text=Apple%20employs%20what%20is%20known,)%2C%20product%20marketing%20is%20another%20. Accessed 11/02/2022.

Thomson, J., 'You just cannot stop': Quantum computing becomes a reality, *The Australian Financial Review*, November 20, 2021–5.00am, https://www.afr.com/chanticleer/you-just-cannot-stop-quantum-computing-becomes-a-reality-20211119-p59ah0. Accessed 08/02/2022.

Thornhill, J., It Is Time to Bet Big on Fusion Energy, *Financial Times*, London, UK, November 19 2021, https://www.ft.com/content/af4a3478-cca3-4610-9325-615716f95a71. Accessed 08/01/2022.

Weber, M., *Basic Concepts in Sociology*, Citadel Press, New York. ibid, 29, 1964.

Wernerfelt, B., A Resource Based View of the Firm, *Strategic Management Journal*, 5 (2), 171–180, 1984.

4 Technology evolution in the Future Corporation

Paul Hunter and Stuart Orr

Introduction

When engaged in future thinking from the year 2020, prevailing conditions reflect periods in time that are unique. Although challenging, many events can change the nature of industries, economies and societies. While these can often be predicted, the exact timing for such events is far less certain. The global Covid-19 pandemic and its economic impact is a case in point. Pandemics form part of the sequence of disruptions that industry will experience in the long term. Pandemics such as Covid-19 are rare; however, it occurred only 16 years after severe acute respiratory syndrome (SARS) was first reported in Asia in February 2003. Many other similarly disruptive factors, such as economic shifts, will also lead to disruption. Immediate future examples include the Global Financial Crisis, continuing integration of Hong Kong's economy into the rest of the Chinese economic system, increasing aggression between superpowers, and changes in social behaviour accelerated by advances in social media technology. The ensuing impact can be expected to be major and permanent.

One factor stands out in its inevitable impact on the corporate world over the next 30 to 50 years. That is the rise in technological capability growth, which is travelling in a singular, upward trajectory. Its future appears to be quite certain, but, at the same time, uncertain in detail and complex in nature. Technological developments are tied to advances characteristic of the Fourth Industrial Revolution (4IR); an elevation in technological capabilities and the basis for adaptive organisational transformation and renewal. As early as 2014, eight central components of the 4IR had been identified (Segars, 2018). Nearly all groups were related to digital technology in one form or another:

i. **Pervasive computing**. Also known as ubiquitous computing, the term applies to the omnipresent, embedded digital processors (microchips) that enable computational activities to take place anywhere and at any time. Illustrative applications are the Internet of Things (IoT), smart watches and self-driving cars.
ii. **Wireless mesh networks**. Enabler of pervasive computing, this is a multi-wi-fi network that enables connectivity between "smart appliances and

DOI: 10.4324/9781003183679-4

machines". It is made up of a combination of software applications installed on smartphones and small low-cost communications repeaters that provide greater access to wireless networks.

iii. **Biotechnology**. Artificially created autonomous biological devices, including body parts.
iv. **Three-dimensional printing**. Digitally configured objects produced using 3D printing. Interesting applications include printing obsolete car parts and the use of moondust to print accommodation infrastructure on the Moon.
v. **Machine learning**:
   - **Cloud computing**. Remote memory storage that allows simultaneous access from different sources, enabling collaboration between remote devices.
   - **Big data**. Automated management of high volume, historical, mostly corporate or government level data feeding and enabling predictive analytics and insight into trends, phenomena and behaviours.
   - **Artificial intelligence (AI)**. Technology that enables machines to analyse and share core data for (1) predicting the future, (2) learning and correcting failure in processes and systems and (3) forecasting outcomes and trends. A practical application of AI is the detection of money laundering from a broad range of sources such as bank transactions, travel documents, telephone conversations and other social media.
vi. **Nanotechnology**. Micro-engineered robots can fill a variety of functions, even travelling through the body for diagnostic purposes.
vii. **Robotics**. Normal-sized machines applied to automated processes and domestic activities. Advanced applications are autonomous driving capabilities installed in cars, trucks and trains and other machines including cordless, autonomous vacuum cleaners.
viii. **Super technologies**. The development, enhancement and combination of each of the foregoing into new applications and platforms. An illustrative application is the enhancement of autonomous machine capabilities through the application of fifth-generation (5G) wireless networks, cloud-based computing, satellite navigation and blockchain. Apart from the convenience that driverless cars will bring to society, it is expected that this technology will reduce the risk of collisions, a result of their (collective) ability to learn from experience. These technologies frequently interact with other technology to provide advanced technological systems, such as blockchain and information networks. As discussed in Chapter 3, blockchains and distributed ledgers enable the encrypted messaging of data. When applied to mobility, information shared between vehicles in motion considerably enhances the safety, efficiency and convenience of autonomous driving technologies (Ross, 2017).

To determine how social change, technical change and the 4IR will shape the corporation of 2040, this chapter provides an analysis of how these factors will interact to drive strategic thinking. This analysis answers the research question: What are the most likely characteristics of the Future Corporation? This chapter uses information collected from presentations given at two conferences organised by the Strategic Management Institute (SMI) in late 2017 (Hunter and Orr, 2019) on the topic of the "Corporation of the Future". Content delivered via presentations was used to identify the factors likely to influence the Future Corporation. A framework for evaluating the types of strategic technology changes that they could produce and how they interact was first developed from this data. This framework was used to produce four different backcast views of the Future Corporation, which were then considered for their relative likelihood.

Methodology

The evidence base used for the backcasting process was drawn from presentations given at the two conferences. Conducted back to back, the first was held in Melbourne, Australia, and the second in London, UK. This approach was designed to introduce an international perspective into the presentations. All presentations were from subject matter experts who had published, spoken on and managed significant organisational change and organisational responses to major environmental changes. The data was cross-sectional, representing the experiences of industries ranging from manufacturing through to government departments. Notes were taken during the presentations, identifying the key themes and relationships proposed by the presenters. Ethics approval for the collection and analysis of this data was obtained through the Australian National ethics framework. Data were collected from 18 presentations made at the two conferences.

The data was then thematically analysed using the qualitative analysis package NVivo to identify the key themes. Coding was independently conducted by two coders. The results were then compared, conflicting codes reviewed and the codes resolved to create the final coding. The themes identified from this analysis were then used to identify a framework for the analysis. The thematic analysis indicated that the dimensions of reactive and pre-emptive behaviours and change were the appropriate dimensions, which resulted in four possible Future Corporation configurations.

To develop the details of each of these configurations, the literature was reviewed to identify the context that would apply to each configuration. The themes from the previous data analysis were then evaluated against this context and allocated to the most appropriate of the four different configurations. A matrix of greatest uncertainty was created for each of the configurations. The matrix was then used to determine which configuration was the most internally consistent and robust. This configuration is presented as the final backcast description of the Future Corporation and the path leading to its development discussed.

Summary of data analysis findings

The analysis findings primarily described four central Future Corporation organisational processes:

1. Strategy process
2. Strategic thinking
3. Strategic innovation
4. Strategic change

Only the strategy process descriptions incorporated the effects of advanced technology, the remaining streams reflected conditions relating to the organisational consequences of strategic thinking, innovation and change. The findings in the first stream confirmed that the broad effect of technological change is reasonably predictable, but not the social impact. This finding also demonstrated several recurrent subthemes which appeared in many of the principal themes:

1. How a corporation manages future technological capabilities and social behaviours
2. How a leader develops an understanding of the future
3. How a corporation plans for the future
4. How a corporation monitors its progress

One of the most surprising analysis findings was the observation that although the presentations primarily identified the current effects, they did not identify what impact current forces on industry would change in the future. In particular, the effect of world-changing factors was not addressed by the presenters. In a post-Covid-19 world, overlooking this type of event effect seems surprising. The themes are summarised in more detail in Table 4.1, along with a range of impact measures. They reveal that change capacity, culture, the ability to transform and communications were key responses, driven by technology and social change.

The culture theme included concepts such as the requirement of leaders to think differently. This required leaders to reframe current perceptions of "what is" to initiate discussions about the corporation of the future. By engaging in exercises of reframing, one participant suggested, "the trick is to avoid the trap of falling into a pattern of autopilot or group think … we should engage in

Table 4.1 Thematic analysis results

Issues	*Measures for each issue reflected in presentations*				
	Awareness	*Importance*	*Opportunity*	*Transparency*	*Disruption*
Technology	Low	Critical	High	Low	High
Social change	Medium	Critical	High	High	High
Networks	Low	Low	Low	Low	Low
Culture	High	High	High	High	High
Transformation	Low	High	High	Low	High
Organisational change	High	Critical	High	High	High
Communications	Medium	High	Medium	High	High

frontal cortex dominated deep thinking that extends beyond the boundaries and constraints of business as usual".

The themes of technology, social change and organisational change were all found to require strategic thinking for successful corporations of the future. The data indicated that corporations are still struggling to adopt this concept. The data relating to the technology theme indicated that a focus on strategic thinking was not sufficient for the sudden changes imposed by the arrival of advanced technologies. The disruption resulting from new, emerging and predominantly digitalised technology requires the capacity for rapid organisational change and strong support networks as well – connecting the technology, networks and organisational change themes. The data also indicated that many of these technologies had been evolving for some time and their application is just beginning to emerge. The participants predicted exponential growth rates for digital technologies, resulting in a rapidly increasing effect on Future Corporations. One important finding in the organisational change theme was that larger corporations were failing faster than ever before and small organisations were surviving longer than ever before, indicating that small businesses possess more of the capabilities required for organisational change necessary to survive in the future.

The data indicated that there were three important drivers of the social change theme, and all were strategic thinking related: (1) the demand for trust, (2) the influence of global forces and (3) the need to redress unsolved problems. The data indicated that these forces had even driven government organisations to consider how they could develop the capacity to change, which started with expressing commitments in concrete and measurable, social and economic terms and removing internal departmental boundaries by merging departments. The third point also included the need to initiate problem-solving through innovation. This was found to be strongly connected to the generation of trust as it provided the freedom for solution exploration.

The transformation theme included addressing unsolved problems. It was also found to require a reduction in internal boundaries to increase collaboration opportunities. Conflicts between cultures across the boundaries were frequently identified as a major barrier to relaxing these boundaries, indicating the connection between the culture and transformation themes. One of the key features of the culture theme in the data was the desire for independence between bounded groups within the organisation at the expense of collaboration. The data also suggested that the lack of coordination between solution-focused endeavours led to conflicting conclusions which stalled change decisions.

Successful organisational change was also strongly associated with the participation of employees from all sections of the organisation in innovation and solution generation. One of the key network theme findings was the importance of involving entrepreneurs external to the organisation in the innovation process in order to generate significantly original ideas. This finding indicated the importance of the network theme for the organisational change theme. The organisational change theme also included the important observation that plans for the organisational change needed to incorporate the possibility of negative outcomes, as well as positive outcomes if the capability to change was to be maintained.

The transformation theme included concepts such as the discipline of seeking growth in key areas and coordination and connected strongly with the communication theme. The communication theme included the importance of conveying the need for transformation from multiple perspectives. This was found to be connected to gaining a shared understanding of the purpose of the change and of the conditions surrounding the change that is to be made among all stakeholders, responding to ambiguity and achieving shared values and beliefs. This theme also included the importance of transparency and simplification. Problems that were to be solved would not result in collaboration if details were not revealed or if they were presented as overly complex concepts. The data indicated that communicating the need for change in a way that was not overly complex was a major challenge for calls for innovation and strategic thinking. Providing opportunities to "think around problems", rather than focusing directly on the problem was identified as one way of reducing the complexity of the idea.

Implications of the findings for technology in the Future Corporation

One of the key findings was that the rate of change in technological capabilities is slow relative to their potential impact, meaning that small changes in technology can result in profound changes in industries. The findings also indicated that technology resulted in both social and cultural change. When technology development is chaotic, organisational change, network change and cultural effects will be similarly chaotic. The "magnified" effect of technology is important for predicting the nature of Future Corporations. In defining a (typical) Future Corporation, there is a risk that the consequences of the capability, applicability and integration of technologies may not be correctly understood, leading to misconceptions about future business environments. Similarly, an adequate understanding of the nature of a particular technology can result in a poor prediction of the rate of change of the technology.

While technology growth is very likely, the speed of its development, along with enhancements of features, attributes and benefits will be chaotic. For example, electric bike componentry and even electric cars can develop relatively rapidly, while the development of a reusable spacecraft moves on a much slower trajectory. The speed of development and the commercialisation pathway that new technology takes are difficult to predict. The development of phone technology provides a good example of how the rate of technology development (and its impact on industry) can change. As demonstrated in Figure 4.1, it required 100 years for the landline telephone system to evolve into a commercially viable, analogue, wireless mobile device. Socially, ten-year increments were only required for significant iterations of mobile phones to develop as a result of the technology and physical infrastructure which had been put in place for the first wireless mobile device.

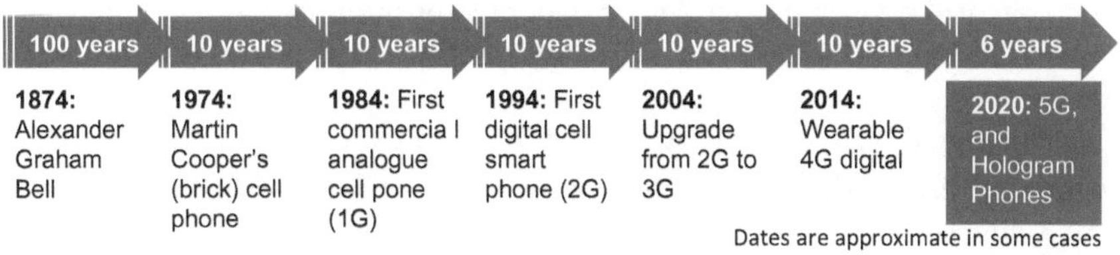

Figure 4.1 History of the evolution of mobile phone technology.

Key themes

In organisational transformation, it is not just the technology itself that will change. Other factors, including the lead time required to translate the idea behind the technology into a commercially viable product, also result and lead to further uncertainty. Similarly, the time required to establish the necessary technology adoption infrastructure introduces another dimension of uncertainty. Examples of critical infrastructure include the development of microchips, mobile telecommunications networks, satellite systems, optical fibre and energy networks.

The data indicated that legal, political and social constraints interact with these infrastructures to encourage or inhibit organisational transformation. As a result, technology such as software applications can also enable evolutionary and sometimes revolutionary social change. The combination of circumstances where advances in technology and changes in social behaviours and attitudes become intertwined was referred to in Chapter 3 of this book as a phenomenon of socionology. This concept is described as the "blending of a future environment that survives through an ability to integrate the hard power of new, mostly digitalised technology with that of increasing demands for greater engagement, awareness and responses to the soft issues of social and societal welfare".

The extent to which socionology impacts society is witnessed through social media giants Facebook, Snapchat and Instagram. Each has influenced generational change in social behaviour since their inception and are good examples of socionological effects. These effect influences can also be seen in local as well as global contexts, even down to local communities. In the 2019 Hong Kong riots, for example, social media was used to "organise, document, and assemble large-scale protests" as well as to "win the battle for public opinion" (Shao, 2019). Socionology can even be observed in the context of organisational competition. In the case of the Hong Kong riots specifically, facial recognition, mobile phone tracking, Facebook postings and closed-circuit television were used to track and publicise protestors, creating a competitive social context.

John Naisbitt was a clear advocate for socionological thinking. In his 1999 book *High Tech, High Touch* he noted that human's attraction to advanced technology influences the rationality of organisational decision-making and redefined strategic thinking (Naisbitt, 1999). This, he proposed, was the process of "dealing with, or interacting with a human being as opposed to transacting with computers". McKendrick confirms this opinion, suggesting that no amount of technology will have an impact if it isn't adopted by innovators or entrepreneurs intent on making lives better for customers or workplaces better for employees (2021).

Technology-driven socially structured behaviours directly affect strategic change and organisational transformation. They will introduce bias in decision-making and lead to both congruous and incongruous decisions. Technology capability optimism is a good example of this phenomenon. Elon Musk displays a high degree of technology optimism which has driven him to introduce unanticipated and extremely disruptive businesses in the domains of space transportation (SpaceX), electric cars (Tesla), neurological implants (Neuralex) and artificial intelligence (Open AI). Whether these advanced technology-driven business decisions lead to sustainable organisations and whether this matters is as yet unknown.

The thematic analysis identified the fact that leadership (and follower) capabilities will also determine whether organisations achieve the transformation necessary to successfully adopt new technologies. This is consistent with a study which found that leadership capability required for advanced technology-based organisational change is uncommon and that 70% of large-scale, advanced technology-driven initiatives do not achieve their required goals (Bucy et al., 2016). Other researchers identified a lack of employee engagement, management support, collaboration and accountability as the major causes. GE's experience with the GE Digital initiative was commensurate with these findings. Despite pouring billions of dollars into this initiative, the company's stock price continued to fall as the organisation became overly focused on short-term goals in an attempt to create success from its technological initiatives (Morgan, 2019).

Conceptual configurational framework for future technology

The themes identified from the research data analysis indicated that strategic technology change was the result of innovation or the need to adapt. To determine the changes that lead to the Future Corporation, a framework is required which captures these two dimensions. As discussed, and illustrated in Chapter 2, within the context of reactive and proactive environmental system responses (Figure 2.1), both adaptation (response) and innovation exist on a continuum. Adaptation can either be reactive (responding to existing forces) or proactive (responding to future anticipated forces). At both ends of the spectrum, this represents a strategic change decision resulting from a force which is initiated externally to the organisation. Innovation can also be a reactive response to existing conditions (such as the novel adaptation of new technology to create a new line of business). Or it can be proactive (such as the invention of a new technology that creates a new market), occurring in the absence of any external stimuli. In this study, we have defined adaptation as a *response* in the framework. Adaptation can include other dimensions, such as evolution, however, response was the most consistently identified feature of adaptation in relation to strategic technology change in the data. The connection between innovation and strategic technology change focused primarily on the creative use of innovation as part of a strategically focused technology change. A term does not exist for this phenomenon, so to be consistent with the use of *response* to represent adaptation in this study, we refer to the creative use of innovation in strategic change as *prosponse*. This reflects the future industry condition focus of innovation-driven strategic change identified in the data.

Figure 4.2 provides an example of how this configurational framework could be applied to the burgeoning space transportation industry and categorises organisations operating in this industry into the four domains represented by the continuums of response and prosponse, ranging from lagging (reactive) to leading (proactive) behaviours. Each of the categories has been given a title and the performance of the exemplar organisation incorporated in italics. The companies listed in each category are all significant members of the space transportation industry.

It is important to note that this framework only represents a snapshot in time for this industry and that changes in strategic thinking can move these organisations into different configurations fairly quickly in an industry as dynamic and rapidly evolving as space transportation. The conditions in each of the four configurations will now be considered.

Configuration 1: Inertia. The European Space Agency (ESA) and the National Aeronautics and Space Administration (NASA) from the United States had been placed in the inertia category because their responses are reactive and even their innovation is a response to external stimuli. Both ESA and NASA

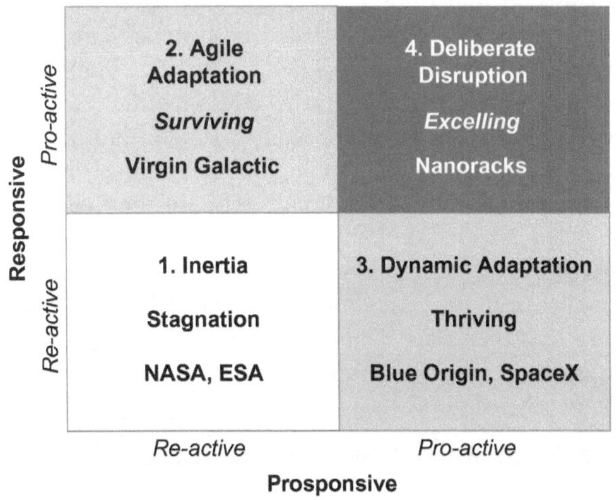

Figure 4.2 A framework of reactive and pre-emptive strategic technology change with examples for the space transportation industry.

function today as enablers of space travel commercialisation, rather than developers of this emerging sector. ESA's website describes its mission as "to shape the development of Europe's space capability and ensure that investment in space continues to deliver benefits to the citizens of Europe and the world" (European Space Agency, 2021). NASA's enabling role was encouraged by US Vice President Mike Pence's demands that they land astronauts on the Moon by 2024 – four years ahead of schedule – and overcome their bureaucratic inertia (Clark, 2019).

Configuration 2: Agile adaptation. Virgin Galactic's mission of providing a space tourism service classifies it as an agile adapter. Virgin Galactic is responding proactively to opportunities to provide commercial space travel in the future, although its innovation is reactive, resulting from an integration of existing innovations in its environment. It has been running years behind its original schedule as it seeks to create an advantage out of innovations existing in the industry.

Configuration 3: Dynamic adaptation. In comparison with Virgin Galactic, Blue Origin and SpaceX are both dynamic adapters. Each is adapting existing technology (reacting) developed by NASA, while proactively innovating their service – becoming a logistics and infrastructure provider on the Moon. Jeff Bezos, founder and former chief executive of both Blue Origin and Amazon announced in May 2019 Blue Origin's objective of transporting people to the Moon by 2024 (Paul, 2019). Similarly, Space X draws reactively on NASA and sister company, Tesla's technologies, but with pre-emptively innovative objectives of facilitating settlement on Mars.

Configuration 4: Deliberate disruption. The less well-known space exploration company Nanoracks is a deliberate disruptor because it is proactive in both its responses and prosponses. As an early investor in the International Space Station (ISS) and specialists in miniaturised satellite launch and management, Nanoracks was already being described by Fast Company as "The UPS of Outer Space Shipping" back in 2012 (Ungerleider, 2012). Nanoracks provides space transportation services to educational and scientific research institutions at much lower costs than Virgin, SpaceX or Blue Origin. Both their service and the way they have created it are highly pre-emptively innovative. Their service is providing a physical interface between their client's miniaturised satellites (called Nanoracks' CubeSat) and the energy source and data processing capabilities of the ISS. They handle all paperwork, book transportation of the satellite to the (ISS) and organise the installation of the satellites in space. Nanoracks is the largest commercial user and private investor in the ISS and has customers from 30 countries.

Features of the four configurations of technology in the Future Corporation

The framework presented in Figure 4.2 shows the multidimensional nature of strategic technology change identified in this study. This framework will now be used to identify the four types of Future Corporation based on the dimensions of response and prosponse. An analysis of the literature was used to identify how the characteristics of the strategic technology change and how their motivations identified in the data analysis could evolve into each of the four quadrants of the framework. The literature indicated that some innovations could take more than 20 years to progress to the level at which they have an appreciable effect. As result, the target date for the categories was set at 2050 to include the initial stages of some of these effects in the Future Corporation backcast.

The context

The key political context for the Future Corporation was emphasised through the recent swing away from the previous 20 years of globalisation trends towards nationalism and state sovereignty. Between 2018 and 2019, the average global democracy score fell from 5.48 in 2018 to 5.44 (on a scale of 0–10), which caused the *Economist* to comment that it was the worst it had seen since its introduction in 2006 (Economist Intelligence Unit [EIU], 2020). The decline was driven by sharp regressions in Latin America and Sub-Saharan Africa. Similar trends towards nationalism have also been evident in other countries, including the United States and within the EU, where anti-immigration lobbies have increased in power. Increased agitation for independence in Spain and the UK's withdrawal from the EU (Brexit) suggest that these specialisation trends will continue for some time. The observation in the data analysis relating to the strategic technology change theme and planning for the future subtheme suggested that this reflects an increased focus on internal processes in response to significant external change effects including climate change, terrorism, cyber-attacks and Covid-19.

The increase in nationalism has exerted both positive and negative influences on the global economy. The tariffs and measures protection imposed from the trade wars have had a significant impact and the need for rapid responses at the national level, encouraging corporations to focus on adaptation to the new economic environments that they are experiencing. The economic changes do not represent a downturn in economic activity (although China's economic growth has diminished in the last five years), they are mainly the redistribution of economic opportunity. They also only remain possible while sovereign states retain an independent monetary system. Moving to an internationally integrated financial system, such as the EU or even cryptocurrencies, will seriously restrict the opportunity to make national-level economic redistributions.

Advanced communication technology is also transforming the social and political conditions as populations have access to unprecedented levels of information about government actions and decisions, as well as the opportunity to publicly express their opinions. Generally, as observed in Hong Kong, the disruptions resulting from clashes between political actions and societal preferences have had a limited long-term effect on business activity. Technical and social combined effects (socionological) are also significant factors affecting the context of the Future Corporation. The interaction represented by socionological effects will lead to more dramatic and greater rates of change for the context of the Future Corporation, creating opportunities as well as demanding responses. Technologies will add to the Future Corporation's capabilities (such as AI), increase efficiency (through automation) and increase control (by allowing for more forms of monitoring, forecasting and analysis). Table 4.2 provides a list of the future technologies which were identified as being able to affect the Future Corporation. These technologies, however, mostly offer the opportunity for increased efficiency and control, leaving responsibility for innovation to the Future Corporations themselves.

The "climate emergency" we are facing will arguably have a greater impact than the Covid-19 pandemic. The changes to corporate behaviour necessary to avert this emergency will make the Future Corporation very different to today's corporation. Many organisations will withdraw from the global environmental reserves instead of repaying the environmental debt already generated. Increasingly, the sustainability of the natural environment is integrated with the sustainability of social impact and even community economic viability. Inevitably, the three forms of sustainability will be dealt with as one by the Future Corporation and this will also have a fundamental impact on the economy, society and industry cooperation. For example, the UK Treasury determined that the cost of climate change to the UK alone was around US$2 trillion (BBC News, 2019).

At present, both these changes and technological innovations have created great challenges for national and international legislation, which is currently inhibiting reactive innovation based on technology. For example, PwC's 23rd Annual Global CEO Survey determined that implementation of innovation is exceeding the rate of development of the regulatory systems and standards designed to maintain control and ensure the safety of society (PwC, 2019). Inevitably, this will lead to legislation being based both on public need and economic opportunity. The Future Corporation is likely to have a much greater role in legislation development. Regulations are also likely to be increasingly internationally focused in reflection of the global effect of many technologies. For example, Mark Zuckerberg (CEO of Facebook, now Meta) was demonstrably aware of what "might be" when he claimed that it was not the responsibility of Facebook to determine the legitimacy of society's free speech (Meta, 2019).

In a broader context, outer space, off-world business operations, offer several advantages including access to low-cost materials, low-cost (solar) energy, new opportunities for scientific research, cold climate data processing (heat generation significantly increases the cost of computing power) and tourism. Many countries are already working towards permanent Moon bases in the next few years (Dovey, 2019). These developments will create even more challenges for international regulation development.

A comparison of context and the identified themes

The context in the section "A backcast view of the corporation in 2050" was compared with the themes identified from the data analysis, using the

Table 4.2 Future technologies affecting the Future Corporation

Application	*Description*
Internet of Things (IoT)	Equipment, maintenance and appliances can connect to optimise organisational capacities via automated interactions, scheduling mechanisms and simple mutual control.
Robotics	With a 40-year pedigree in manufacturing, the introduction of advanced computing and AI capabilities will enable this technology to operate in uncertain environments in most business contexts which only staff can currently navigate.
Automation of knowledge generation	Intelligent software capable of changing big data into knowledge and predictions to produce contracts, financial reports, schedules and logistics.
Autonomous vehicles	Taking the form of private vehicles and commercial transportation, these systems will increase transportation efficiency and reduce risks to create new opportunities and reduce costs.
Augmented Reality (vision)	Computer-driven systems that enhance existing perceptual information to facilitate work activities such as logistics network management, product and infrastructure designs and accounts management.
Energy storage	Increased efficiency and reduction of energy costs made possible by cost-effective localised energy storage, coupled with renewable energies such as wind, solar, thermal, hydro and hydrogen will make smaller and more localised operations viable as well as providing greater flexibility in the selection of business locations.
Blockchain, internet trading payment systems and other advanced financial transaction mechanisms	The security, networked capability and simplicity of transactions provided by these systems further reduce the significance of location for many types of business. This frees organisations and industries to establish in locations which offer more attractive operating costs or access to critical resources.
3D printing	A constantly expanding technology that allows an unprecedented level of customisation and operating location freedom to Future Corporations. This technology is already expanding into many unanticipated industries such as medicine (e.g. production of tissue/organs), instruction in extreme environments (e.g. construction of buildings on the Moon) and high-value manufacturing (e.g. jewellery).
Medical technologies	Rapidly increasing medical manipulation enables the impact of health on society to be reduced, creating new business opportunities.

response–prosponse framework. The insertion of the context information derived from the literature into this analysis produced findings that enabled the two conceptual dimensions of response and prosponse to be expressed as future industry condition dimensions. The first dimension, legislation, emerged as the most important motivator of adaptation in a future where emerging technologies create opportunities at a rate greater than the evolution of the regulations necessary to control them, or the evolution of economic conditions or customer demand. It reflects the consequences of several other significant adaptations requiring future conditions, such as social, natural and economic sustainability demands on the organisation, as well as changes in national and global politics and trade groupings. The second dimension, socionology (introduced earlier), represents the prosponse feature of innovation, resulting from technical and social development, and interactions between these two factors. The data identified a few other prosponsive contributions to strategic technology change that would apply to the Future Corporation. These two dimensions are presented in Figure 4.3, along with some exemplar contextual evidence, which includes business organisation, operational format and forms of control.

The configurations shown in Figure 4.3 represent a range of social and organisational impacts, ranging from a simple trajectory of existing technology effects to a radically new environment where the effect of independent artificial

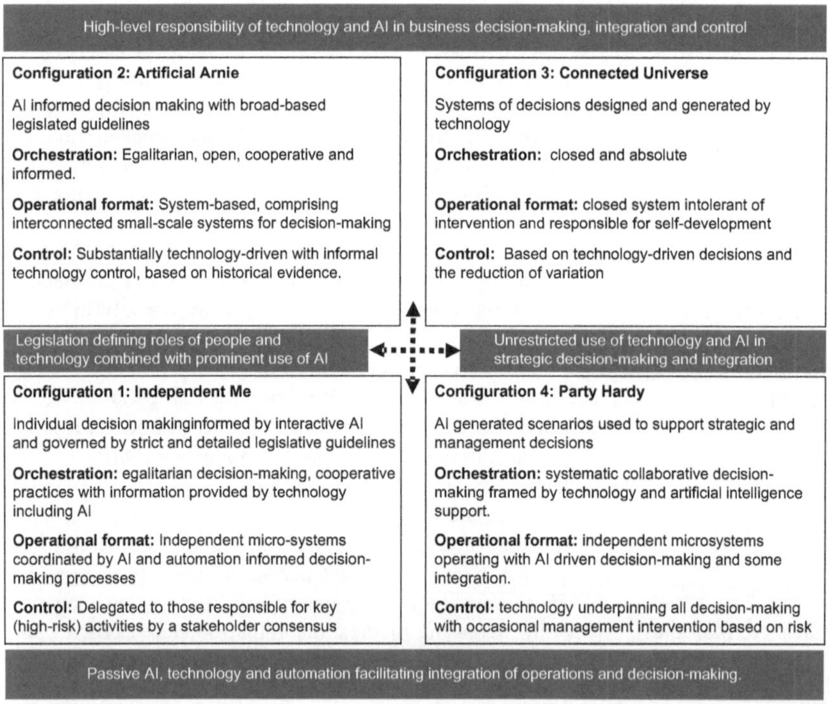

Figure 4.3 Configurations of the future corporate environment.

decision-making systems has led to significant social and organisational change. Whether this extreme is realistic is not important, it represents the boundary condition identified for the socionogical conditions affecting strategic technology change in the Future Corporation. It also demonstrates, however, that the changes occurring today can lead to the emergence of very different decision-making perspectives in the future. Already, for example, brain/machine interfaces (BMIs) are being used to combat neurological disorders (Neuralink, 2021). Quantum computing technology has already enabled some computerised activities that would have taken 10,000 years to complete in 2010 to 200 seconds in 2020 (Wall, 2020). These types of technology developments in the future will create a different context for strategic thinking in the Future Corporation. Responding to Covid-19 and its profound effect on industry is already shaping future perspectives and enabling many strategic technology changes that would otherwise not have been accepted. The experience of hospitals being constructed for pandemic victims in ten days will create permanent changes in viewpoints about the types of organisational change that are possible (Wang et al., 2020). It is important to determine how far viewpoints can change, which is why it is important to identify the boundaries of likely changes to strategic thinking in Future Corporations.

Configuration 3 represents the boundary of likely future organisational conditions for training and environments in which conditions reflect an unconstrained input from technology, including AI, into decision-making. This represents a possible, although radical, future context. On one hand, organisations can be expected to continue to impose controls on all decision-making processes (for example, a CEO would require board approval to make a significant change). On the other hand, the influence of governments and regulatory authorities on technology integration in decision-making for social and political reasons (including in detecting corporate crime) may significantly hamper the future firm's ability to control such inputs. The difficulty that organisations had in controlling the potential for the year 2000 (Y2K) bug to disrupt business and influence business decisions is a salient reminder. Externally prescribed technology is much more integrated into business operations now than it was then and will be much more integrated in the future.

By comparison, configuration 1 is not a radical future context, although it is still highly disrupted. This configuration reflects the trajectory of factors being experienced at present. The data analysis for this study determined that the greatest impact of advanced technology on the Future Corporation will be to increase efficiency, productivity and effectiveness. This is consistent with our experiences of the effect of technology over the last 40 years. Increases in efficiency through technology are likely to continue to draw the focus of decision-making towards cost-cutting, which has been a primary focus of strategic thinking for the last 20 years. Increasing interconnectedness is a key feature of this configuration which, through technologies such as the Internet of Things, creates a demand for connecting systems in manners which may or may not be predictable. While this will create more opportunities for internal improvements, it will also reduce the barriers protecting the organisation from competitors. It is quite plausible that these tensions will lead to an increased focus on the impact of internal technology commitments in strategic thinking. At present, technology is not a significant component of corporate governance, however, high degrees of integration and the potential to affect it are likely to change this in the Future Corporation.

The other two configurations also provide the basis for flow-on effects to the types of strategic technology changes which will be adopted by Future Corporations, stemming from technology and disruptive factor collaborations which affect strategic thinking. It is now necessary to identify the most likely of the configurations for use in the backcast analysis of the Future Corporation.

Configurational likelihood analysis

The data and literature relating to each of the configurations were assessed using a framework of orchestration, culture, strategy, governance, operational format, leadership and control to identify the key features of each configuration. The identified key features were then used to distinguish the uncertainty elements associated with the eventuation of each configuration. The results are shown in Table 4.3.

A comparison of the dimensions of uncertainty for the four configurations suggests that the impact of the uncertainties for configurations 1 and 2 are low, however, the inherent benefits associated with these configurations are also lower than the benefits of configurations 2 and 4. While the uncertainty-based barriers to configurations 1 and 3 are low, the motivations for these configurations are also low. These two configurations were dismissed as being unlikely. Configurations 2 and 4 offer a variety of significant benefits, especially egalitarian and creative opportunities, and the uncertainty is not very much greater than that of configurations 1 and 3. Overall, configuration 2 offers the greatest potential value relative to the uncertainties and is the most likely candidate for the Future Corporation. This configuration is used as the basis for backcasting the Future Corporation.

The following backcasting commences in 2050, addressing the path back to 2020. The depth of this timeframe allowed the authors to emphasise the key stages of the evolution process. It also provided a perspective that enabled the assumptions, objectives and interdependencies to be more clearly identified, leading to a clear description of the characteristics of the Future Corporation.

A backcast view of the Future Corporation of 2050

The backcast analysis of the Future Corporation (2050) according to configuration 2 describes the pathway through which this form of Future Corporation emerged. The following analysis will not only identify the path that led to this configuration, it will also identify the barriers to achieving this configuration and its negative features. As the analysis will demonstrate, the selected configuration

Table 4.3 Dimensions of uncertainty for future configurations

Configuration 1: Independent me	*Configuration 3: Connected universe*
Individual decision-making; informed by interactive AI and governed by strict and detailed legislative guidelines. **Orchestration**: egalitarian, open collaboratives informed by AI. **Culture**: organisation dominated; defined by an open, informed leadership team. **Strategy**: driven by technology created and predicted trends, team decisions dominate. **Governance**: focused on stakeholder outcomes. **Operational format**: interconnected, independent microsystems controlled by AI-informed management decision-making. **Leadership**: open decision-making, collegiate input, public results. **Control**: risk-focused, technology-supported, consensus-based.	Systems of decisions designed and generated by technology. **Orchestration**: closed and absolute. **Culture**: reflective and portfolio-based decision-making criteria. **Strategy**: based on predictive analytics based opportunity identification. Board function reduced to quality control. **Governance**: focused on continuity. **Operational format**: closed system intolerant of intervention and responsible for self-development. **Leadership**: implementation of technology-driven decisions, limited capacity for change. **Control**: alignment with technology-driven decisions and reduction of variation.
Dimensions of uncertainty	
• The extent of legislated definitions of distinctions between the authorities of people and technology. • The ability of passive technology to interface with communities and provide machine-based intelligence support.	• The ability of independent machine-based decision-making to influence independent organisations. • The effect of interaction between independent machine-based decision-making and social activities. • Legal structures to support the use of technology for decision-making.

Key configuration features

(*Continued*)

Table 4.3 (Continued)

Key configuration features	
Configuration 2: Artificial Arnie	*Configuration 4: Party hardy*
AI-informed decision-making with broad-based legislated guidelines **Orchestration**: egalitarian, open, cooperative and informed. **Culture**: open group behaviours determined by technology limitations and constructs. **Strategy**: corporate culture responsive, influenced by analytics and technology, hierarchical. **Governance**: focused on shareholders and stakeholders. **Operational format**: system-based, comprising interconnected small-scale systems for decision-making. **Leadership**: open and consensus-based, but filtered decision-making processes, with high levels of hierarchical authority. **Control**: substantially technology-driven with informal technology control, based on historical evidence.	AI-generated scenarios used to support strategic and management decisions **Orchestration**: systematic collaborative decision-making framed by technology and artificial intelligence support. **Culture**: team-based cultures making up a portfolio organisational culture influenced by informed decision-making. **Strategy**: rule-based strategic decision-making informed and evaluated by group leaders using AI analytics. **Governance**: stakeholder focus and secondary owner focus. **Operational format**: independent microsystems operating with AI-driven decision-making and some integration. **Leadership**: consensus processes moderated by centralised decision-making. **Control**: technology underpinning all decision-making with occasional management intervention based on risk perceptions.
Dimensions of uncertainty	
• Reliant on the advancement of technology into an interactive form. • Reliant on appropriate legislation for each industry that facilitates the role of technology-based decision-making. • Intolerant of histories of technology failure. • Dependent on the application value of technology design.	• Ability to capture high-level needs and decision-making processes in evolving technology design. • Acceptance of highly specified technology and decision-making support in an arbitrary management decision-making context. • Regulatory constraints on technology domains, effects and connections.

of Future Corporation still represents several familiar characteristics, however, the strategic thinking and social space focus represent substantial differences, resulting from changes in the accountabilities and boundaries of advanced technology, AI capabilities and the associated legislation. To explain this process, a sequence of steps will be presented, starting with 2050 and stepping back in sequential decades to 2020. Consistent with the same approach to backcasting as that adopted in Chapter 3, the SMI "Cycle of Organisational Transformation and Renewal" is deployed as the backdrop to the transformation journey underway. As a reminder, the stages of that framework are illustrated in Figure 4.4.

As a backcasting exercise, the discussion commences in Stage 4 and follows a reverse trajectory towards Stage 1. The discussion of each decade will explain the processes that occur at that point and provide a summary of the strengths of the corporation at that time. The data analysis described earlier and the theoretical frameworks in "Conceptual configurational framework for future technology" were used to create these descriptions.

By 2050 operational efficiency and effectiveness have improved dramatically since 2020 due to dramatic changes in the automation immobilisation of data and materials processing, designing, moving, storage and removing (waste in particular). Backoffice functions have been completely automated, however, to create greater certainty in the interface between humans and AI in these areas, legislative requirements had been imposed for all industries, across all of these activities. The development of this legislation was somewhat turbulent, reflecting the desire for sovereign states to retain power. By 2050 however, the openness of government decisions through social media resulted in a level of coordination which made controlling legislation for AI effective at an international level. Interestingly, the combination of this openness and the transparency of AI operating under this legislation significantly reduce the opportunities for fraudulent and corrupt behaviour globally.

From a 2020 perspective, the Future Corporation is a finely tuned, regularly renewing entity where strategic transformation projects are implemented continuously under the guise of adaptive and inventive programmes where deliberate disruption forms the dominant strategic technology change agenda. Similar to the corporate structuring methodology introduced in Chapter 3, corporation 2050 is centred around a systematic collaboration capability that produces combined product and service offerings. Strategy focuses on adapting to unforeseen change while simultaneously creating and introducing deliberate change, contributing

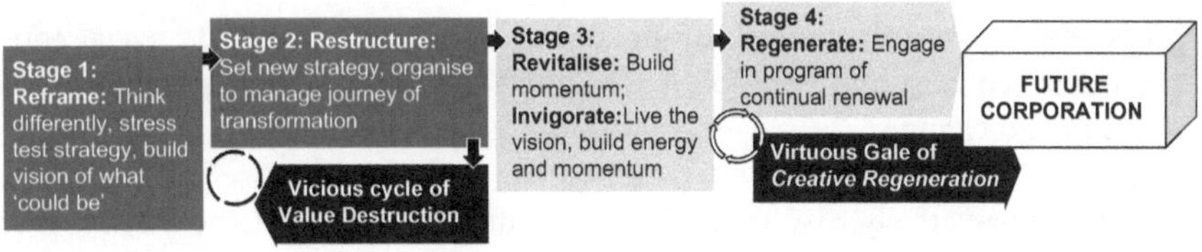

Figure 4.4 Cycle of organisational transformation and renewal.

to the achievement of strategic outcomes. The corporate office is lean and agile, enabling it to oversee a dynamic portfolio of corporate collaborative systems. Each system is independently managed by a dedicated leadership team using AI to integrate operations and decision-making. Each leadership team manages their area as a portfolio of subsystems in a larger business system, rather than through internal competition because the interaction between the systems is transparent.

The focus on agility, efficiency and effectiveness of the corporation in the year 2050 has created a single organisation-wide management system that is efficient, effective and constantly evolving through self-generated, machine-learning mechanisms and high levels of internal integration. Corporation 2050 is heavily dependent on automation and AI for both efficiency and integration. It continually reviews and renews its short-term strategic actions against a long-term strategy supported by a unified organisational purpose. Its core competences are design-focused, research-oriented, customer-centric and systemic. These competencies function in an organisational system and subsystems (referred to in Chapter 3 as core competence platforms), which are open and managed through significant AI input, without being dominated by the AI. The efficiency, depth and flexibility of the organisational system minimise the constraints on the design and makeup of the subsystems.

Structured as an Integrated Value System (refer Chapter 3), the Future Corporation comprises both internal resource-oriented core competencies and dynamic, external, dynamic market systems. This platform of market systems and core competence platforms is supported by an automated, integrated corporate management system, a global supply chain, a knowledge-based, organisational learning capability and analytics-based management control capability. Table 4.4 summarises the main features of the Future Corporation using the categories in the preceding configuration analysis used to select configuration 2.

2040s: An era of revitalisation

The key focus for the Future Corporation (2040) was the consolidation of the technological platforms and service solutions that resulted from plans for an envisaged future initiated some ten to 20 years prior, when:

- practical applications of AI had started to emerge;
- the global pandemic, ruthless and devastating, produced a "black swan" moment and triggered substantive, generational change and political reform; and
- intolerance towards the lack of global action on climate change, racial and gender inequality and homophobia resulted in large-scale political and social action and change.

Although it is relatively easy to envisage this utopian future in the 2020s, the practice of achieving this at the organisational level was difficult. The data determined that, in 2018, essentially none of the organisations were planning changes

Table 4.4 Summary of corporations in the 2050s

Environment: monitored by interactive AI under internationally accepted legislative guidelines for use in continuous strategic decision-making.
Orchestration: egalitarian, open, collaborative decision-making strongly supported by automation and AI. Basic operational decision-making and systems controlled extensively by AI.
Culture: characterised by cooperative decision-making with a high level of transparency and dependence on AI for all decision-making and routine processes.
Strategy: system-driven input resulting from all aspects of the organisation, based on AI-generated data and scenarios. Team decisions are significant and dominate, however, corporate level control by key stakeholders is maintained along with a strong commitment to maintaining integration of the organisation's system.
Governance: governance comfortably balances social responsibility, performance and harmony among stakeholders.
Operational format: compilation of systems connected and controlled by AI and other technologies which make basic operational decisions but do not contribute to strategic decision-making.
Leadership: all stakeholders contribute and all contributions are acknowledged. Open decision-making is used for most issues; however, major issues are still resolved at the senior committee level. Sole leader decision-making does not exist.
Control: conferred on groups of individuals with decision-making assigned to those carrying the greatest risk. Nominated individuals agreed by all stakeholders.

to their strategy in response to the above forces. By 2040, however, these strategic choices were commonplace, and leaders were focused on a future 30 years hence. The decision-making process was still reasonably centralised, however, it was now concise, balanced and well informed. Relative to 2020, frustrations with the lack of achievement had dramatically reduced because decisions were made on a much more reliable and extensive evidence-based knowledge platform. The remaining frustrations experienced by boards primarily resulted from the slow pace of establishing legislation, which was still catching up with social changes that had driven it.

Unsurprisingly, only ambitious organisations from 2020 survived to 2040. The challenges of finding a good balance between strategic thinking and a rapidly evolving technology environment encouraged many organisations to be too cautious or too ambitious to embark on the journey to 2040. Individual corporate ambitions were also disallowed by an increasingly powerful social consciousness. Accordingly, legislation imposed ever more strict conditions on corporate entrepreneurs. As an interesting consequence, however, this legislation also created a more encouraging environment for start-up entrepreneurs taking advantage of new applications and technologies as they arose. Downsized career ambitions became increasingly common as opportunities for personal opportunism decreased in major corporations. This brought more high-level level skills into the small business environment. As a result, caution and reflection were significant components of strategic choice in the 2040s.

Responding to the newly introduced legislation created a range of other challenges, including constraints of AI applications both for information and competitive purposes. In many ways, it would have been better if the legislation had been introduced in the 2030s as the preceding decade had been characterised by an uncontrolled application of AI wherein some of the legislation lagged the capabilities of the technologies deployed in the 2040s. Many felt that there was a lack of synchronisation between societal expectations, technology capabilities and legislation in this period. This resulted in the establishment of resources within organisations directed at finding a path through this lack of synchronisation. Special taskforces were also established, aimed at accelerating and correcting legislative developments.

This dynamic adaptation led to a higher degree of external uncertainty. Perhaps this period of caution and consolidation was necessary anyway, given the extent of change that had already occurred, which resulted in an average of 30% of all work being automated across industries (Manyika et al., 2017). Despite this caution, this era was, as noted above, also a time of the development of new industries and newly industrialised countries and cities – coupled with new distributions of human settlement. Off-world colonies had been established; however, they were almost fully populated by robots as the cost and disadvantages of human occupation made human colonisation unattractive. On the other hand, the African continent had evolved into a thriving economy, along with the Middle East where economic pragmatism had finally replaced warfare. The Eastern Bloc, India, Indonesia and China had predictably migrated into mature economies with correspondingly lower growth rates. Table 4.5 provides a summary of the Future Corporation using the same categories as for Table 4.4.

2030s: A period of restructuring

This was a very difficult decade for strategic thinking. Plausible perceptions of what "could be" brought about an understanding of the enormity of changes that would be required to achieve those outcomes. Strategic thinking and choice were categorised by dynamic adaptation, although the outcome was actually derived from transformation through self-imposed disruption. The restructuring required in this era focused on a long-term transformation as short-term performance improvement was all but abandoned in preference or perception of an envisaged future and interpretations of what "could be". Strong parallels with the responsible organisations to the dot-com boom are apparent, however, this time, the opportunities that the future offered were much more clearly defined and tangible. Consulting firms that had enjoyed several decades of providing efficiency improvement services found that the demand had moved on to long-term strategic thinking and transformational change support services. Enterprise-wide management information systems such as SAP and Oracle along with increasingly

Table 4.5 Summary of corporations in the 2040s

Environment: semi-inclusive decision-making; informed by interactive AI operating under broadly accepted, but lagging legislative guidelines.
Orchestration: egalitarian and open, collaborative concerning social matters and informed by AI. Plans underway for increased use of AI for the control of basic operations not requiring strategic decision-making.
Culture: still organisational in focus but influenced by the standardisation effects of technology and increasingly open in response to social demands. Inclusive decision-making restrained by old habits but increasingly trusting of AI-based decision-making. A clear pattern of delegation of control downwards and towards AI.
Strategy: short-term in focus in response to the uncertainty in the external environment and changes made in the previous era of decisive restructuring. Where long-term strategy was developed, it was predominantly focused on 2070 – a world that can only be imagined. Strategic thinking was cautious as a clear vision had emerged from the previous years of transformation and the emphasis was on preparing for this.
Governance: corporations had adapted to the new legislation as much as possible and were impatient for the remainder of the legislation to be formalised as well as attempting to influence it where possible. The distinction between shareholder and stakeholder was rapidly diminishing and societal obligation was taking its place.
Operational format: comprised of independent microsystems operating as part of a larger macrosystem facilitated by technology, operating under uncertain and rapidly changing constraints. Reasonable level of management trust in AI and parallel technology developments, but still very much in control of decision-making.
Leadership: all stakeholders contribute and all contributions are acknowledged. An open decision-making process was used for most issues, however, senior management determined the final decisions.
Control: substantial control allocated to intra-organisational project teams and determined by the level of risk. Team management generally nominated by all stakeholders.

sophisticated AI capabilities became the backbone for corporations seeking to institutionalise efficiencies and branch out into more systems-based, collaborative enterprises.

Organisations not engaging in the long-term development transformations continued to focus on cost reduction efforts to support an ever-decreasing level of competitiveness. This focus drove those organisations into a spiral of continual downsizing and eventual closure. The data collected for this study provided significant evidence to suggest that this cycle had already begun for many organisations, suggesting that the roots of this path to demise were to be found in the 2020s. Although the timeframe for these transformations was not excessively challenging, the level of change required was both demanding and resource-intensive. Over the decade, the cost of these transformations became very significant for most organisations and represented a challenge to their survival. Even organisations focusing on transformation experienced significant downsizing in this period.

One of the major challenges was transforming systems in a way that had not occurred before. It required new approaches and ideas for handing over decision-making processes which had always been handled by humans to machines. Career transition was also an important part of this decade as familiar jobs became redefined or disappeared entirely. Overall, this period was extremely challenging for staff as well as for their organisations. Appendix 2 provides further reflections on why corporate life during this decade was one of extreme frustration.

One of the biggest challenges in this era was the difficulty of translating the context for strategic decisions into needs that could be supported by advanced technologies. The greyness of strategic decision-making, its supporting evidence and assessment of its outcomes did not match the capabilities or design of the advanced technologies which could be used and had been selected for these purposes. In the 2020s, software was standardised and supported existing strategic decision-making processes. The customised software available in this era challenged many of these decision-making processes, requiring a rethink of the fundamental philosophies behind them in every organisation and every area. This proved to be quite daunting as well as exposing the subjectivity of strategic decision-making in the 2020s.

In addition to corporate objectives, social objectives had also become a significant factor in this era. Social expectations were on a trajectory that would give them a high degree of influence over future organisational strategic decision-making. Incorporating increasingly dualistic objectives added a further challenge to this time of transformation. The trajectory of social expectations was as dynamic as it was strong, creating the need to revisit prior strategic decisions which no longer aligned with social expectations during this period of transformation. Without a doubt, the Covid-19 pandemic was the breakpoint which enabled social expectations to enter into the trajectory experienced during this period. It was a time of significant social order rearrangement when the adage "you can't predict the future, but you can influence it" became a reality.

In addition to the challenges, opportunities also emerged. New industries providing opportunities for those displaced by automation were born. One of the most exciting developments was the establishment of significant operations on the Moon, Mars and orbiting space stations towards the end of the 2030s. Overall, however, the key challenge for this period was resolving the increasing conflict between the capabilities of advanced technology and strategic thinking. Table 4.6 summarises Corporation 2030 using the same framework as for Tables 4.4 and 4.5.

2020s: A period of reframing

From 2020 to 2030 was a period of deep and critical strategic thinking. It began with the disturbance generated by the Covid-19 outbreak and the subsequent

Table 4.6 Summary of corporations in the 2030s

Environment: AI is limited in this period, being limited by the fact that the environment for which it is intended is envisaged, but not yet present. Semi-inclusive decision-making makes use of AI that demands more clarity than contemporary strategic decision-making and thinking can provide.
Orchestration: egalitarian, open collaborative behaviours that are increasingly influenced by social expectations. Constant change underway leading towards increased use of automation for basic decision-making and control purposes, which is proving to be very disruptive and challenging to develop in practice.
Culture: organisation focused, with increasing technology dimensions and social responsibility features. Leadership teams are quite authoritative as a result of the pressures of the transformations underway.
Strategy: focus is short term as transformation demands considerable resources and effort at every stage. Strategic choices are driven by the shared and understood need for the transformation and regeneration of industries. Organisations intending to survive in the future had no choice other than to commence their transformation.
Governance: legislation for the use of AI-created challenges in interpretation and adaptation, particularly as the legislation was also continually evolving. Organisations sought to influence the development of the legislation to increase flexibility and certainty. Social responsibility had also become mandated as a component of decision-making and customers were prepared to pay more for goods and services provided in a socially responsible manner.
Operational format: independent but facilitated microsystems. Still reliant on management intervention to integrate and coordinate. Trust from management within the microsystems of AI is increasing, but not to the point of allowing AI to replace management decision-making.
Leadership: all stakeholders contribute and all contributions are acknowledged. The decision-making process is open for the majority of issues, however, it is still within the absolute control of senior leaders. Decisions must also be signed off at board level.
Control: substantial control is assigned to individual project teams assigned specific projects of contributing to transformation. Senior leaders responsible for appointing transformation team members and still have oversight of existing operations.

economic downturn experienced across the globe. Organisations and economies focusing on global growth revisited the fundamentals of their strategy and organisational purpose. On top of this, aspects of AI and other forms of automation continued to develop in the background, although overshadowed by the human toll of the virus and the economic challenges that followed.

By 2025, the world had returned to economic equilibrium; however, organisational perspectives, national priorities and technologies were no longer the same. In addition, some hasty implementations of advanced technologies deemed necessary to cut costs had resulted in several significant disasters, especially for major organisations. The reality of these eventualities underscored the need for greater strategic thinking about the future. Appendix 1 provides a discussion of some of these eventualities.

The period is notable in history as the point at which the social reforms that achieved full strength in 2030–2040 commenced. This was combined with a clear trend towards a global societal view and the beginning of a downturn in the role of national politics due to its inability to function effectively on a global scale. Without a doubt, technology stood behind much of the early stages of this social revolution as it allowed for greater localisation of goods and services, while at the same time, eliminated the significance of international borders. Each was facilitated through technology-enabled communication systems, a capacity for, and expectation of sharing, and accommodation of common causes – at a level never before possible (and outside political boundaries). This period was also notable for the uncertainty that surrounded business, strategic thinking, transformation choices and the practical aspects of the path that technology was taking. Strategic decision-makers were highly challenged by the clear and unavoidable pressure to change and the uncertainty of the immediate future to which they were attempting to adapt. In response, successful organisations focused on increasing their agility while preparing for a wild strategic journey.

The lessons learnt from the erratic ride over this period proved to be invaluable for the period 2030–2040, when the nature of the Future Corporation became much clearer, as did the extent of transformation that was still required for organisations. From a positive perspective, this era could be described as one of awakening and substantive reframing, even if transformation outcomes were limited, compared to the following decade. Table 4.7 summarises Corporation 2020 using the same framework as for the previous tables.

Summary of findings

The proceeding backcasting indicates the significant emphasis on leadership, strategic technology change, thinking and decision-making, culture, the role of AI and automation and organisational transformation in the data collected for this chapter. Interestingly, despite the emphasis on the role of AI and automation, the expressions of understanding of how this would work and be implemented in the Future Corporation were very limited. The understanding of the role of these technologies in the organisation focused mainly on their operation within existing systems and for process-oriented applications. Their role as a source of integration, influence and even an informing mechanism was, however, notably absent. This is reflected in the uncertainty predicted for the period 2020–2030. Increasing consolidation of strategic thinking and the demands on the Future Corporation due to global factors, which had increasingly limited country-level differences, especially the natural environment, social expectations and technology drove much of the development described in the backcast. Although the data preceded the advent of Covid-19, it was evident that a tipping point was

Table 4.7 Summary of corporations in the 2020s

Environment: the development and acceptance of AI increased significantly over this period, although its effectiveness remained limited. It was not until the end of this period that the true functional capability of AI and other forms of automation were fully understood and a focus transformation business to take advantage of its capabilities could occur. Social turbulence over this period was also evolving towards a level of influence that would ultimately change the nature of organisations in the decades to come. The pressures for change in business practices globally and its inevitability became increasingly evident as the decade progressed.

Orchestration: the uncertainty in this period caused leadership and strategic decision-making to remain fairly closed. Towards the end of this decade, as an understanding of the future for organisations had begun to coalesce and viewpoints converged, leadership and strategic thinking became more open to support leaders as they struggled to interpret environmental changes around them. Interestingly, this created some opportunities for the effective use of AI, especially in dealing with complex and uncertain interpretations.

Culture: organisation focused, especially during periods of closed decision-making. The shift towards more open strategic thinking and decision-making, combined with the sense of social change and an increased but focused use of AI for decision-making, led to more egalitarian cultures.

Strategy: the uncertainty prevalent in the first half of this period promoted a strong focus on long-term strategy, combined with short-term tactical behaviours. The short-term tactical behaviours reduced in frequency towards the end of the period as long-term goals became clearer and AI started to assist with making more informed long-term strategic decisions.

Governance: initially even more shareholder focused than the previous decade due to the pressure of the economic downturn, governments swung almost 180° by the end of the decade towards the interest of a broad range of stakeholders.

Operational format: most business activities focused on consolidation, revival and increased agile flexibility. Growth was limited or even negative and many organisations stumbled either due to the economic challenges or achieving sufficient agility and flexibility to respond to the rapidly changing conditions. The individual systems remained independent as rapid changes made integration challenging.

Leadership: strongly united leadership teams took responsibility for strategic decision-making with consultation among stakeholders in an attempt to understand the dynamic changes afoot. Hierarchical leadership resulted from this effect and the difficulty of decision-making in this environment, although increasing delegation of decision-making was apparent towards the end of the period.

Control: control was strongly defined by organisational structure and hierarchy, relying heavily on traditional control methods. The effectiveness of this control approach was highly challenged by the rapid rates of change in most organisations, which constantly rearranged structures and capabilities. Extensive use of specialists to assist with decision-making and some focused use of AI for decision-making were also apparent from early on in this period.

inevitable. In the backcast, the subsequent effects of Covid-19 on social thinking, politics and the economy were cast in this role.

It is also interesting to reflect on the timeframes required for this evolution. The data collected for this chapter was surprisingly consistent in descriptions of the time it takes for social change to affect strategic thinking and decision-making and the transformation of organisations to adopt new internal systems, respond to the external environment and fully integrate external influences such as technology. The data was also very consistent in the observation that legislation and policy would lag even the rate of corporate response to these conditions. Management and organisational responses to the various stages in the backcast were reflections of responses observed to similar conditions in the data. The inevitability of the social change described in the backcast, together with the inevitability of the corresponding change to organisational behaviours, structure and strategic decision-making described was also an interestingly consistent perspective in the data. Evidence of this change is, however, fairly evident in media and social behaviours.

Could organisations have responded more rapidly than the backcast predicts? Logically, this is quite possible, however, the absence of proactive behaviour in industry and the reliance on reactive responses is the main reason that the backcast was commenced as far out as 2050. Although it is proposed that Covid-19 represents a tipping point, resulting in a consolidation in the number of factors already in play (any similarly disruptive event could have the same effect), the effect is not likely to be short-term. For example, the 2003 SARS outbreak had major global effects; however, organisational responses to the subsequent changes in the global economy and business behaviours were slow. In many cases, slow responses reflect a deep-seated doubt about global changes. In this backcast, we propose that the conditions are such that a sufficient global change will occur to make organisational change inevitable. Unfortunately, the 2020–2030 period of uncertainty and confusion in the backcast results from the time in which it takes organisations to acknowledge these changes and develop the agility to be able to respond.

This is a key lesson from this backcast. The evolution of any corporation will demand that they are in control of their strategic change. Controlling strategic change encourages adaptive rather than inventive responses. The level of transformation required in the backcast, however, clearly requires invention more than adaptation.

An interesting feature to emerge from the backcast was the interactive relationship between corporate enterprises responding to global pressures and the slow rate of legislative change that followed. This created a window of opportunity for Future Corporations to influence legislative change, creating some degree of tension between the corporate view of where these legislative changes should proceed and the social and global issues driving them. This represents an unanticipated level of influence in global affairs by the Future Corporation, and also a surprising convergence of attitudes among corporate organisations globally. The likely convergence of corporate views regarding the backcast global legislation also represents a convergence on the future of organisations among the current corporate community and leaders. This step from this convergence to the accommodation of legislation and social pressures and integrating technology in a fundamentally new way is not great.

The British Academy's first report on the Corporation of the Future (Mayer, 2018) makes a compelling case to encourage corporations to change at least the societal aspects of this issue. The action required Mayer proposes, takes aim at the fundamental need to re-imagine and redefine the primary reason why a corporation exists, a notion he describes as corporate "purpose". Over a long period of time Mayer has observed, a corporation's purpose has become focused solely on profits (shareholder value), a concentration which in itself has created a considerable loss of trust in corporate integrity. Although an admirable objective for those who have invested in the business, a focus on shareholder value alone can come at a considerable expense to all the other stakeholders that may be more, or at least conscious of a need to take an equal responsibility for the environment within which the corporation operates. No doubt, technology in the form of social media and subsequent legislation will follow pressures from society as is so often the case.

Conclusion

The backcast presented in this chapter describes a transformation journey, commencing in 2050 and describing a Future Corporation that ultimately is not so different from the corporation of today. Corporation 2020, however, must be prepared to remain connected to an evolved world order that makes use of technologies in a way that will require it to undergo a significant and sometimes challenging evolution. This evolutionary process will require it to manage the dual process of managed, adaptive decline, while at the same time, evolving an invented future enabled by socially acceptable technological advances and agreeable legislative boundaries. Legislation, suggested by this backcast, will not drive this development. Ultimately, social and technical environmental pressures will create both the desire and the requirement for the Future Corporation to undergo this journey. The indicators are already in place and, as we move out of the immediate effect of the Covid-19 pandemic, with a degree of global disarray, the journey has already commenced.

Appendix 1

Artificial Intelligence as a source of efficiency, effectiveness and competitive advantage

Although extremely powerful, there have been many warnings against the use of AI technology as scientists and practitioners of the highest standing express their concerns. That "AI has the capacity to send people to jail even when they haven't committed a crime" (Hao, 2019) – money laundering is a case in point. According to the Australian Crime and Investigation Commission (ACIC), criminals intent on hiding the proceeds of crime can readily do so through money laundering activities undertaken through legitimate means. Although many devious money launderers have been captured, the ACIC observed that many were unjustifiably suspected of the crime as a result of inaccurate interpretation of AI data (ACIC, 2020).

Using historical data to train risk assessment tools could mean that machines are copying the mistakes of the past. The same outcome can be applied to facial recognition, which although promising in concept, has failed in many practical and moral applications. *The Guardian* has reported findings of its research into the use of facial recognition technology by the Metropolitan Police in London. According to academics from the University of Essex who conducted the research, the system regularly misidentified people who were then wrongly apprehended (Booth, 2019). Despite this, the private sector's use of AI and other machine-learning technology is outpacing the development of regulatory systems and standards necessary to mitigate the risks. Organisations interested in global cybersecurity and internet governance are fragmented. No global framework exists that can control attacks on digital technology, and in many areas, digital dominance is increasingly seen as both an economic competitive advantage and a national security imperative. Guidance on this matter can be obtained; however, it is already evident from contemporary trends that reflect changes in social behaviours, attitudes and ultimately sources of power from AI; and its application to social media in particular. Critical to the success of the introduction of new technology, and indeed anything that is new, is the user's acceptance of change. For every person excited by the prospect of travelling to the Moon, there are likely many more who will oppose it. Although technological advances carry with them an automatic momentum for change, the extent to which the change agents will be successful in convincing the doubters to adapt to the proposed change will be reliant on their ability to influence cultures and attitudes. In some cases, these will have lasted a lifetime, if not many lifetimes The uncontrolled growth of AI therefore can be seen as the *cat among the pigeons* in the introduction of digital technology in corporations of any size. This eventuality, therefore, along with unkempt influences on its impact on social behaviour, society in general and the ecology of the environment are representative of the first combined areas of greatest uncertainty in the generic corporation transformation to a "brave new world" of 2040/2050.

Appendix 2

The politics and opportunity from mining the Moon, Mars and other planetary systems

The first person to physically mine the Moon, albeit with a shovel, was an astronaut from Apollo 17. The flight was made in 1972 and was the last Apollo mission flown. Samples taken from the Moon at that time weren't overly impressive. That is because the mining wasn't very deep. Subsequent unmanned missions have found a bountiful supply of water and a vast inventory of heavy and valuable metals. They are, however, expected to be found deep in the mantle of the Moon, an area impossible to access (Byrne, 2019).

Even so, considerable interest in mining the Moon and surrounding asteroids is strong, but competition is increasing dramatically. The United States, India, Russia, Europe, South Korea and Japan all plan to send robotic and manned spacecraft into space in the next few years (Dovey, 2019). NASA is aiming to land people on the Moon by 2024 while China plans to build its own lunar base by 2030. At the same time, the likes of SpaceX and Blue Origin are actively striving to establish commercial operations on both the Moon and Mars. These ambitions, however, inevitably lead to the question of who will determine the ownership, laws and mining/development rights for the Moon, Mars and beyond. Similarly, it is necessary to know who will be responsible for the policing of those laws. Further, the question must also be asked if it is safe to travel in space in the long term and will the environment of the Moon, Mars and other planets sustain our Earth-like behaviours. It is not until these questions are resolved that significant investment in Moon- and Mars-based infrastructure can proceed. In the meantime, little is being done to prevent rampant preparation for the exploration of space on a commercial scale.

Recognising this as a key issue at the time of the first landing on the Moon, in 1967, the United Nations developed an Outer Space Treaty (OST) that sought to protect any unauthorised pillaging of the Moon and other celestial bodies. Under this treaty, signed by every country that engaged in space research, it was agreed that "no nation can claim sovereignty over Earth's lunar satellite … and other celestial bodies" (Cowing, 2014). As with most legal documents of this nature however, the wording is exposed to challenge as a result of ambiguity in interpretation and questions of relevance of both fact and timing. This eventuality played out in reality following the landing on the Moon by American astronauts in 1969. Subsequent to that event, a new "Moon Agreement" was proposed, and it received unanimous approval from the UN General Assembly in 1979. Regrettably however, the Moon Agreement has only 18 states as parties to the treaty; none of the spacefaring nations with a crewed space programme would sign it (Dovey, 2019). In contradiction to this agreement, the Obama government introduced and passed the 2015 Commercial Space Launch Competitiveness Act. This dictated that US companies held the right to ownership of any resources that they found *off-Earth*. This ratification was adopted and embellished further by the Trump government in 2020.

References

Australian Crime and Investigation Commission (ACIC), Accessed 18th Feb 2020. https://www.acic.gov.au/about-crime/organised-crime-groups/money-laundering

BBC News, Climate change: Emissions target could cost UK £1tn, warns Hammond, 6 June 2019. Accessed 21 Jan, 2020.

Booth, R, Police face calls to end use of facial recognition software, *The Guardian*, Thu 4 Jul 2019 04.00 AEST. https://www.theguardian.com/technology/2019/jul/03/police-face-calls-to-end-use-of-facial-recognition-software

Bucy, M., Finlayson, A. Kelly, G., and Moye, C., The 'how' of transformation, *McKinsey & Company*, May 2016, Accessed 20 Feb 2020. https://www.mckinsey.com/industries/retail/our-insights/the-how-of-transformation

Byrne, P., Mining the moon, *The Conversation*, Mar 5, 2019, https://theconversation.com/mining-the-moon-110744

Clark, S., Pence calls for NASA to land astronauts on the moon within five years, *Spaceflight Now*, Mar 26, 2019, Accessed 17 January 2020. https://spaceflightnow.com/2019/03/26/pence-calls-for-nasa-to-land-astronauts-on-the-moon-within-five-years/

Cowing, K., Who owns the moon? *NASA Watch*, http://nasawatch.com/archives/2014/02/who-owns-the-mo.html, Feb 18, 2014. Accessed 21 Jan 2020.

Dovey, C., Mining the moon, *The Monthly*, July 2019, Accessed 19 Feb 2020. https://www.themonthly.com.au/issue/2019/july/1561989600/ceridwen-dovey/mining-moon

Economist Intelligence Unit (EIU), Global democracy in retreat, Tue, 21st Jan 2020, Accessed 25 Jan, 2020. https://www.eiu.com/n/global-democracy-in-retreat/

European Space Agency (ESA), About us, Accessed 4 Apr 2022. https://www.esa.int/About_Us/Corporate_news/ESA_facts#:~:text=Us%20%2F%20Corporate%20news-,The%20European%20Space%20Agency%20(ESA)%20is%20Europe's%20gateway%20to%20space,organisation%20with%2022%20Member%20States

Hao, K., AI is sending people to jail—and getting it wrong, *MIT Technology Review*, Jan 21, 2019, Accessed 14 Jan, 2020. https://www.technologyreview.com/2019/01/21/137783/algorithms-criminal-justice-ai/

Hunter, P., and Orr, S., Strategic Management Institute, Accessed 3 Apr, 2022. https://www.smiknowledge.com/resources

Manyika, J., Lund, S., Chui, M., Bughin, J., Woetzel J., Batra, P., Ko, R., and Sanghvi, S., Jobs lost, jobs gained: What the future of work will mean for jobs, skills, and wages, *McKinsey Global Institute*, Nov, 2017, Accessed 3 Mar, 2020. https://www.mckinsey.com/featured-insights/future-of-work/jobs-lost-jobs-gained-what-the-future-of-work-will-mean-for-jobs-skills-and-wages

Mayer, C., *Reforming Business for the 21st Century; A Framework for the Future of the Corporation*, British Academy, London, UK, Nov 2018.

McKendrick, J., High tech/high touch: The more we rely on machines, the more we need humans, *Forbes*, Dec 29, 2021, Accessed 3 Apr 2022. https://www.forbes.com/sites/joemckendrick/2021/12/29/high-techhigh-touch-the-more-we-rely-on-machines-the-more-we-need-humans/?sh=1e664a5167e8

Meta, Mark Zuckerberg stands for voice and free expression, meta web site, about us, Accessed 2 Jan 2022. https://about.fb.com/news/2019/10/mark-zuckerberg-stands-for-voice-and-free-expression/

Morgan, B., Companies that failed at digital transformation and what we can learn from them, *Forbes*, 30 Sep 2019, Accessed 20 Feb 2020. https://www.forbes.com/sites/blakemorgan/2019/09/30/companies-that-failed-at-digital-transformation-and-what-we-can-learn-from-them/#4ab63761603c

Naisbitt, J., High tech, *Hi Touch*, 1st Edition, Broadway Books, New York, 1999.

Neuralink. Accessed 8 Sept, 2021. https://neuralink.com/science/

Paul, K., Blue origin: Bezos company aims to take people to moon by 2024, *The Guardian*, San Francisco, Accessed 10 Nov, 2022. https://www.theguardian.com/technology/2019/may/09/blue-origin-jeff-bezos-moon-announcement

PwC, 23rd Annual global CEO survey, Navigating the rising tide of uncertainty, PwC Global, Accessed 29 Jan, 2020. chrome-extension://efaidnbmnnnibpcajpcglclefindmkaj/viewer.html?pdfurl=https%3A%2F%2Fwww.pwc.com%2Fgx%2Fen%2Fceo-survey%2F2020%2Freports%2Fpwc-23rd-global-ceo-survey.pdf&clen=26063636&chunk=true

Ross, P., Toyota joins coalition to bring blockchain networks to smart cars, *IEEE Spectrum*, 24 May 2017 | 14:02 GMT, Accessed 22 Feb 2020. https://spectrum.ieee.org/cars-that-think/computing/networks/toyota-joins-coalition-to-bring-blockchain-networks-to-smart-cars

Segar's, A. H., Seven technologies remaking the World, *MIT Sloan Management Review*, Mar 2018

Shao, G., *CNBC*, Thu, Aug 15, 2019 7:57 pm edt updated Fri, Aug 16 20195:41 am edt, Accessed 15 Jan 2020. https://www.cnbc.com/2019/08/16/social-media-has-become-a-battleground-in-hong-kongs-protests.html

Ungerleider, N., Nanoracks is the UPS of outer space shipping, *Fast Company*, 8 May 2012, Accessed 2 Feb 2020. https://www.fastcompany.com/3000152/nanoracks-ups-outer-space-shipping

Wall, M., 'Supremacy' achieved: Quantum computer notches epic milestone, *Space Inc.* 23 October 2019, Accessed 8th Feb 2020.

Wang, J., Zhu, E., and Taylor, U., How China built two coronavirus hospitals in just over a week, *Wall Street Journal*, Updated 6 Feb 2020 12:37 pm ET. https://www.wsj.com/articles/how-china-can-build-a-coronavirus-hospital-in-10-days-

5 Internal purpose in the 2040 Corporation

Claire Tomlins

Introduction

The essential driver of a company is its purpose. Aligning everyone and everything with a corporate purpose means that streamlining is easier and highlights those areas where innovations can create an effective and efficient service that adds value. Whilst also considering advancing technology, economic, social and governmental factors that have an impact. This chapter looks forward to how a company will exist and operate in the year 2040. Backcasting (Bibri, 2018), a strategic problem-solving framework is used to research the topic of *creating a company with purpose*. This method looks forward to 2040 and then backcasts to 2020. Thereby establishing the steps required to achieve goals set for the 2040s. Factors and their relationships are found within secondary and primary research to allow the construction of causal linkages between the backcasted years. During this 20-year period, there is an increasing emphasis on creating a fair and equitable future for everyone, while also addressing climate change and pandemic outcomes around the world. A rich tapestry of occurrences with many factors to consider.

The structure of the chapter starts with an explanation of the strategic problem solving method and framework. The second part sets the scene in “A Day in the life of a core company member” at home and at work, where the meeting agenda highlights key changes occurring and existing in 2040. The third part discusses the 2040 model created from primary and secondary research findings relating to core company executive roles and contributory ecosystems. Then moves on to the fast moving 2020 *new normal* occurrences. The fourth part categorises the factors that facilitate the steps from 2020 to achieve the 2040 existence. Each factor is examined by exploring the following: situation description; key decisions; key-problems – what caused the problems; key successes; and what were clear revelations, thereby elucidating how leaders and managers can align their company’s 2040 purpose and existence conclusions.

Method

In this chapter, backcasting is applied to establish the steps required to achieve the conditions that lead to the 2040 Corporation (Bibri, 2018). Factors and

DOI: 10.4324/9781003183679-5

their relationships are found within secondary and primary research to allow the construction of causal linkages between the backcasted years.

Secondary research started by searching business literature and academic peer-reviewed articles using the keywords and phrases: future of corporations, corporate purpose, innovation and creativity. This research resulted in an array of subjects: world geography, economic, social policies and; online and offline business and working environments; climate change; and latterly pandemics and civilian space travel.

Primary research is grounded in the real world. There is much speculative futuristic and science fiction literature, but this chapter considers how the creative use of developing technologies will impact future companies' purposes; people's personal and work lives; and environmental sustainability topics. A questionnaire was compiled from the secondary research to be referred to when conducting structured interviews with business people. The interviewees worked in the subject areas and faced the realities of innovations and their impact on key systems within their own businesses. These C-suite executives, mostly CEOs and specialists, work in the following sectors: business and innovation technology, brand design, financial investment and accounting, building design and connected technologies, healthcare and climate change. Thereby having wide and practical knowledge of what is currently working, happening and things that are likely to change how, why and when. Apart from solving problems and situations, they also prepare corporate strategies and outlooks on what is realistically going to happen, be required and used by companies in the future.

To cast a light on future possibilities between the years 2020 and 2040, questions were grouped into topics as follows:

- Definitions: innovations and creative topics; corporations between 2020-2040.
- Internal factors that will influence a corporation's structure, corporate identity and brand.
- Organisational: structures, leadership, culture, products and services.
- Designing the future of the corporation, new and existing technologies.
- External ecosystems that will collaborate and influence the corporation.

It must be borne in mind that during this 20-year period, commercial, pandemic and environmental existences are in continual upheaval and renewal mode throughout the world. Hence, the following three concepts have relevance:

i. The *Kondratiev curve* illustrates the economic cycle of expansion, stagnation and recession, formally every 50 years now reduced to a few decades.
ii. *Creative destruction* – when ageing industries and businesses that are no longer profitable fail and new industries are able to take over. The economist Joseph Schumpeter describes this as recurring revolutions relating to the

incessant destruction of old economic structures to create new ones. Netflix[1] is a good example of creative destruction.

iii. The *technology adoption cycle* depicts the market's adoption and acceptance of innovations and new products or services advancing from innovators and early adopters to the late majority and laggards.

To set the scene, a 2040s situation: A day in the life of a core company member

Background setting

Diary date: 2nd January 2040. Today I have a human conversation at the company core team (CCT) HQ. Normally I would be working at home in my quiet office pod reading the latest corporate business reports and watching company videos on my *danky*, a flexible square of digital genius that fits into a tube. On awakening, I press the health and emotional diagnostic sensor, my results are normal and therefore no remedial action is required, only the peak performance dietary requirements. As it's a weekday I verbally instruct the robot to make my usual breakfast. Occasionally we order a special breakfast by drone delivery. I activate deVoice and listen to my selected news and music streams. During the day there are so many frenetic electronic voices and sounds relating to market flow and adverting. I enjoy a more soothing introduction to my day at breakfast. As the family are arising and taking over the living area and performing their routines, I assist my mother into her active life chair and leave for work.

We live in a company housing ecosystem, so I call for a fully charged fly/drive vehicle with the HQ directions set. Some team members prefer the solo-jet, but you cannot listen to music as there are many regulations in place to ensure your craft does not hit a delivery drone or another solo-jet. When the destination is reached – the CCT building – I walk through the security clearing space. After my CCT membership is identified, I sit at the CCT world table and a hologram introduces me to the other executives, including those online.

The business agenda highlights key changes that occurred during the period

Those at the CCT table are experts in their fields, each having a clear working knowledge of the company's requirements and objectives and can step into a variety of roles when required. There is no CEO as collaborative teamwork is found to be the best approach. Our knowledge and skills are complementary and individually we have been screened, tested and analysed since birth. After the pandemic of the 2020s, an overhaul of the health system occurred. Now the health ecosystem regularly monitors us to ensure we maintain a healthy lifestyle by eating nutritiously and exercising regularly both physically and mentally. After catching up on each other's news, time is set to read the business, artificial intelligence, societal, space, economic, environmental and governmental (BAISSEEG) information displayed on the dynamic dashboard. Sometimes the hologram appears to tell us of a crucial occurrence and its implications.

Perhaps you would benefit from some background information to understand the necessity of having this meeting. This is a key human decision-making event in the company's calendar to ensure the central core and ecosystems are working effectively and are in alignment with the corporate purpose and values of maintaining our survival and defence systems.

There have been several computer system, new technology and data disasters during the last 20 years. Now the Technology Ethics Board guidelines specify the types of decisions that computers can make and those that require human CCT input. Computer decisions are now forbidden in the resolution of high-level BAISEEG problems and issues. Artificial intelligence can answer complex questions at great speed by analysing large data sets sourced in robotic and other computing systems. It does not understand the nuances of human interaction, how solutions are achieved or the best approach or solution. To widen access to opinions non-executives, governments and large corporations' representatives, trade or industry body delegates are available. Having these contacts is helpful when engaging or interacting with global issues that require specific knowledge, expertise or insight.

Large data centres run all major operations. If anything goes wrong, we have a set procedure to follow: ask what, how and why the situation occurred. Find a solution and decide on the best implementation action. This is primarily used for blockchain processes as reviewing, examining and recording solutions are required for regulation, legal purposes and future reference.

The CCT avatar activates the meeting's recording system and checks water and food supplies. Our agenda discussion begins:

i) On Earth, blockchain reports detail all project workflow in qualitative, quantitative and financial terms. This dramatically reduces the number of audits that previously took up so much time and effort. We still must agree on the percentage accuracy rating as some businesses do not wish to comply with blockchain requirements for various cultural reasons. It is useful to ensure that the team know the blockchain protocols in case a problem arises. If the problem is significant, we engage with the blockchain company representative for more in-depth discussion and action.
ii) No longer earthbound, we have an increasing number of moon and interplanetary projects requiring creative ideas and innovations to sustain the business. The CCT moonbase on the southern arc of the Moon is our first outpost and was developed in the mid-2020s as a stopping point for interplanetary travel, particularly to Mars. Fortunately, we developed technologies that allow tolerable conditions for human to survive in a lunar bubble environment, with fuel conversion capabilities, which enable rockets to be launched and travel the lengthy and time consuming distances to Mar and other planets.

    Currently, we are making decisions on our Moon operations as the space travellers' moonbase is fully operational. A staging post for staff and collaborators before travelling further afield to our Mars company's main office and mining operations. Recently, we received instantaneous data to say that one of the vehicles needed a part modification. The prototype must be tested, certified and financial approval signed off by the CCT. An augmented reality (AR) image appears in the centre of the room and descriptive texts appear on our individual digital displays. A 2030s campaign to reduce computer clutter and improve Earth's digital environment resulted in a one digital device per person policy. The Mars vehicle part's AI results are positive but the CCT wish to discuss the flexibility and manoeuvrability of the vehicle on Mars terrain when driven by a human or drone power. To facilitate the final decision, we contact the design part company representatives and government certification agency for further advice.

iii) The geography of design and manufacture is now worldwide as human and computing creativity influences innovations and inventions. Key centres exist in countries in Africa, Brazil, China, Mexico, Russia and the United States. These countries have high manufacturing capabilities with huge populations that use and create products and services. To improve national and business relationships, delegates often attend meetings in addition to online video calls. European design and manufacture have a long cultural history and now inspire new specialist technologies on a small scale. Another outcome is that intellectual property legislation is a prime source of income and knowledge for the European creative industry with other parts of the world following. We highlight where successes and problems are arising across a wide range of interests from large and small countries and check the dashboard to determine potential problems and how to resolve them.

iv) As climate change is always high on the agenda, we have many rehabilitation projects across the planet. Monitoring changes is a necessity for weather patterns, fires, floods and volcanoes in both deep subterranean trenches and on land. Air pollution is clearing across all continents but there are pockets of high pollution that require attention, particularly in large conurbations. Electric vehicles and hydrogen energy technologies are in daily use with a carbon allowance in place for each traveller.

v) The fragility of the planet's existence became apparent after a reappraisal of the world's geography and ecological landscape, both in human and environmental terms in the mid-2020s. This work still impacts daily and business life today as everyone is aware of the planet, its natural inhabitants, environments, ecologies and, not least, pandemics. We consider relevant topics relating to our company's purpose and concentrate on selected aligned activities.

vi) As digital communications engender higher engagement, popular voting and uprisings across the world, we need to be risk aware of occurrences arising from changes in political ideologies and democratic affairs. Extinction Rebellion, Simplicity and Raison d'être are mainstream movements providing alternative lifestyles and making contributions to reducing global catastrophes.

vii) Our operations are worldwide and we have people from many origins. Diversity and remote collaborative working enabled us to solve problems quickly during the low yield years, 2020–2023. At that time, governments introduced strict financial controls and fewer paid jobs were available. Families had to look after themselves and appreciate what they had. As a responsible corporation, we provide aid to staff and local work locations as required.

viii) New ideas, creativity, innovation and invention still abound. Alas, only a select few innovations survive the now rigorous hurdles. Today, adventurers dive into the deepest depths of the oceans and travel into outer space further afield than ever thought possible. New and exciting strands to our operations are being progressed, such as exploration and exploitation of the Moon, Mars and Earth's deep-sea trenches for new mineral resources required for electronic manufacture.

ix) Computers use continuous learning to provide precise, accurate and efficient adaptive feedback. Hence, humans now have more time and resources to resolve problems, address human issues and undertake learning and creative projects to service manufacturing and the environment. New medical conditions are still arising that require research as some people, for example, have an adverse reaction to electronic devices or require an adjustment to their computing system to work and enjoy life to its full potential.

x) Learning is a key human activity as the natural world, business and learning ecosystems increase opportunities. Human intelligence ratings have increased, particularly in digital natives educated through access to infinite resources, communication and play sources at their fingertips and voice.

xi) Millennials and Gen Zs are now the decision-makers, resolving problems quickly through unique approaches and clear cohesive actions. Their tacit knowledge of a wide range of computing systems both strategic and operational in nature being a contributory factor. At long last, we have resolved many of the AI-related problems, but we are still wary of new issues arising.

xii) Our teams of ecosystem collaborators are encouraged to remain agile. Training and educational initiatives support learning and imagination projects as design, ecological and outer space developments become central to our business. We provide computer processing power for large data volume experiments and prototyping to progress research and creative endeavours. This creates new products and services which then require manufacturing, business ordering and distribution systems using blockchain.

That's our meeting over, on travelling home I catch up on the family's news and activities and check that everything is going well with granny. She had a stroke a few years ago and recovered remarkably. Soon after the stroke, a thread-like robot was guided through her brain's blood vessels to clear the blood clot and administer drugs. Her aftercare requires repetitive hand and body movement so that the neural pathways rewire quickly. Her therapist prepares the exercise plan and granny regularly sits in her wellbeing chair with a robotic attachment that repeatedly exercises her limbs. The children are now signing into their learning ecosystem, a result of the radical education system changes in the mid-2020s.

Each child is expected to attain their highest potential with lessons, downtime and nutrition guidelines set and monitored to recognise progress and exceptional talents.

Everyone is now settled. After the early 2020 pandemic, people wanted to meet up more as isolation manifested a need for human activities often related to environmental projects. We are having a family event soon. What should I wear to the event? Brand names of my youth have disappeared along with many others from the pre-pandemic time. Big brands and company-own brand suppliers provide all the daily necessities – housing, food, energy and clothing. My ***danky*** enables me to access brand e-booths. I select an outfit with an AR display. The dress and surface design appears, and I review other patterns. Eco-credentials, fabric details, prices and cleaning instructions are listed on my ***danky***. By clicking the digital payment spot, the transaction appears and the blockchain supply and delivery are initiated. The dress arrives by drone within one hour. Day journal entry completed.

So that is a glimpse of corporate working life in 2040. The next section looks at what the corporation will look like in 2040 by considering the main elements of the corporation's 2040 core and contributory ecosystems.

The 2040 corporations' core and contributory ecosystems

The 2040 corporation comprises a central core team (CCT) placed within the organisational structure at its core (see Figure 5.1). The 2040 model of a corporation's core and contributory ecosystems deals with internal functions and external ecosystems' ephemeral existence. The following sections discuss each of these organisational and central core team elements and ecosystems.

Core teams

To ensure the company's success, a core team (CCT) oversees the whole running of the operation, making decisions as situations and emergencies arise. Leaders and managers must align and attend to creating a clear purpose, appoint leaders and create an awareness of culture and ethics, with an unequivocal company ecosystem comprising of corporate, learning, natural, lifestyle and space skillsets and databases.

Purpose

A company's purpose looks at the organisation from the outside, satisfying the customer above cost. Defining what the company does, its values, why it has taken that approach and how it aims to achieve its goals[5]. It is central to business success informing the corporate strategy or outlook.

Aligning all company strategies and operations is key and leaders must define and enthuse the corporate purpose throughout the organisation.

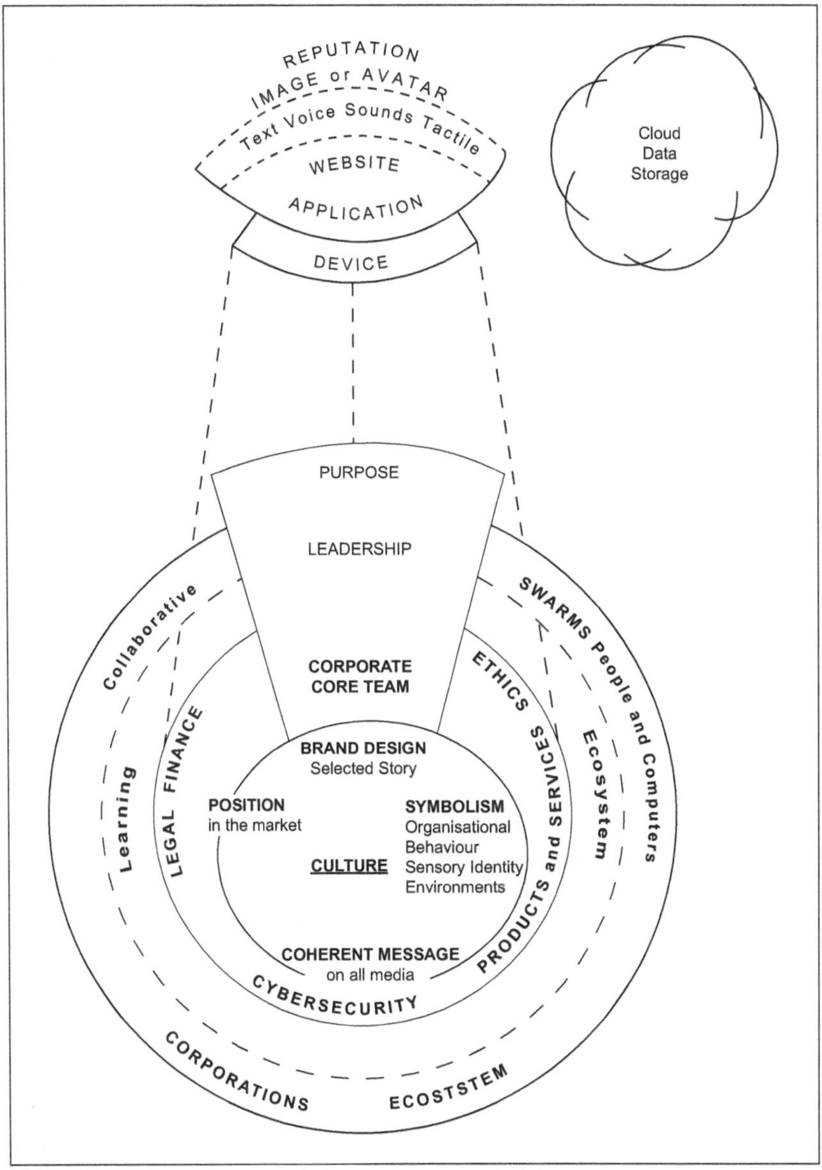

Figure 5.1 The 2040 Model of a corporation's core and contributory ecosystems.

By placing purpose in the centre, staff know what is expected of them and form a cohesive cultural unit that recognises and removes non-value adding elements so that operations are streamlined. This contributes to the business thereby guaranteeing value creation and societal objectives (Harrington, 2019). As technology advances, *being* a *driver for change* regardless of the organisation's size is the key purpose of a corporation.

Leadership

Leaders, whether appointed in person or on a rotating basis, are necessary to orchestrate the business's interwoven roles and activities (Ostergaard, 2018; Hudson Searle, 2020). A hybrid of democratic leadership exists in 2040 with people from a diversity of backgrounds. The leadership role requires a reputable person with good communication skills who serves their employees by using their powers to open doors. Thereby ensuring clear communication channels to the CCT core and ecosystems.

There are three types of leadership in the hierarchy (Ancona et al., 2018). The lowest being entrepreneurial, the middle enabling project leaders and at the top architectural leaders who deal with the big picture or helicopter viewpoint. This formation is a key feature as teams work across versatile ecosystem computing platforms.

Culture

The creation of a coherent corporate culture is central to purpose, setting the tone and way of working with cultural awareness, organisational behaviour and values being important business differentiators. Corporate culture can be structured or organic with approaches ranging from authoritative to democratic as technological and societal changes are played out throughout the world. Nevertheless, being respectful of culture is important even for small things, for example, the Chinese design style of the Johnny Walker's whisky logo must be culturally relevant in China and Taiwan with a Chinese design aesthetic.

Ethics

How people from different cultures interpret situations at work or elsewhere can vary widely. There may be no right or wrong version but ethical guidelines ensure approaches, actions and interpretations are aligned. A Technology Ethics Board is now in place as the implications of human existence alongside computing advances highlight the fact that there are political or cultural reasons why individuals or organisations do not wish their data to be used – whether people have a choice depends on where they reside.

Creativity

In daily life, while at home, travelling, at work or at play, we often overlook the creativity involved in visioning, planning and making our environments. Forming something new is particularly human, but computers have caught up forming an additional creative and business sector. Humans and computers now contribute to the design of clothes, the formation of mathematical formulae and the construction of vehicles and rockets that transport and support us in the deepest ocean or outer space. Human creativity finds solutions to problems that artificial intelligence cannot and therefore people with creative skillsets are in demand. Particularly in highly competitive markets, for example, composing sounds, music and jingles (du Sautoy, 2019), when suitably implemented, can differentiate a business online and offline, facilitating a good corporate reputation and social media recommendations. This business reputation then progresses through future introductions, contracts and staff acquisition as required.

These organisational and central core team elements are surrounded by supporting ecosystems. The next section considers the development of these ecosystems.

Ecosystems

As companies became aware of the necessity to extend their corporate purpose with the expansion of operational considerations of people and planet, strategies had to include all stakeholders' requirements and objectives. Ecosystems are the result of this expansion. This section starts with "Corporate ecosystems" for all business activities, including stakeholders. Second, "Learning ecosystems", which include those for business, education and leisure activities. Third, "Natural ecosystems" for the wider world. Finally, there is a section on "Lifestyle and outer space ecosystems".

Corporate Ecosystems

Within the corporate ecosystem, there is a complex fluid of networked companies and people, where various collaborative working protocols and programmes operate. The word corporation has its derivation from *corpus*, the Latin for a body of people. In 2040, this term still applies to swarms of people and computers working on projects collaboratively, within portfolio careers, with three to four companies. There is still an innate need for people to be around people for social interaction and to bounce off ideas to advance innovative thinking and products. Hence, co-working places are now accommodating backroom staff, tech geeks, creatives and engineers, under one roof, on temporary or full-time contracts.

A clear corporate purpose is important to ensure that potential and new employees establish alignment, or not, with the organisation's values and operate efficiently within the company's environment and ecosystem. Company representatives frequently discuss the company's culture when determining business, financial, creative, engineering and communication skill requirements, particularly when the human resource index and skillset database, popularly known as the digital nomadic database (DND), needs updating. This is referred to when a vacancy needs filling. The system enables a faster matching of a candidate's skills, qualifications and culture fit with the company's style and staffing requirements. Allowing companies to select and recruit the best person for a job, or for an individual to self-select themselves to contribute to a company's operations anywhere, anytime. This increases flexibility, making life easier for everyone but it does require trust, intelligence, intuition, transparency and learning capabilities to be successful. While facilitating lean and agile corporate ecosystems to maintain their market share.

Workflow performance and financial results appear on blockchain reports. This system dramatically reduces audits that previously took up so much time and effort. A percentage accuracy is required as some businesses do not wish to comply with blockchain requirements for various cultural reasons. Knowing blockchain protocols is also important for fast problem resolution that we undertake ourselves. Occasionally, if the problem is significant, we engage a blockchain company representative for in-depth discussion and action.

Learning ecosystems

Like biological ecosystems, businesses will either grow or die, consequently, continuous learning and gaining subject knowledge is important as technology advances and its application assessed. As knowledge and expertise increase, this corporate memory benefits the company, employees and collaborative workers (Johnson, 2019). Ultimately, the knowledge database within a learning ecosystem provides resilience and versatility, which allows arising problematic situations to be recognised and resolved across natural, learning and corporate ecosystems.

This ecosystem is not solely corporate but includes further education and access to leisure and hobby databases. By 2030, many companies run their own universities conducting research according to their specific requirements across joint technological and art projects.

Natural ecosystems

The annual Earth Day highlights planet Earth's existence and fragility, both in human and environmental terms. There are many contributors to this ecosystem: animals, birds and insect habitats, including plants, trees and urban environments. All of which can be used for healing purposes, new foods, product development or recreational pursuits. Meanwhile, AI can examine and analyse samples by comparing them against natural history records to identify potential uses, advantages and disadvantages. This work contributes to medical advances, enabling diagnoses to be made and treatments progressed.

Through time it became clear that some people have side effects from working with or being close to computers, including those using digital technology overzealously. This ecosystem provides alternative living, working and learning opportunities for these people and those interested in the natural world in general.

Related ecosystems

Lifestyle ecosystems

People choose different lifestyles to suit their needs. Many makers and creatives select this route often, initially through the learning ecosystem, as it provides freedom outside the corporate system to explore and exploit their own talents and skills.

Space ecosystems

Space environments and ecosystems are expanding as outer space travel increases for business and leisure. Space travellers undertake the most research into their trips as they must pass a test on all elements of outer space travel before gaining their special access pass. This could be the start of a new job, research opportunity or make that vacation trip to the Moon more interesting.

So that is how the core company executive roles and contributory ecosystems relate to internal functions and external ecosystems existence and contributions. The next section explores the *new normal* - the initial 2020 situation and then the 2020 business year's exploration of the *new normal* situation and experience.

The new normal – the 2020 situation

Initial conditions in 2020: The sudden new normal

The New Year and holiday period of 2020 are over, everything is back to normal with people travelling to work, reading newspapers and books online and as broadsheets. Shoppers and tourists going to the end of winter sales and new spring season fashions appearing. People travelling around the world for business and vacations to ski resorts or for some sunshine. Schoolchildren and students returning to classrooms and lecture theatres. Exhibitions and entertainment in full swing.

During the previous two decades, a constant increase in digitalisation crept into work and personal lives with lifestyles becoming frenetic. By 2020, most people are familiar with the internet, smartphones and smart meters, buying online and conducting business digitally, while AI is creeping into research and corporations. Video calls and webinars are popular in business. While viewing and learning from YouTube videos and TED talks for hobbies and work are popular. Yet there is still an element of “its digital” for younger people, for work but increasingly for shopping, entertainment and getting the latest sports update on social media but *the real thing* is much better. Many people are reluctant to have too much digital in their homes, especially older people.

We must talk and act as climate change issues are arising. So many major catastrophes are occurring across the globe: sea levels rising as icebergs and glaciers melt, volcanoes erupting and temperatures rising to over 40°C in Europe. The Climate Change Conference held in Glasgow, Scotland, in November 2021 debated these events.

China *closed up-shop*. They have coronavirus and everyone must stay at home – everything is being sprayed with disinfectant. The virus is said to be spreading. I am waiting for a train and looking down on this central London station concourse from a balcony. Why is everyone standing separately? Almost a metre apart front, back and sideways. Is someone making a film in the station?

March 2020, UK lockdown – *The New Normal: Everyone must stay at home.*

- Healthcare services are stretched to the limit as doctors try to keep people alive and scientists research vaccines. People of all ages are very ill and dying, particularly the elderly and vulnerable.
- Lifestyles change as businesses close and can no longer function unless they are online. Staff are furloughed, that is they are retained and paid 80% of their salary by the government. Many businesses close never to re-open and staff are made redundant.
- Children must be home-educated, so classes and teaching materials move online. Parents become temporary teachers for their children. Meanwhile, university students' courses and communications are put online. Many students go home or stay inside student residences.
- People declutter their homes, revisit old hobbies or start new ones, cook, bake and sing in online choirs, increasingly most activities move online by virtue of necessity. All those Zoom calls –where are the make-up websites? New businesses appear.

Massive strides in digital advances occur. Families and friends communicate through Facebook, Zoom calls and WhatsApp. Online buying, selling and deliveries soar. Supply chains are stretched to the limit and through time become disrupted, problems being resolved as fast as possible, if at all. Banking and financial transactions are only online or by phone. Young and old are taught how to use online banking. Through numerous local and online communities available to help or instruct people.

This pattern progresses across the world as each person, each country and every government grapple with their best approach for keeping citizens safe by lockdowns, curfews, social distancing and face masks across China, Europe, India, Africa, the United States, Canada, South America, Australia, New Zealand, Indonesia and so on. Meanwhile, scientists are developing Covid-19 vaccines. In the UK, a vaccine is developed in one year – a tenth of the normal vaccine development programme. Within the next year, by September 2021, over 70% of the UK population over 16 years old are vaccinated twice. This enables people to resume a *new normal* life with the caveat of being careful as we may have to have further lockdowns as winter approaches.

Yet with fast and furious change, economic, societal and governmental (ESG[2]) strategies continue to ebb and flow to achieve the best result by combining human and digital information and increasing the use of AI decision-making processes. By the end of 2020, most people are familiar with the internet and smartphones. Integrating training and education with digital and human activity becomes an everyday occurrence and seamless learning a necessity.

The 2020 business year

The Covid-19 pandemic certainly sent shockwaves around the world, testing leadership and staff capabilities to the ultimate.

Suddenly, everyone works remotely and collaboratively, while optimising their online and offline operations. Situations and occurrences such as supply chain disruptions, employee self-isolation and home-schooling changes occur frequently as regulations and legislation are put in place within short time spans. Business leaders are literally drivers of change navigating their way through this global crisis by combining helicopter viewpoints and detailed analyses. CEOs review their company's situation – systems, stakeholders and shareholders as digital communication facilitate fast pivots. By concentrating on values and purpose, the CEO and staff can speak directly with each other on video calls. Decision-making is faster and communicating to all staff is instant, fostering collaborative engagement. This enhances the corporate culture to survive and prosper in difficult times.

Through this experience, a resilient and agile digital business transformation model took a five-year leap forward, achieving a better fit for purpose status. Employees working from home (WFH) quickly developed remote IT communication skills and knowledge of cybersecurity through online skills training, attending Zoom meetings and collaborating on Trello and suchlike. Meanwhile, households receive daily deliveries from Amazon worldwide, with its Trusted Brand status, customers feel safer in registering bank details to this platform and ecosystem, which now caters for 90% of deliveries. On the healthcare front, often seen as slow-moving, specialist small agile businesses start feeding into the larger health system, becoming key contributors. Keynote being the development and manufacture of vaccines to combat the virus in a tenth of the normal vaccine development period. Throughout this period, it soon became apparent that business continuity planning and investment in operational resilience are always paramount if the corporate purpose is to be satisfied in a crisis.

Brand positions and reputations alter as business models become irrelevant or dramatically change. Health, education and community become more important as travel, hospitality and familiar department stores, badly impacted, disappear as do many middle market brands. Online and offline grocery, gardening, DIY and clothing enterprises rise to the challenge. Many expanding physically yet having to ensure staff can work safely. Companies identify new markets and business concepts and develop relevant products and services to fill customers' new real needs. A relevant customer query being *Do you do what you say?* A clear alignment of activities, products and services with purpose and its internal and external customer stakeholders.

Business creativity manifests itself through a clear brand strategy and corporate identity management by the alignment of a coherent message across all brand channels. The backdrop being that often customers like to know a business's evolution and progression by its story as it reinforces its philosophy, values and ethos forming a basis for its purpose and brand expression. Customers then decide whether to buy into the brand and become loyal to its values. This clarity of purpose centres and engages staff, attracts loyal customers and ensures cooperation online, offline or both. To attract attention and engagement, a brand's image and corporate identity is communicated through sensory channels, primarily visual and sound. Current visual auditing technologies provide quality benefits for the symbolic visual design process, as elements such as name, typeface, colours and logos can create an identity, with suggestions on colours and shapes. While products can be viewed from many angles at their various design stages. Nevertheless, the human soul and intuition cannot be replaced and usually has the final say on design output.

Creative industries now have a greater reliance and accessibility to technology and resources across a wide range of makers' and thinkers' work. The key advantage being ease of access to online sources relating to consumer requirements and source of materials. In any creative idea, the scope of change may be high but if it delivers value, whether this is by reducing costs, providing cheaper services or a new benefit, then the proposal can be viable and flourish.

Millennials and Gen Z working in the gig economy have an unforeseen opportunity to thrive in this *new normal.* Key to good results is productive creative and digital technology skills training with a note that creativity arises across a wide range of media and landscapes, talents and skills. Yet, returns on investment tend not to be high.

Before continuing, funding must be mentioned as creative industries and R&D technology progress in their symbiotic relationship. Funding is a necessity to enable the manifestations or purpose of an artefact, system or design to be successfully found. Crowdfunding is a strong contributor in this aspect. Governments are becoming more aware of funding as they realise solutions to arising problems must be found. An important note from an interviewee is that the development of creative and technological advances is not only about funding, if at all. The removal of impediments to change and increasing regulations that slow down or reduce creativity are thought to be more pertinent. With the point being made that sometimes the artistic and technology mix and crossover can produce exciting developments. Funding is also required for training children as they are most creative in their younger years.

New business models arose around 2020 as the Marvel Cinematic Universe (MCU) (Harrison et al., 2019) offset business stability with renewal when companies adapted to customer expectations as the human or digital worlds merged. Companies must maintain growth and regeneration by using creativity and innovation as key drivers to ensure the companies continue their services and products existence, reputation and purpose.

Central banks waver and debt structuring becomes stringent in the early 2020s. Many people look for alternative financial approaches and start to consider bitcoin as part of their financial portfolios. The creation of bitcoin and the blockchain concept was initiated by Satoshi Nakomoto (2008) as a decentralised ledger maintained by anonymous consensus. This decentralisation and people-run approach enhanced by bitcoin, which is not a physical asset, is held in a digital wallet with layers of security. Cryptocurrencies are digital assets representing the value of different blockchain protocols. Further cryptocurrencies are appearing, two of the original being altcoins and Ethereum. Token representations of an asset or utility reside on top of another blockchain representing any asset that is fungible and traceable ranging from loyalty points, commodities or other cryptocurrencies. Many people see these currencies as the future of money and digital natives considered them more appropriate to their needs as anyone can access the bitcoin network and transact.

During this period, cryptocurrencies rose and fell frequently in the markets. By June 2020, there were 6000 cryptocurrencies but most fell within five years. Bitcoin remains, becoming fully public, with investors continuing to conduct research as to whether bitcoin can fulfil their requirements. In February 2021, bitcoin reaches its highest valuation and then fell again. Meanwhile, payment systems such as Libra, backed up by reserves, create a global financial system based on blockchain technology with security being a key driver.

Having now considered the backcasting strategic problem-solving framework and the 2020 *new normal* occurrences, the next section addresses the actions and decisions to reach the 2040 position.

Actions and decisions taken in the period 2020–2040 that resulted in the 2040 position

By 2040, massive changes occur. The central core team concept is operating with the corporate, learning and natural ecosystems working in a gig-like basis. Between 2020 and 2040 some monumental and some small disruptions impact both personal and business life across the globe. To identify these occurrences, the backcasting strategic forecasting framework is applied to establish the necessary steps in achieving the goals set for 2040. Topics and their relationships are sourced within secondary and primary research to allow the construction of causal linkages between the backcasted years.

SPE³C²IAL Schematic global factors showing linkages and relationships

By combining the literature and interview survey results, Figure 5.2 shows factor clusters and their linkage and interrelationships with one another. Resulting from this, the following corporate strategy factors arose: sociological, political geography, environmental, economic, exploration, creativity, computing and cybersecurity, intelligence and data, aid and legal, which form the mnemonic SPE³C²IAL. Company leaders and managers can address each factor and add others according to their own company's situation.

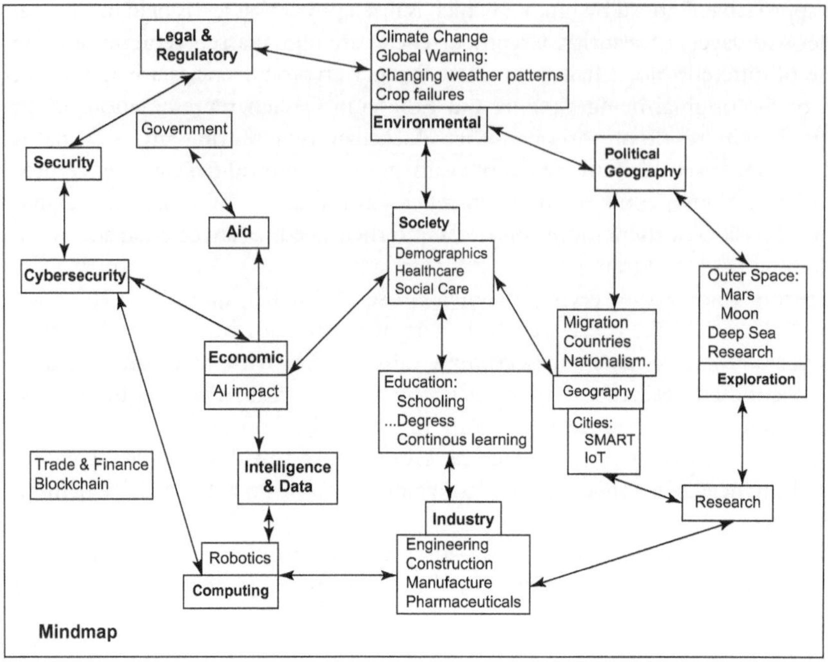

Figure 5.2 Mind map to identify corporate strategy factors likely to impact companies by 2030 and 2040 with linkages and interrelationships.

Actions and decisions made between 2020 and 2040 using the SPE³C²IAL mnemonic

In this section, individual SPE³C²IAL factors are shown with discussions and evaluations by relevant contributions and requirement ratings addressing each of the following:

- Describe the situation
- Key decisions
- Key problems – what caused the problems
- Key successes
- What was a clear revelation?

A rating is attached to each contribution:

High-risk requirement – must have
Necessary requirement – must have
Key requirement – good to have

1. Sociological

(i) **Situation: Healthcare and pharmaceutical research** *High-risk requirement – must have*

Key successes: After the success of Covid-19 vaccines, pharmaceutical research on unresolved medical issues gain higher precedence as malaria and tuberculosis thought eradicated saw a resurgence in early 2020.

Key decisions: To keep people healthy in 2040, the World Health Organisation (WHO) upgrades its health and emotional diagnostic systems to ensure wider usage. Apart from Covid-19, no further pandemics occur – only local sporadic epidemics. Robots are treating stroke patients by following a human therapist's instructions.

Key problem: The Covid-19 pandemic impacted millions of people in 2020 and 2021 – it took time for vaccines to be developed, costing lives. AstraZeneca and other pharmaceutical companies used AI and the latest research technology, creating a successful vaccine in one-tenth of the normal research period.

Clear revelation: People accept serious situations and adapt to another safe existence until vaccines or solutions are found. Each country takes its own approach in preventing the spread of coronavirus. Vaccines are not always top of the list. Nonetheless, by September 2021, 70% of the UK population was vaccinated.

(ii) **Situation: Education and corporate learning ecosystems** *Necessary requirement – must have*

Key successes: Life-long learning is necessary to keep skills current within a competitive market as technological developments, subject knowledge, behaviours and skillsets are required for future business and outer space projects. Government initiatives encourage people to retrain or learn a new hobby to keep active, especially if between paid jobs or retired.

Key decisions in the late 2020s to early 2030 were:

- Online education must be accessible for children to continue their schooling and university education and for those in outlying areas.
- Human intelligence is far more perceptive of nuances and understanding of cultures than AI. Hence, universities continue to hold classes on campus and actively encourage students usually studying online to visit the campus once a term or to attend either the summer or winter academic weeks. It is important to meet people face-to-face to develop cultural awareness and good communication and negotiation skills.

Key problem: Home-schooling across primary, secondary and tertiary education became a necessity during the pandemic. Educational establishments re-evaluated their digital strategies and content creation, becoming their own ecosystem. Progressing a route expected to occur in the future. There is much trial and error.

Clear revelation: Age is not a barrier to learning and can be a benefit.

(iii) **Situation: Demographics** *Necessary requirement - must have*

Key successes: Demographics contribute to establishing better emergency services.

Key decisions:

- Children's medical records begin at birth and are logged for screenings, tests and analyses.
- Elderly and multigenerational activities, entertainment and learning new hobbies and skills are encouraged.

Key problems: Birth rates and ageing populations always vary. The birth rate was dropping in 2020 but as the pandemic and environmental issues arose, nurturing within family units is increasing. The ageing population and care homes crisis during the pandemic meant that people became more aware of older people and their needs.

Clear revelation: Elderly people can contribute to society far longer than expected if allowed to do so – the Captain Tom approach.

2. Political geography

(i) **Situation: Migrations** *Necessary Requirement - must have*

There is no clear success on migrations as it is an ongoing human condition.

Key decisions: There are many reasons why people migrate and therefore the decision was made to try to understand key problems and motivations. Some migrations are long-running, while others are sudden. To stem the flow or offer refuge requires decisions and organisation as many people die attempting to travel to a safer country.

Resolving problems and conflicts should be the first objective. In the early 2020s, migration was a huge problem as people from Africa, Afghanistan, Hong Kong and other countries fled in fear of their lives.

Clear revelation: New immigrants from different countries help one another.

(ii) **Situation: Voting** *Key requirement – good to have*

Key successes: Estonia became an e-country launching a highly successful digital programme and becoming a flagship e-country with e-passports and services. Other countries follow on.

Key decisions:

- New opportunities arise and people reassess how to lead their lives and make decisions on their future through voting. By 2030, voting is online for election of UK members of parliament and local county councillors.
- The internet engenders higher popular voting and uprisings across the world, nevertheless, solutions to problems are often found quickly. By 2040, Simplicity and Raison d'être movements provide alternative lifestyles.

Clear revelation: By 2030 into 2040, life is calming down as the *new normal* is firmly in place and people have learnt how to work and live in the digital world, while carving a human lifestyle.

3. Environment

i) **Situation: Climate change global impact** *High-risk requirement – must have*

Key successes: In the 2020s, climate change gathered momentum as large areas of the planet became uninhabitable through shifting weather patterns, fires, floods and volcanoes in both deep subterranean trenches and on land. The COP26 Conference in Glasgow, November 2021, discussed the problem and how to protect natural inhabitants, environments, ecologies and possible pandemic recurrences. A raft of initiatives occurred as thinking and actions had to change faster than the climatic change impact.

Key decisions: Between 2020 and 2040, specific objectives and purposes were set in mainstream thinking.

- An appraisal of the world's geography and ecological landscape requests nations to join forces to maintain their existence and safety. This is a continual assessment programme of Earth's survival status. By 2040, Earth had been mapped in detail with risk factors calibrated. Global communications contribute to this exercise, applying culturally diverse knowledge and approaches to data collection and records
- Decisions were made to stop diesel fuels in the 2020s and deliberate burning of forests to reduce pollution. New technologies such as electric vehicles are now in daily use.
- UN Sports for Climate Action Frameworks encourages sports teams and organisations to sign up to promote greater environmental responsibility, such as taking air and car mileage and converting this to financial terms to be contributed to environmental change projects.
- The COP26 Climate Change Conference in Glasgow raised several problems and decisions were made, but India and China are not reducing coal usage in the near future.

What caused the problems: David Attenborough warns that the world warmed by more than 1°C in the last 150 years, which could send global temperature spiralling higher. While Mark Carney explained that action is necessary as floods, fires and irregular weather patterns are destroying vast areas of the planet. Various groups form in the 2020s such as the Extinction Rebellion. Originally being problematic by blocking main roads and causing life-threatening occurrences for many people.

Clear revelation: The pandemic lockdowns travel stoppages across air, land and sea transportation allows people, particularly younger generations, in large conurbations to breathe clean air and see blue sky. The climate change agenda is successful with the planet beginning to rejuvenate in small ways by 2040.

4. Economic

(i) **Situation: Leadership** *Necessary requirement – must have*

Key successes: In the 2020s, autocratic leaders were thought to be disappearing but recent political events show this is not the case. As collaborative working becomes normal staff need to trust their leaders as project leaders revolve, depending on merit, skillsets required and stage of a project.

Key decisions: Leadership changes with an expected democratisation trend up to 2030, as collaborative working becomes the norm. Opening doors to access networks became another element of a leader's role.

What caused the problems: Many skills are required to lead an online company. The pandemic instigates rapid digital transformation requiring urgent online training.

Clear revelation: Leaders can take on many roles as situations arise.

(ii) **Situations: Decision-making – frameworks and scorecards** *Necessary requirement – must have*

Key successes:

- The British Academy's Future of the Corporation[5] aims to revitalise the purpose of a company that allows people and communities to survive and thrive.
- A new ESG framework adds non-financial to traditional financial performance metrics and integrates a strategy map to visually represent the company's strategic objectives (Kaplan & McMillan, 2021).
- Decision-making is a key skill for any leader. Through the 2020s and 2030s, topics and content change. The 2040 CCT dynamic dashboard presents BAISSEEG information related to current problems and issues. A hologram appears to explain the occurrence and its implications.

Key decisions: In 2021 companies are encouraged to work with the wider world's SMEs, charities and social community projects to create economic and other value adding attributes. The British Academy Policy and Practice for Purposeful Business (2021 Report)[6] encompasses this approach and includes Covid-19 and technological impacts.

Key problems: Reducing poverty, social exclusion and environmental issues must be addressed.

Clear revelation: Historical information systems approaches can still be relevant.

(iii) **Situation: Employment and skills** *Necessary requirement – must have*

Key successes:

- Multigenerational companies with personalised learning and development programmes exist in 2040. Company learning ecosystems create resources that staff can access for continuous learning. Government grants are available for a one-person digital access device with training allowances.

- Many Gen X and millennials lost their jobs in the pandemic. Forcing them into setting up their own businesses. Social media and networking platforms such as CONNECTS[3] facilitate business networking.

Key decisions: Generational and trans-generational skills and knowledge are harnessed to combine pre-digital and digital working methods and training. In 2020, the following assessments were made:

- *Baby boomers* can work until 2030 as more than half will remain in employment until 70 or over. Patience, generational knowledge and skills requirements can provide better products and services.
- *Generation X* in their late 30s to early 50s during the pandemic stretched staff loyalty, except when furloughed. Yet their combination of digital skills and traditional leadership enabled numerous problems to be overcome and new opportunities to be detected.
- *Millennials*, the first generation to grow up in the digital era, are technology-driven, use social media for research and communicate continuously on TikTok, Instagram and WhatsApp. The digital world with its continuous updates, values and networking often encouraging them to start their own business.
- *Gen Z*, those between eight and 25 years are still at school, start work in their mid-teens or have just left university. Most are shaped by the pandemic, climate change and the financial crisis. They have become inured to a shrinking state and support network. Gen Z aligns with the gig economy networks and ecosystems. They are perceived to be brighter, as there is a greater emphasis on knowledge and qualifications in all vocations. Access to the internet provides an infinite knowledge source and facilitates worldwide conversations with like-minded people.

Key problems – what caused the problems

- Underemployment and unemployment rose in the early 2020s during the pandemic and as the use of artificial intelligence advances.
- The digital divide became clearly apparent during the pandemic when children had to be home-schooled. The unequal distribution of computers was clear. Charities and government contributions began to provide funds and services to alleviate the development of a backwards subsection of society but vigilance is still required.
- Government grants allowed people to retrain or develop additional skills.

Clear revelation? Many people like travelling to work as it places a break between home and work life and there is an opportunity to exercise and see the outside world.

(iv) **Situation: Skills Index** *Key requirement – good to have*

Key successes: To ensure success, organisations need to adapt fast as opportunities arise. A nomadic database and human index of employees' and collaborators' skills and knowledge are created and by 2040, filtering technology will identify suitable projects and clients for a company.

Key decisions: Many people retrain or diversify in the 2020s as uncertainty breeds versatility, encouraging people to develop wider skillsets as the job-for-life mentality dissolves.

What caused the problems: Lifestyles and personal goals re-evaluation occur as pandemic fiscal regimes are implemented and pensions and social security diminish. Self-reliance becomes the *modus operandi*.

Key changes: Loss of white-collar jobs resulting from the introduction of AI and the demise of many middle-range brands and SMEs during the pandemic.

What was a clear revelation: Through time it became clear that human nuances override AI in social interaction and problem resolution resulting in new job roles, where human empathy skillsets are superior.

(v) **Situation: Blockchain transactions** *Key requirement – good to have*

Key successes:

- Blockchain ensures credentials remained uneditable and fraudproof while streamlining business transaction traceability and transparency, both qualitatively and quantitatively. Reducing the necessity for audits. By 2025, the blockchain system of authenticity, traceability and trust exists. Large construction and property development projects (Tapscott and Vargas, 2019) use the system to automate contractual processes and paperwork requirements to support complex undertakings. Project delivery is faster and reduces costs and allocation of costs and resources is more effective. As public scrutiny of blockchain increases, it gains acceptance as a useful system.
- Cryptocurrencies have various incarnations, yet bitcoin survives. By 2040, advances ensure that financial systems and currencies use a cryptocurrency unheard of in the early 2020s.

What caused the problems:

- Bank notes and coins were slowly taken out of circulation during the pandemic and 2020s. Initially, old notes were replaced. By 2030, printing stopped.
- Technology may change but industries have their own cultural practices and relationships that present hurdles. To overcome this, a reliability and validity-rated percentage is assessed.

What was a clear revelation: Initially, blockchain was moving towards a near miss but persistence prevails and through design iterations, it becomes mainstream by 2030. A new cryptocurrency appears around 2040.

5. Exploration

Situation: Space and deep ocean exploration *Key requirement – good to have*

Space travel to the Moon, Mars and outer space in the 2020s and 2030s advances exploration as communication, rocket and vehicle construction gain greater flexibility in form and movement. Exploration of the ocean depths and deep-sea trenches as part of Earth study are benefitting from these technological advances. Both ventures are searching for new minerals and natural life to exploit or to establish bases for further exploration.

Key successes: Mars saw a drone drop in, on 18 February 2021, with a rover called Perseverance to scout the planet's surface. Four previous rover missions explored the geology and climate, providing evidence that it had been a warm, water-rich planet with possibly microbial life before becoming a frozen desert. These expeditions test new technologies to open the pathway for human exploration of Mars.

Key decisions: The International Space Station stops operations in the late 2020s. Travel to the Moon is commonplace in 2040 as it is now a base for interplanetary travel to Mars and beyond.

What was a clear revelation: Elon Musk bought redundant oil platforms with the objective of using them as space travel launch pads. In September 2021, he and his company SpaceX took part in the first civilian crew to go into space and launched a new era of space tourism. Richard Branson's Virgin Galactic spaceship took a flight to the edge of space in July 2021.

6. Creativity

Situation: Multidimensional *Necessary requirement – must have*

Creativity is foremost in the years 2020–2040 across many dimensions, resolving problems and ensuring the survival of the planet, be this high specification computing systems or part of the climate change and green revolution requirements. Often, each enabling the other to perform more effectively.

Key successes: Creative people have played a massive role in recent years, creating unique designs and thinking outside the box – more literal today. Examples of this from interviewees include:

- The mathematician Alan Turing created the first computer. Emphasising the requirement to have good mathematical training, as often writing rigorous spreadsheets proficiently, is key to finding solutions to problems and overcomplicated processes.
- Much of a CEO's work requires original thoughts, suggestions, ideas and sources to aid the generation of solutions, approaches and systems. Design thinking facilitates this work by applying research and intuition that creates new or renewed activities and products.
- Brand designers go beyond the superficial by making connections not made before and finding the spaces between the change points that are just as important at the moment of change.

The geography of design by 2040 is worldwide as the internet becomes accessible in remote areas of Brazil, Russia, India, China and South Africa (BRICS) countries. Creativity often being driven by necessity. In India, the potential to see and create new things is awe-inspiring. In August 2021, 1.37 billion Indians have access to the internet,[4] a rate of three people per second signing up for access. Greater access to investment facilitates training people, thereby establishing and increasing manufacturing possibilities but this is not always accepted.

Key decisions:

- Companies can no longer have 100 per cent intellectual property rights, so they are choosy. On the other hand, creatives now have assured income from their work. New legislation and regulations are part of purposeful company initiatives.
- Funding has always been a tricky subject in the creative sector. The developed world gains income from established intellectual property

Table 5.1 Actions and decisions made between 2020 and 2040 using the SPE^{3}C^{2}IAL mnemonic

	Factor		*Contribution*	*Rating*
1	Sociological	i.	Healthcare and pharmaceutical research	*High-risk requirement – must have*
		ii.	Education and corporate learning ecosystems	*Necessary requirement – must have*
		iii.	Demographics	*Necessary Requirement - must have*
2	Political Geography	i.	Migrations	*Necessary requirement – must have*
		ii.	Voting	*Key requirement –good to have*
3	Environmental	i.	Climate change global impact	*High-risk requirement – must have*
4	Economic	i.	Leadership	*Necessary requirement – must have*
		ii.	Decision-making scorecards	*Necessary requirement – must have*
		iii.	Employment and skills	*Necessary requirement – must have*
		iv.	Skills Index	*Key requirement –good to have*
		v.	Blockchain transactions	*Key requirement- good to have*
5	Exploration	i.	Space and deep ocean exploration	*Key requirement –good to have*
6	Creativity	i.	Multidimensional	*Necessary requirement – must have*
7	Computing	i.	Business technologies	*Necessary requirement – must have*
		ii.	Websites	*Necessary Requirement - must have*
		iii.	Devices	*Necessary Requirement - must have*
8	Intelligence Data and Cybersecurity	i.	Data and intelligence	*Necessary requirement – must have*
		ii.	Privacy and cybersecurity	*Necessary requirement – must have*
9	Aid	i.	Disasters	*Necessary requirement – must have*
10	Legal	i.	National jurisdictions	*Necessary requirement – must have*
		ii.	Ethics	*Necessary requirement – must have*

rights (IPR) of long-standing in Europe and the United States. As the BRICS countries increase their design and production capabilities, IPR rises. presenting problems to those long established.

- A reappraisal of regulations is instigated as many hinder creative projects just as much as funding.

Key problem:

- In the 2030s, the downside is that companies now have rigorous selection processes as many people pursue the maker and inventor career route. Nations with varying styles of governance and legal jurisdictions petitioned to maintain their individual stance on IPR.
- Intellectual property discussions arose when AI began to create images and music.

What was a clear revelation: In the past, China was a manufacturing centre for copying and delivering visions. In the 2020s, the axis of power was over Europe moving east to China, and by 2040, China is becoming the innovator's country with a high innovative capability.

7. *Computing*

(i) **Business technologies** *Necessary requirement – must have*

Key successes: The 2020s pandemic saw computing technology advance rapidly as the *new normal* forced people to realise the positive contributions it could make to their lives. Communication technology and use of data advances five years in a matter of months as business models change rapidly to cope with people working from home.

Table 5.2 is based on primary and secondary research findings for the decades 2020s, 2030s and 2040s.

- Showing the advance in ecosystems and technologies that interviewees expect to occur.
- Websites and devices take a great leap as digital communication in the 2020s becomes key to daily life, work, education, shopping and leisure in the UK and around the world with increasing attention being given to privacy and cybersecurity, developments.
- As the decades progress, data storage, analysis and AI are expected to increase as the pandemic recedes and people look forward to new lives and lifestyles in the decades to 2040.

(ii) **Websites** *Necessary Requirement - must have*

Early 2020 websites are a company's online anchor, communicating its market position, information and a place for companies and customers to meet online 24/7. By 2030, there is a 50:50 chance that websites may not exist. Whether apps become a subset of websites or websites become a subset of apps remains to be seen. Changes occur during and after the pandemic:

Table 5.2 Pace of expected technological advance

Technologies	*2020s*	*2030s*	*2040s*	*Comment*
Ecosystems				
Natural ecosystem	*	**	***	Greater knowledge of the natural world
Learning ecosystem	*	**	***	Smart ecosystem access; increasing IQ
Corporate ecosystem	*	**	***	Swarm computing and collaborative projects
Communications				
Websites	***	**	*	Front door or similar function on a new system
Data storage	**	***	***	Increasingly massive: there is value in data
Devices	***	**	*	One multipurpose device or entirely new system
Data and information				
Artificial intelligence	*	**	***	Contributing to home/business life using data
Data analysis	*	**	***	Statutory requirement
IoT and smart technology	*	*	**	IoT usage increases as the world goes digital
Environmental				
Renewable energy	*	*	**	Better education and new technologies
Electric vehicles	*	*	**	Environmentally friendly
Financial				
Blockchain	*	**	**	Large project transactional tracking system
Cryptocurrencies	*	**	***	Digital currencies require legal/political acceptance

*Low usage
**Medium usage
***High usage

- NHS and news websites are vital for local and national information on what to do, when and how. Telephony, call centres, websites and social media are critical resources for healthcare challenges. Patients can log on, get opinions and access home exercises and improvement programmes set by therapists. Within the health sector, websites will continue to exist with added useful services.
- Business websites become more important as staff are furloughed and customers wanted to buy online. Online working becomes a necessity with Zoom, Trello and Slack being popular apps. Hierarchal business structures are levelling as CEOs can speak directly to and with all staff. Both parties realised the necessity to focus on the business' core purpose of why the business exists. Achieving its goals by streamlining operations and realigning duties impacting business culture often for the better as trust and communication became key enablers.
- Websites are part of the gig economy, expanding rapidly in this period as those laid-off try to find alternative employment or turn hobbies into a business.
- Brands require differentiation as influencers and bloggers have their say and digital marketers create business by introducing customers to the brand and vice versa. Digital brands are likely to become one-stop shops with AR pushing towards visual and auditory as portal interaction increases.
- Metadata will be read on websites as they become machine readable, that is, machine-to-machine interaction rather than individual apps. Agents will do the negotiating.

It is unlikely that websites will disappear by 2030. Then a technology creep or step will introduce a new device, data and security as changes become more fluid at the edges and computers take a mobile form. Identifiers will be avatars and holograms in a moving environment – Instagram Plus. The term website could change as did the term *wireless* for early radios. Wireless has a different meaning today within digital technology. Websites could become the 2040s' library.

(iii) **Devices** *Necessary Requirement - must have*

Computing devices are always changing. Table 5.3 shows how interviewees expect devices to exist in the UK and elsewhere.

- 2020s: Desktop, laptop, smartphone and tablet
- 2030s: All combined into one device, a smaller iPad with voice
- 2040s: Implants or digital handkerchief that you can fold up or no physical device at all

By 2040, a step change in computing and a computer's fabric is expected as research advances on what humans require computers to do. There could be an

Table 5.3 Evolution of present devices and introduction of inventions and innovations

Device	*2020*	*2025*	*2030*	*2035*	*2040*
Desktop	*				
Laptop	*	*	*		
Tablet	*	*	*		
Smartphone	*	*	*		
Internet of Things	*	*	*		
Implants				*	*
Eyeball implants, Neural smart glasses				*	*
Holograms				*	*

element of computers taking on various roles but the previous 20 years highlight unforeseen problems and advantages particularly as the cost of developing, selling and distributing products and services becomes too expensive in both carbon footprint terms and economics (Newport, 2019).

Internet of Things

The Internet of Things is expected to increase through to 2040 with wide applications within the public and private sectors such as in healthcare, energy management, safety and crop yield management. These smart technologies will advance services by communicating with one another and generating information by analysis and sense-making. Thereby creating value. This information creation will be an infinite cycle of activity, recorded by sensors, with data analyses being conducted in the Cloud, which ultimately contributes to decision-making. There are hurdles to be overcome such as devices will have to be compatible to enable data connection both geographically and through time. This will be an urgent requirement if gig-like work and learning collaborations are the future.

8. ***Intelligence, data and cybersecurity*** *Necessary requirement – must have*

(i) **Data and intelligence**. AI transforms the speed and accuracy of administrative tasks that humans could not emulate. AI provides answers from complex datasets, sourced in robotic and other smart Internet of Things (IoT) (Birkenshaw, 2019). Through time AI gains acceptance with rising generations who better understand what is happening and overcome the obstacles. In the early 2020s, AI is recognised and applied within government, education and resolving pandemic problems. AI innovations will progress through 2030–2040 and beyond as it becomes cheaper and makes business operations more efficient.

Key successes:

- Live chatbots and AI stimulate human dialogue in the pandemic, which means that people are growing accustomed to interacting online.
- AI advances Covid-19 vaccines research into one year, which previously would have taken ten years.
- China is aiming to become a world leader in AI by 2030, accounting for 17 of the top 20 academic institutions patenting AI. Baidu and Tencent, two of China's largest companies, are investing in high-potential start-ups in other countries.

(ii) **Privacy and cybersecurity**

In the early days, website security breaches were frequent. General Data Protection Regulations (GDPR) were implemented in the UK (May 2018), making people aware of the basic requirements with similar systems being implemented in other countries. The pandemic made cybersecurity imperative as everyone realises how important their data is to their data lives. Economic, societal and governmental impacts and their resolution varies according to each country's situation and approach to the topic.

Data storage in the Cloud is expected until 2040 permeating everything in some format. People initially thought the Cloud was a clever marketing ploy, all hype and market-driven, and were dubious, as its ephemerality meant you did not actually own anything yourself and the record could be lost. In the future, data storage will have massive value and most likely to rapidly become a utility with cybersecurity and websites becoming part of a meshed network and street furniture of the future. Cloud storage and data security could see a more reliable system arising.

Key successes: New roles will appear as data requires cleaning, checking and inputting for insights to be found. Salaries in this field will have to increase as this work requires high calibre people.

Key problems:

- Data: People, particularly older age groups, are becoming aware of how insidious computing systems are and how their data is being used. Data privacy and ownership are an important part of daily life and cybersecurity is a key requirement. As millennials and Gen Z become key corporate leaders and decision-makers, this could be an evolutionary stage.
- Business technology is making rapid advances in creating necessary products and services. Yet further suggestions are that governments should underwrite technology costs and a policy commitment to enable open source data.

Key decisions:

- As profound advances in machinery occur, an ethical code/ dimension should be clear and influential in a manner to ethical standards required for medical science research. As a wide and contentious subject area, a new body should form to handle worldwide implications.

- Fears that AI will take over white-collar jobs are realised, requiring human resource departments to reassess their function by redirecting it towards a human development department at the intersection of the corporate and learning ecosystems. The importance of this step is recognised when it becomes apparent that humans are better at empathising, intuition, making decisions, creativity and visual recognition. AI's tipping point could be state control and excessive use of personal data.
- Personal data requirements and their safety are key issues. Yet, to ensure results are reliable, algorithms and data still had to be checked and cleaned. Resolving near-miss problems and inputting safety systems are legal requirements alongside constant vigilance and upgrading.

What was a clear revelation: The speed and pace of digital transformation particularly during the pandemic.

9. *Aid*

Situation: Disasters *Necessary requirement - must have*

Key successes: Drones and AI now source and deploy quick reaction teams delivering supplies and surveying disaster areas faster than any other vehicle, while improving forecasting of catastrophes.

Key decisions: Pandemic relief and vaccines are paramount in the early 2020s.

What was a clear revelation: That the Moon and deep ocean exploration research and development has further application in aid relief.

10. *Legal*

Situation: National Jurisdiction *Necessary requirement - must have*

Key successes: The global pandemic instigates unique interventions by government and regulatory agencies worldwide. In the UK, The Centre for Corporate Governance was established in June 2020 to reorient governance priorities towards environmental, society and governance (ESG) issues with working groups on sustainable capitalism, stakeholder governance, implications of artificial intelligence and emerging technologies.

Situation: Ethics *Necessary requirement - must have*

Key successes: Ethics are an important contribution in this area, described as a voluntary contribution undertaken by a company when there are no laws in place and interpretations differ. This changes as new laws, regulations and approaches are introduced in the early 2020s with increasing interest in multicultural values arising from the Black Lives Matter campaign, which highlights racial inequalities within organisations and the wider world. Ethical policies within the business environment are often associated with corporate social responsibility (CSR) policies. Alas, there are many projects where corporate values are not aligning with policies, resulting in conflicts of interest or mixed messages. Another rising ethical stance is that many people regard technology as a power for good and encourage its usage without thinking about data implications. A Technology Ethics Board is expected to be formed.

Key decisions: Intellectual property, employment contracts and regulations. Global information framework and regulations provide clarity for fluid business operations.

Key problems: Ethical standards require attention, while profound advances in machinery occur and have an impact on individual and business existences.

This section describes the SPE^{3}C^{2}IAL factors' findings. It is difficult to say when these occurrences are likely to occur but the list is fairly comprehensive being based on interview findings and secondary sources, so it is safe to say that there is a strong likelihood that many of the factors and contributions will appear in some form in the next 20 years.

Conclusions

Creating a company with a purpose for its 2040 existence is the aim of this chapter. It is hypothetical, set against future assumptions and possibilities. Nevertheless, through the primary and secondary research findings, it does make leaders and managers aware of core activities at the centre of an interwoven tapestry of ecosystems, crisscrossing time, space, technologies and environments. To set the scene, a description of A *day in the life of a core company member* in 2040 shows a business executive's working day at home, travelling to work with a meeting's agenda items indicating changes over the period to 2040 with situations and decisions that executives will have to resolve in 2040. Backcasting, a strategic problem-solving framework looks forward to 2040 and then backcasts to 2020 to identify the required factors and steps between 2020 and 2040 to be considered.

The *New Normal*, in 2020 and 2021, rapidly transforms people's lives, livelihoods and digital advances. A company's purpose requiring reassessment from the outside to facilitate satisfying the customer above cost. Realigning its company strategy and operations became a necessity, often on a daily if not hourly basis. Leaders and staff had to ask basic questions. Defining what the company does, its values, why it takes that approach and how they aim to achieve its new survival goals: What? Why? Where? and How? actioned Now! and fast. Purpose enables everyone to know what is expected of them, resulting in a cohesive cultural unit that recognises and removes non-value adding elements to streamline operations. Through creativity and application of innovative digital technology, working methods change and drive effective and efficient added value services within this constrained environment. Many businesses survive, appear, go online or disappear.

To identify discussions and decisions to be taken in getting from 2020 to 2040, the fourth part presents the research findings dividing the results into two sections: the central core elements and ecosystems that contribute to the organisation's workings in a gig economy manner.

To capture pertinent aspects of the 2040 company's core elements Figure 5.1 has been created from the primary research questionnaire interviews and secondary research literature. The key points being:

i) Defining a clear company *Purpose*.
ii) *Leadership* through the 2020s was expected to be more democratic as collaborative working turns into being the *new normal* and project leaders revolve depending on the project's stage. Workers need to trust their leaders to open networking doors and support them in gaining and contributing to projects.
iii) *Culture* sets the tone and way of working with diverse cultural awareness, organisational behaviour and values being important business differentiators and key elements in recruitment. *Ethical* corporate guidelines are important here. To ensure approaches, actions and interpretations align.
iv) *Creativity* – forming something new is inherently human, often providing solutions to problems that artificial intelligence cannot. In highly competitive sectors, creative skillsets are in demand.

Ecosystems – the three ecosystems identified are:

i) Corporate ecosystem – a complex fluid of networking companies and people applying collaborative working protocols and programmes in a gig-like economy. Results indicate that people need social interaction to bounce off ideas and progress in innovative thinking and products. This results in digital and real-world networking hubs.
ii) Learning ecosystem – subject knowledge and continuous learning on technological advances are necessary for businesses to be resilient, versatile and grow in the marketplace.
iii) Natural ecosystems – searching and researching new plants and ecologies contribute to medical advances and food nutrition. While makers and artists take this route for inspiration in creating innovative products and services, perhaps for application in interplanetary projects.

After considering the corporation 2040 formation above, how can answers be found to the situations occurring over the period 2020 to 2040? To accomplish this, secondary research academic peer-reviewed articles and business-related literature contributed to the identification of the initial factors, illustrated in Figure 5.2. A questionnaire designed from the initial findings becomes the reference sheet in structured interviews with C-suite executives and specialists. The results from readings and the survey are combined and factors clusters expanded forming the mnemonic SPE^3C^2IAL: sociological, political geography, environmental, economic, exploration, creativity, computing related, intelligence, aid and legal.

Actions and decisions made during the period are described in detail by answering the questions: What are the key successes? What are the problems? What are the key decisions? and What is a clear revelation?

From this list there are three main concerns:

- *A wish for a fairer and more equitable existence for people across the globe*
- *Concern over climate change and its impact on the environment*
- *The impact of the Covid-19 pandemic on peoples' attitudes to health, caring services and medical research*

The following illustrates how the SPE^3C^2IAL factors are applied to such concerns, situations or problems that require a resolution by senior managers or leaders. From each factor in Table 5.1 select the most relevant factor heading and then the contributory element. The requirement rating then determines the important actions to be taken in order of impact. This list can be aligned with the corporate purpose to provide a solution direction. For example:

Wish for a fairer and more equitable existence for people across the globe.
Factors: Sociological, Political geography, Economic and Computing
Necessary requirements:

Sociological: Educational with corporate, learning and the natural world ecosystems.

Demographic data – current and relevant.

Political Geography: Migrations try to understand the problems and motivations.

Economic: Leadership, decision-making scorecards, employment and skills. Skills Index – by 2040, personalised learning and development programmes exist and can be used worldwide by 2030.

Computing: AI and continuous learning provide accurate and relevant data, but human intuition cannot be replicated and therefore both are required.

Climate change and its impact on the environment
Factors: Environmental natural ecosystems:
High-risk requirement

Environmental: Monitoring weather patterns, air pollution, fires, floods and volcanoes.

Climate change: Reappraisal of the world's geography and ecological landscape.

Necessary requirement

Computing: AI has given humans more time to be actively involved in solving problems. Innovative technologies for electric cars and hydrogen energy.

Creativity: Lifestyle changes e.g. Simplicity group.

The impact of the Covid-19 pandemic on peoples' attitudes to health, caring services and medical research.
Factors: Sociological, Computing, Economic
High-risk requirement
Sociological: Healthcare, disease identification with vaccine and therapy research
Necessary requirement
Sociological: demographic data
Computing: AI, computing and data can contribute to problem resolution.
Economic: decision-making scorecards. Accessing networks and enabling connection and engagement is key.
Key requirement – Skills Index – by 2040, possibly earlier, personalised learning and development programmes

This process can direct many situations towards a solution.

Throughout this chapter, several *words* from the interview findings occur frequently and it is how these words are applied that has the greatest sway and therefore they are included here: Peoples, technology and science *create* a harmonious society with better *problem-solving* capabilities to reduce the likelihood of dysfunctional societies. *An open attitude* would be transparent, honest, ethical and authentic. Working methods would revolve around *trust* instilled in business, government and society. *Accessibility* to housing, work, education and technology. *Creativity* is a key requirement of humans and computers, as worldwide design and manufacturing centres in the BRICS countries and specialisations in smaller countries. *Cross-cultural knowledge and wellness* awareness are essential differentiators in the workplace and at home as international work becomes commonplace. *Innovative technologies and methods* overcome previous catastrophes and new ones yet unrecognised require all our imaginative capabilities.

Between 2020 and 2040, a company's existence and purpose are to better people and the environment. In the 21st century, agility and lean management are key, taking over from formal strategy and forecasting approaches. Artificial intelligence dramatically changes people's lives yet human intelligence and creativity are still important. Insufficient thought was put into the risk factors of computing development and many AI problems are addressed in hindsight. This situation raises an alarm in some quarters where groups like Simplicity and Raison d'être including artists, designers and engineers, maintain a human maker's online ecosystem, thereby becoming the go-to people when practical problems need to be resolved. As ecosystems become more fluid and company ecosystem memberships increases, competition intensifies. Learning ecosystems now focus on adventure and creativity so that new discoveries and inventions occur in extreme locations such as in Earth's deep oceans, on the Moon and now on Mars where discoveries continue.

By 2030, it is expected that *people will be leading more fulfilling lives*, although employment may not be full time, opportunities are available for further education and skillsets necessary for the evolving technologies and working environments.

By 2040, questions will arise as to whether this way of life is worth pursuing as new ways of life and technologies become mainstream. Yet, these technologies can take you to the Moon and beyond. Many people think that technology has been embraced with insufficient reflection on the outcomes and impacts of future technological advances or addressing the expectations that technology should meet. People are asking when will humanity regain control.

Notes

1 www.ae1.org, AEIdeas blog post, 6 August 2015, "The Netflix effect": and an excellent example of "creative destruction".
2 Reimagining the Balance Scorecard for the ESG Era. By Kaplan, R.S. and McMillan, D. 3 February 2021.
3 CONNECTS is a digital business matchmaking platform created by TIAO where companies can find, create and promote online business opportunities and communities through a global network of chambers of commerce: www.connects.world
4 www.Statista.com; accessed 12 October 2021.
5 Principles for Purposeful Business (2019 report).
6 Policy and Practice for Purposeful Business (2021 report).

References

Ancona, D., Backman, E., & Isaacs, K. (2019, July–August). Walking the line between creativity and chaos. *Harvard Business Review Magazine*. 27(3).

Baldwin, R. (2019). *The Globotics Upheaval Globalization, Robotics and The Future of Work*. London: Weidenfeld & Nicolson.

Bibri, S.E. (2018). Backcasting in future studies: A synthesized scholarly and planning approach to strategic SMART sustainable city development. *European Journal of Futures Research* 6(13). https://doi.org/10.1186/s40309-018-0142-z

Birkenshaw, J. (2019, 8th August). Ecosystem businesses are changing the rules of strategy? *Harvard Business Review Magazine*.

Birkenshaw, J. (2019, 13th August). What's the purpose of companies in the age of AI? *Harvard Business Review Magazine*.

du Sautoy, M. (2019). *The Creativity Code: How AI Is Learning to Write, Paint and Think*. London: HarperCollins.

Harrington, H.J. (2019) *Creativity Innovation, and Entrepreneurship: The Only Way to Renew Your Organization*. Abingdon: Routledge.

Harrison, S., Carlsen, A., & Skerlava, M.H. (2019, July–August). Marvel's blockbuster machine. How the studio balances continuity and renewal. *Harvard Business Review Magazine*, pp. 136–145.

Hudson-Searle, G. (2020, June). The age of compassion post Covid-19. AMBITION The Association of *AMBA*.

Johnson, W. (2019, 22nd July). Your organization needs a learning ecosystem. *Harvard Business Review*.

Kaplan, R.S., & McMillan, D. (2021, 3rd February). Reimagining the balance scorecard for the ESG era. *Harvard Business Review Magazine*.

Newport, C. (2019). *Digital Minimalism: On Living Better with Less Technology.* London: Penguin Random House.

Ostergaard, E.K. (2018, 22nd February). *The Responsive Leader: How to be a Fantastic Leader in a Constantly Changing World.* LID Publishing.

Ostergaard, E.K. (2019, 15th Nov). *Teal Dots in an Orange World: How to Organise the Workplace of the Future.* LID Publishing.

Satoshi, N. (2008, November). Bitcoin: A Peer-to-Peer Electronic Cash System, *Whitepaper.*

Tapscott, D., & Vargas, R.V. (2019, 26th July). How blockchain will change the construction industry. *Harvard Business Review Magazine.*

The British Academy Policy and Practice for Purposeful Business Report (September, 2021): The final report of the Future of the Corporation Programme, The British Academy. DOI: doi.org/10.5871/ba-fotc/9780856726699.001

6 UK local and national government in 2040

Mike Donnelly

Introduction

UK Prime Minister Harold Wilson when facing the sterling crisis in 1964 reportedly briefed journalists that "a week is a long time in politics". The Liberal politician Joseph Chamberlain in 1886 reportedly said, "in politics, there is no use in looking beyond the next fortnight". Both Wilson and Chamberlain highlight the seemingly impossible task of trying to accurately predict what might happen, let alone how to react, in a political environment over even short periods of time. The task of backcasting the future of government in 20 years or so, however Herculean, is the focus of this chapter.

Here we make estimates of the desired 2040 government purposes, contexts and actions that might be taken to achieve them, using a Delphi Panel of government "experts". The Delphi Panel approach, developed by Project Rand in the late 1950s, is based on the assumption that group judgements are more valid than those made by individuals. Both can be wrong, of course, but insights can be developed into complex situations where traditional research methods fall short.

Although the national focus of this study is the UK, there may be similar possible futures and lessons for other countries, as well as alliances and political unions, across the world. It is a challenge for these countries and alliances to assess the relevance of the following analysis to their own national and international context, and perhaps to conduct a backcasting study in that setting.

Method

Individual experts were identified and invited by the facilitator to participate in the Delphi Panel. The facilitator had previous engagement as a political colleague or as an expert or special adviser to potential Delphi Panel members.

The backgrounds of Panel members who accepted the invitation to participate are given below. The participants comprised:

Three national government politicians
Eight national government civil servants

DOI: 10.4324/9781003183679-6

Four local government politicians
Three local government officers

All three national government politicians had served at senior ministerial and cabinet level; of the eight civil servants, one had served as permanent secretary, two as head of departments and five as senior advisers during periods of significant change; all four local government politicians had served as local authority leaders; and finally, two of the three local government officers had been heads of service, the remaining person as an adviser. The Panel, therefore, had a range of relevant expert experiences in national and local government.

The rules of engagement required participants to remain anonymous, with Panel members communicating with the facilitator their views on issues and questions without any direct interaction with other Panel members. The initial views of Panel members on each issue were analysed and summarised as a synthesis and this summary was reflected back to Panel members for further comment. The process was repeated until an acceptable level of agreement, a consensus, was reached on the issue involved. Email correspondence was used to invite member views and to reflect back to members the resulting synthesised summaries.

Delphi Panel members were briefed on the project and invited to consider three issues over a period of six months from October 2018 through April 2019. They were asked to vision (i) the purposes of government in 2040, (ii) the contexts of government in 2040 which would support these purposes being achieved and (iii) to backcast the actions that could or should be taken to help create these 2040 contexts.

Delphi Panel: Round 1 – purposes of government in 2040

Panel members were invited in Round 1 to consider what the purposes of government in 2040 should be and the contexts that they felt they would ideally want for the UK government in 2040.

ROUND 1: TASK FOR DELPHI PANEL

Vision yourself forward to the year 2040. Making whatever assumptions you feel are required about what might happen between now and then, and thinking about both local **and** national governments:

(i) Describe what you consider the purposes of governments **should be** in 2040.
(ii) Identify the contexts you would **ideally want** for governments in 2040.

Following exchanges with the facilitator in response to (i) of the Round 1 task for the Delphi Panel, eight synthesised purposes were identified and agreed upon for government in 2040. These were:

A. To protect and defend citizens' well-being, individually and collectively
B. To ensure the effective provision of public goods and services
C. To secure, manage and control public resources
D. To set and implement legal standards and regulations
E. To make laws and ensure an independent and fair legal system
F. To promote citizenship, social cohesion and community capacity
G. To provide democratic leadership and define our place in the world
H. To anticipate, plan and coordinate priorities and actions for uncertain futures

These purposes are likely, now and in the future, to be acceptable to most citizens in a liberal democracy and are broadly reflected in existing administrative government and political science literature. The core purpose of protecting citizens in a global context is complemented by national and local public services provision, within agreed resource demands and funded through general and specific taxation and borrowing.

As national, regional, and local legislatures and regulators, governments in the UK will continue to support the development of civic society, all within a framework of democratic accountability.

Interestingly, the purpose (H) of anticipating and addressing uncertain futures was included by the Panel as a key purpose for a 2040 government. Interesting because of the uncertainty that is often *generated* by governments, as well as the pervasiveness of systemic change and uncertainty that shows little prospect of settling in the coming 20 years. Indeed, this will probably become more agitated and serious, perhaps beyond the control of national governments, thus requiring international cooperative and collaborative action.

The 2040 desired contexts of government

The Panel was invited in Round 1(ii) to explore the desired contexts within which the complexity facing governments in 2040 might be addressed in achieving the identified, agreed purposes. Panel members were free to make whatever assumptions they felt appropriate in getting to 2040 – their specific task was to identify the contexts they felt would best support government to achieve its core purposes.

This exploration resulted in the synthesis of seven *context* factors for government in 2040, illustrated in Figure 6.1.

The following descriptions involve interesting overlaps between these factors as the 2040 desired picture begins to emerge. Written in the style of the contexts actually being in place, the description includes some personal vignettes as illustrations of the different ways individuals might be impacted.

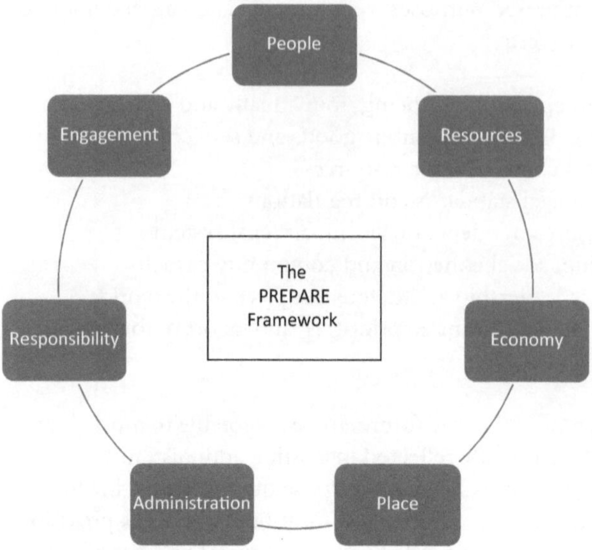

Figure 6.1 The prepare framework.

People. In 2040, the UK population will be well-educated and well-informed with high, and realistic, life expectations. People will see themselves as citizens as well as consumers and producers in the economy, equipped with transferable skills as well as knowledge.

There will be a national culture that is tolerant, respectful and outward-looking based on an understanding and acceptance of the value of difference. The early 21st-century conditions of loneliness, depression and social isolation have largely been eliminated and there has been a shift in the balance towards leisure from work – citizens understand that it is their duty to be healthy.

People will have a strong sense of belonging as well as individual identity and group affiliations.

MO

Mo's day really begins with his morning exercises and health check. Loaded with a good breakfast and his meds, he makes his way from his personal bed-sit unit to the family room on the same terrace to catch up with the "kids". With his personal social services mentor, Mo reviews his "daily living" plan of leisure, work, social, recreation and solo activities for the next few days. His mentor logs the plan with the council for its records and follow-up actions to make sure all the services he needs are available at the right times. Mo is looking forward to a game of walking football in the afternoon with some of his old pals. But before that, he heads off with his grandchildren to the local education centre for the Citizen Action class – Developing Community Health and Well-being. *This should be exciting since they'll get to meet ex-Celtic and ex-Rangers players as well as the current UK Olympic head coach.*

Resources. In 2040, the allocation of public resources will be needs-driven and will follow decisions on public service activities and actions.

Resources decisions will be taken with a long-term, global perspective. Decision-making will be timely and take competing demands and limited resources fully into account. Accountability and performance assessments will be conducted across a broad range of metrics including economy, efficiency, effectiveness, equity and environmental sustainability – the Five Es.

Existing and emerging digital and other technologies will be better understood, sensitively exploited, and with individual. personal as well as aggregated data effectively protected. Access to information and communications technologies will be universal and "fake news" free. Applications of AI and automation in the economy and society will be assessed for impact before introduction, managed throughout their useful life, and controlled in their retirement from service. Wider use of communications technology will be achieved by developing and enhancing the "technological capability" of the wider population through specially developed education and training courses, especially for underrepresented groups, so that everyone can have "universal access".

There will be security in the availability and protection of life essentials such as energy, shelter, food and water supplies. Effective systems will be in place to prevent cyber-terrorism and to protect an open, unregulated internet.

Economy. The economy in 2040 will be growing sustainably and there will be excellent supporting digital and physical infrastructure. There will be a focus on soft and creative skills development as well as the technical skills needed to complement significant advances in AI and robotics in the economy.

Public services will be resourced on a sustainable tax platform that has consensus agreement based on wealth, income and business volume as well as value surplus.

Corporate behaviour will be based on ethical and long-term principles as well as shareholder surplus; it is adequately regulated and there will be effective systems in place to prevent tax evasion and minimise tax avoidance.

Age will not be a factor in the world of work and the extremes of poverty and wealth will be monitored and addressed.

With an ageing population and a second baby boomer generation, retirement has been redefined and work and leisure have been rebalanced towards leisure.

NORMA

Norma's main job is updating and analysing data collected and captured across the city by mentors and online monitoring bots. She loves this job since it contributes to the decisions taken by authorities in every aspect of life. But the bit she likes best is the conversations she has with ordinary people about the big, and sometimes quite small, issues that are thrown up by the analysis before final decisions have to be made. All of this information is checked and verified before it is made available through the open community information "net" and feeds into the national "net" to inform decision-making at that level too. Norma doesn't get as much time as she'd like to meet or listen to her elected representative, but she is confident that they will respond in good time to the voicemail request and points of view that she has sent them. It's good that politicians seem to be able to work together even though they are in different parties.

Place. Governments and devolved authorities will be coordinated, and respectful of each other and their place in a global community of governments. There will be effective conflict resolution processes within and between governments and authorities.

There will be strong, effective international collaboration to meet global challenges such as climate change, pollution and humanitarian crises. Specifically, there will be a comprehensive UK Environmental Charter requiring environmental impact assessments to be conducted of government plans before final decisions are made.

There will be effective measures – respecting international law – to identify and combat a wide range of existing and new external as well as internal threats to the country.

Administration. Government at all levels have reliable systems in place to exploit big data so that they have a deep understanding of individual, community and societal needs. Government decision-making at all levels is based on evidence, is taken with a long-term perspective in mind and within appropriate budgetary timeframes.

There is transparency and effective regulatory and public scrutiny of decisions, decision-makers and rules and contexts for exercising power.

There is a genuinely representative electoral system in the UK that is subject to an agreed system of elected member recall. There are effective limits to campaign funding and adequate controls on the various influences on election processes.

Societal changes such as family structures, employment participation and increased value on individual independence are recognised by governments. These factors are embedded in public services design and delivery which meet personal needs as well as public and community interests.

The provision of vital health, education and social housing services are economically and efficiently produced, individually tailored to meet personal needs and based on the principle of a secure safety net for all citizens. Specifically, the focus of health services is on prevention rather than treatment – a "health protection" rather than an "illness treatment" service; homelessness has been eradicated through appropriate levels and a mix of social housing provision; and education at every level is available to all and is based on preparation for living.

CHUCK

Chuck has been a Member of the People's Parliament (MPP) for five years, half a term under normal "Bill of Rights" regulations. As well as his role representing his constituents, Chuck has responsibility for environmental policy coordination with MPPs nationally and internationally to ensure compliance with, and implementation of, the Environmental Charter. He is proud of the government's responses and the technological, AI and human behavioural solutions to the big environmental challenges we face. Although personally held to account by the scrutiny of the Select Committee and People's Fora, Chuck always looks forward to engaging with them to consider upcoming as well as current issues – he has the professional resource support he needs to be able to answer most questions and actually make things happen! He is particularly proud of the alignment of budgetary decisions with policy determined by government.

Responsibilities. The allocation of duties, responsibilities and decision-making authority is based on the principle of subsidiarity and is agreed upon and systematically reviewed. There is an agreed written UK constitution with a Bill of Rights and Responsibilities for citizens that enables effective participative as well as representative democratic engagement. There is effective cross-party collaboration and common interest working.

Citizens take citizenship seriously and take responsibility for failures as well as successes. Social and welfare services incorporate and embed leisure and recreation activities. It is a citizen's duty to be as healthy as possible.

Engagement. Citizen engagement with governments in 2040 is multidimensional – achieved through representative processes as well as individual citizens and communities, including businesses engaging meaningfully with government. Communities of interest as well as geography have an effective method of engaging with integrity in government decision-making. Individual citizens and communities also have effective access to political processes and decisions – before they are made.

There are mechanisms available to citizens and groups to express dissent and effectively resolve differences.

There is trust in, and respect for, elected representatives and in the system of government which welcomes effective engagement, participation and two-way communications between citizens and their elected representatives.

ROSA

Rosa is a part-time teacher and a part-time government regulator responsible for ensuring access to information, communications and decision-making at all levels of government. Trained as an economist, Rosa is an expert in digital and physical infrastructure. Her research has underpinned the government's taxation platform and systems that accurately and efficiently calculate, record and collect the tax due from all citizens and organisations in the country. Rosa also sits on the Security Commission which oversees arrangements for data, energy, as well as personal security of citizens. She is impressed with the effective international collaboration this involves. Her "busy-ness", however, allows enough time to enjoy regular physical workouts, as required by the health and well-being compact. But her real love is teaching – working with students from all backgrounds and abilities using state-of-the-art learning technologies.

From Panel members' initial responses and subsequent commentary on the reflected synthesis, it was clear that there was a shared concern, sometimes hope, around the potential impact of information and communications technology as well as developing an effective response to the climate crisis.

Also, the peculiar economic, political and social history of the UK was occasionally highlighted by Panel members as constraining their analysis to the UK, and therefore its applicability to the UK and not beyond its shores. Arguably, any comparable analysis and solutions will be different for the different historical (and future) circumstances of emerging economies and democracies. Again, arguably, the analyses and futures of the international community of nations will inevitably impact on what happens in the UK.

Delphi Panel: Round 2 – Actions that can be taken now

Round 2 invited the Delphi Panel to suggest strategic actions that might be taken now to achieve the desired 2040 contexts reported above.

A summary of the purposes and contexts agreed upon by the Delphi Group was shared with Panel members and the rules for making suggestions for strategic actions are given below.

1. Select one (or more) of the contexts which you feel are not present at the moment and which you believe are most important in achieving the 2040 "Purposes" agreed by the Delphi Group.
2. From your personal experience and knowledge, identify one or more strategic actions that might be taken to create, or help develop, the desired context from where you feel it is just now. For each proposed

strategic action, outline in as much detail as you feel is needed: what you think should be done; who or what institution should do it; how it should be done in terms of the mechanics of the action; how long you think it will take to implement the action and to succeed; and any other factors that you feel might need to be taken into account.

3. You don't need to justify your choice of action(s) nor to explain any assumptions that you are making about the proposed strategic actions or the other details provided. It is enough that you make your choice and provide any details that you can.
4. Finally, colleagues might want to review and comment more generally on their responses to this round and to the Round 1 considerations and documentation.

Due to time constraints on Panel participants and the facilitator, the full Delphi Panel process was not followed in this second phase of the research project, that is, the synthesis, reflection and iterative refinement of suggested strategic actions did not take place. Panel member contributions were accepted simply as they were presented and it is these unrefined data that are the platform for the following report which, by necessity, can therefore only be illustrative.

What follows is neither a coherent nor an exhaustive set of strategic actions that need to be taken since Panel members did not make submissions on *all* of the desired contexts. It is not possible from the work of this Delphi Panel, therefore, to define what might be regarded as the necessary and sufficient strategic actions to deliver *all* of the contexts identified in the first phase of the work. That is a huge task which would present a significant challenge for the most talented team of policy and strategy government advisers, experts and researchers.

However, there were some common themes in the Panel submissions. These themes illustrate some of the approaches and strategic actions that might be taken, over time, to achieve the desired contexts in the areas of:

- Education, skills, information and the world of work
- Community engagement and capacity
- Economy, infrastructure and key public services

The choice of these three themes generally reflects the nature and number of responses prioritised by Panel members in their responses.

Education, skills, information and the world of work: Strategic actions

1. Review, reprioritise and recast education and training at all levels with an appropriate resourcing plan
2. Develop citizenship and access to reliable public information
3. Review, redefine and legislate for the new world of work and invest in digital and physical infrastructure

An early systematic and thorough review of education and training will have surfaced of the exact nature and true scale of the knowledge and skills challenges to be met by 2040. Making some brave assumptions about the outcome of such a review, Panel members developed ideas and suggestions about how these might be addressed to achieve the "contexts" described above.

EDUCATION, TRAINING AND SKILLS

In education and learning, the starting point for action would likely be a substantial increase in preschool places and a raising of standards in primary schools to ensure that all children proceed to secondary education with well-developed social skills as well as good reading, writing and arithmetical abilities. A renewed focus on early years *education for all* will be adopted. This doesn't necessarily mean formal education for two-year-olds but should contribute to closing the opportunity gap that existed previously.

Small cohorts in primary schools, with additional support for less able children and those with additional learning support needs, will be in place. A key goal will be to create a true partnership with parents, encouraging and supporting them in talking and listening to their children, reading to them and exercising discipline over "screen" time. It will be acknowledged, and acted on, that realistic life expectations begin to be formed at an early age, with schools and families playing their part. Children and young people will have equal access to opportunities, and guidance will be there to support choices.

At secondary school level, there will be high-quality leadership by head teachers and stretching learning and teaching standards which embrace technological innovation and exploit educational research findings to engage meaningfully with students. Teachers will be given the freedom to teach and the burden of bureaucracy on active teachers will be reduced through the training, development and professionalising of school administration and management. Teaching will be appropriately compensated, with manageable workloads and career packages which will attract good quality graduates. Politicians will appreciate teaching as a valued profession.

Achievement of schools will be measured not by crude league tables, but by the progress made by students and other outcome measures. This should take into account the demographic and educational attainment performance of the school catchment area and of individual student progression, meaningfully aggregated to support continuous improvement in the school.

More attention will be paid to those schools that might be struggling. The last 20 years will have provided evidence that, with the right combination of funding and focused action, schools serving traditionally deprived communities can deliver for children and the communities themselves.

Standards of teacher training will have been reviewed, with confirmation that entry qualifications are pitched appropriately and university and college programme exit standards enhanced.

Controversially, perhaps, the obsession with higher education will be recast. More focus on the different options for entering professional roles, through apprenticeships, for example, will be properly promoted and resourced.

Routes into higher education will be available for those progressing via non-advanced further education or through work in later years, using evidence of academic credit for work-based learning. Non-traditional modes of higher education participation and innovative approaches to learning will have been trialled and evaluated – with actions taken based on their findings. In particular, investment should be made to support remote, part-time, articulated and workplace-based higher education.

Further education, including apprenticeship training, will be appropriately resourced and well-regarded. Lifelong learning at all levels will be promoted by employers, government and education providers, who should have an obligation, as a condition of funding, to ensure opportunities are available within their workplaces and their geographical areas.

Higher education will not be accessed only by incurring a vast debt burden. Tuition fees, where they exist, will be abolished or substantially reduced – with consequences for public expenditure.

All this will require increased investment by government, realistically either through a combination of public sector borrowing, a substantially increased tax take or by switching money from other areas of public expenditure. A comprehensive, rolling budgeting system will be developed which supports ongoing strategic decision-making and tracks the financial and other outcome performance measures of the education system as a whole. These actions will require consideration, assessment and decisions based on the long-term economic and societal benefits and not narrow, politically partisan, short-termism. That means that there will be a long-term service and budgetary strategy, to which single, fixed-term parliaments with one- or two-year budget horizons are unsuited. This approach will have attracted cross-party consensus – arguably a requirement for any long-term attempt to change the country for the better.

In Scotland, a national stakeholder Citizens' Panel or Jury will have considered the different roles and responsibilities of local, regional and national government in relation to education and training. This will have followed a mature debate where the interests of students and parents carry as much weight as those of business and other education and training stakeholders. The outcomes or decisions by such citizens' juries will have the full force of legislation to ensure their recommendations are implemented.

CITIZENSHIP AND INFORMATION

Having a better-educated population does not mean people will necessarily be better informed, but it is a good start – people have to *want* to be informed. That is possibly the biggest challenge and the hardest to do anything about apart from pinning the nation's hopes on education. Introducing "citizenship" into the entire education system as a continuous stream will have been a good early action. If people *do* want to be informed, they will need to have the information sources to hand. In that regard, they will have never been better served with news, information, knowledge and comment, literally in their own hands.

However, robust public information campaigns will be developed and delivered to support people's understanding and awareness of ambitious as well as realistic life options ahead, both for themselves and their children. These campaigns will be based on future as well as current opportunities, highlighting available skills and knowledge development opportunities to meet forecast economic activity and support enhanced life chances. Gender stereotyping for future roles will be challenged by adequately targeting and upskilling entrants into non-traditional role occupations.

It will, however, be important that the mainstream media continues to give prominence to news and has not turned itself over entirely to entertainment. There must continue to be a free press. That said, some curbs on social media and "Fake News" will have been increasingly inevitable for a variety of reasons. This is dangerous territory and will have required careful handling by legislators.

It will also be important that people continue to have access to information on health and other public services on reliable and authoritative government websites. Government and its agencies will adopt a policy of continuous improvement in web-based information to the public. Alongside this, ministers and politicians generally will neither over-promise nor give people false expectations as to the quality of services they can expect without significant shifts in service priorities or taxation or both.

THE WORLD OF WORK

National economic modelling and analysis of different, flexible working practices and the length of the working week will have been tested and piloted in key industrial sectors and economic regions. As a result, employment laws will have been reviewed, amended and developed to encourage and support a shorter working week, where appropriate. There will be more flexibility in where and how people work, and support will be provided for people's engagement in voluntary activities and leisure – for all generations. This will not only lead to "better" lives for everyone but will also make sound economic sense. Compensation and remuneration will reflect the real value of voluntary work, home building and third sector efforts and activities. The welfare and social benefits system will have been recalibrated to ensure that people are not economically disadvantaged in "working" fewer days in the week or in non-traditional work contexts such as volunteering.

People will therefore be working hours that are healthy, desirable and productive. There will be more opportunities for younger people coming through and taking on key leadership roles in an economy where technology has redefined the world of work. The full impacts of AI and automation on the economy and society will have been researched and met with policy responses and government decisions taken to mitigate the negative consequences in the 2040 workplace. It will have been recognised that retirement as traditionally understood is not good for older people's physical and mental health and that continuing in fulfilling employment and engaging in voluntary, leisure and cultural activities will lead to happier and healthier lives all round. The experience and wisdom of previous generations will be shared with the new and upcoming workforce through documentation as well as mentoring and work-partnering schemes which will have been developed during the 2020–2040 period.

Ultimately, there will be a demise of the concept of "retirement" with all ages – young and old – leading satisfying, productive and engaged lives where the boundaries between work, volunteering, learning and leisure are truly blurred.

Community engagement and capacity: Strategic actions

1. Strengthen and underpin existing representative democracy and develop and implement methods of participative democracy underpinned by a comprehensive Bill of Rights and Responsibilities.
2. Review community engagement practices across governments and their agencies; develop a new and comprehensive community engagement policy for all public service organisations.
3. Introduce a comprehensive national training and development programme to support this substantial community engagement change process.

Government and public authorities' methods of operating will have been rebalanced between representative and participative democracy. Government bodies will be tasked with providing leadership and effective actions to deliver meaningful public engagement. There will have been investment in the participation and development of the capacity of communities and the people living in the communities they serve.

PARTICIPATION AND ENGAGEMENT

Following a review of existing engagement and participation practices, a national policy will have been determined which will provide a framework for public agencies to engage effectively with their communities. The implementation of this policy will be supported by a national training and development programme, available to people working in all sectors in the field of community development and engagement.

Just as with government decision-making, there will be general agreement that decision-making by representative bodies will be focused on achieving long-term outcomes as well as short-term deliverables. This will involve a more participative approach to decision-making which will clearly relate to public interests and community needs. The nature of democratic decision-making processes will therefore have shifted to long-term successful outcomes – a significant improvement on alternative short-termism where quick (though often suboptimal) results and winning elections were sometimes the main objectives.

The use of citizens' panels/juries mentioned in relation to education and training would be extended to help develop the full range of public service provision. This will include public health services, encouraging a deeper public engagement and better alignment of the services with the needs of the public they serve. The principle of subsidiarity – decisions taken as close to where they impact – will guide those responsible for making the final decisions on which a government department or agency has the duty, responsibility and authority for specific public services.

It will be the responsibility of public agencies to reflect the demographic and service needs profile of the communities they serve in their governance arrangements, workforce structure and decision-making processes.

People's engagement with public service provision will be stronger both through the support available to obtain meaningful work and by actions that public services will take to encourage people to eat, play and enjoy culture together across the generations. Public participation and engagement with decision-making will radically change both the services people help to design as well as their perceptions of the services they receive. Health and social care services will be more integrated into local communities and not necessarily the first port of call for help. Live music and cultural activities will be encouraged in communities — outside shops, schools, transport hubs and eating places. Public transport and other public infrastructure regarded as essential will be free at the point of use – or be used with targeted support and made available to all. Community asset transfers will be made more straightforward so that smaller, less formal groups will be able to use an expanded range of public premises for their activities. Better connections will be made between places where people might go for support – doctors, housing offices, council service points and local public utilities. Intergenerational activities will be promoted and arranged. Libraries will have meeting points as well as quiet areas and act as community hubs.

Citizens previously distanced from democratic processes and authorities will be able to meaningfully participate through an acknowledgement and mitigation of the constraints they might face. For example, people will be supported where their employment conditions and status, family commitments, educational attainment or category of disadvantage is recognised as a barrier to their direct participation. The significance of disadvantaged groups of people being further disadvantaged through exclusion from influencing the decisions that impact on their lives will have been comprehensively addressed through access rights for groups with protected characteristics at every level of government.

This "inclusion" principle will also apply to specific service areas such as health and social services. Examples of these protected characteristics or groups which might be affected may include trade unions, BAME, gender, LGBT, professional bodies and business organisations. The electoral system will be transparent and efficient, supporting meaningful representative governance with clearly defined functions and responsibilities. There will be parity of esteem across elected public authorities and their participants, each respectful of the rights and responsibilities of others. Dignity, respect and equity will be built into major policy and service developments.

GOVERNMENT, ITS AGENCIES AND THE CONSTITUTION

Government leaders will recognise the need for their agencies to operate collectively and in concert, and to engage with national and international partners, when appropriate, to identify areas where a long-term, collaborative, overview is required. Examples will be in the areas of public health, the natural environment and migration where decisions and actions by one authority might impact on the work of others, or where collective actions are genuinely needed to make a difference. This will have been done initially through inter-agency projects and ultimately through the development of agreed protocols, operational mechanisms and appropriate exchanges of resources between authorities. The mechanism of citizens' juries will also be applied to these inter-governmental decision-making areas, again with forceful legislative backup.

Rebalancing public services will meet the twin challenge of changing mindsets and taking difficult decisions on the application of resources. The assessment of these will have been made by a Government Commission on the Rights and Responsibilities of individuals and institutions. Its terms of reference and *modus operandi* will have been informed by both public as well as expert opinion. Over a significantly long (say five years) period, the Commission will have taken evidence from academics, expert opinion and public voices and the experience of national and international agencies to deliver meaningful outcomes.

An area of significant challenge will have been implementing one of the Commission's recommendations, namely the creation of a National Constitutional Convention to review the architecture of government in the UK. The Convention, representative of civic society in the UK, took evidence from a wide range of stakeholder organisations and individuals. It had participants from communities of interest representing business, trade unions, churches and academia, similar to the Convention that underpinned the creation of the Scottish Parliament in 1999. Representations and evidence were taken from regional citizens' assemblies across the UK, created for the specific purposes of reviewing government at that level and assessing the implications of any changes to national government. Contributions to the Convention's considerations were also invited from existing local governments, non-departmental public bodies and representative and learned organisations across civic society. The Convention explored the range of different governmental structures and democratic accountability for citizens wishing to participate in public decision-making processes. At the end of the five-year life of the Convention, a consensus on key recommendations and the way forward had been reached and attracted wide support across the political spectrum.

Central UK government will continue to reserve powers to itself, and non-reserved powers will lie with devolved institutions. This "federal" framework will include governments with autonomous powers in the Scottish, Northern Irish, Welsh and English nations of the UK, regional government in London and some cities and regions of England, and local governments throughout the UK – each with its own electoral processes and public access arrangements based on agreed democratic principles.

There will also be a number of quasi-governmental authorities, some with an elected representative element in leadership roles, responsible for specific regulatory, resource distribution and other government-determined functions.

Finally, in terms of government agencies, there will also be institutions and non-governmental organisations (NGOs) with specific authority in their areas of competence. These will have appropriate governance, accountability and reporting arrangements and some will have directly appointed executive or non-executive members.

Any tensions over who has authority and power and ultimate responsibility for public service roles and functions will have been reconciled on the principle of subsidiarity, underpinned by written protocols and constitutions. Functional organisation and democratic control of decision-making at every level of governance will have been redefined, alongside refinements to the various electoral systems, to allow full participation in decision-making across a coherent and consistent framework of accessible, accountable government. Representative democracy will have been reconfigured to ensure it truly represents the profile and needs of citizens who will be able to engage with the processes of decision-making, monitoring and review. There will be a legal obligation on devolved institutions and authorities to govern, with due consent and consultation, on relevant issues affecting people and communities of interest as well as of geography.

Referenda, when they take place, will have clear rules about their calling; wording and clarity will be given, in advance, on the legitimate and acceptable level of votes in order to make decisions of major importance.

Inclusive voting systems will recognise the agreed constitutional right of citizens' eligibility for participating in the elections to all government decision-making bodies. Positive action or quotas will apply to some authorities to ensure barriers to representative participation are minimised. There will be a balance of engagement with citizens from all social strata, knowledge and expertise to provide the essential skillsets to address the good governance of representative bodies across government. This will be supported by a comprehensive citizen participation programme of courses delivered by education and training institutions, and "citizenship" streams in formal education.

Devolution of power will therefore reach every place of decision-making with a constitutional right to engage in meaningful assemblies for all citizens irrespective of their place in society and different histories, cultures or traditions. The sense of belonging will be a key factor in determining the shape and structure of advisory and decision-making forums from national to local and across functional service areas of government.

These principles will also apply to the composition of the civil service supporting the democratic process. It will require transparency and open access arrangements for engagement or employment at the heart of decision-making. There will be a consultative participation requirement, prior to decisions being made, given to relevant communities of interest that will be embedded into public authorities' constitutions. The extension of democratic engagement will also be seen in the character of NGO participation where the use of public resources is a key element of their decision-making powers.

The interdependence between all tiers of government will have clear systems of arbitration and conflict resolution for strategic, governance and operational issues. A key purpose of government for all our citizens will be to find a place for them in the landscape of political processes that shape their destiny and that of future generations after 2040.

Economy, infrastructure and key public services: Strategic actions

1. Introduce comprehensive community and regional development plans which integrate local, regional and national priorities and services
2. Review and develop a strategy to mobilise resources with a common framework for performance assessment, review and development
3. Revitalise health and housing services

First, we reflect on economic developments since 2020.

Economic and social fallout from the Brexit era will continue to affect life in the UK. There will have been a managed UK exit from the EU, which, although experiencing some "bumps" on the way, will have been as smooth as it could have been. Any initial damage to the relationship with the reformed and expanded European Union will have been repaired by 2040 and a constructive, positive approach to the future will be taken by both.

As a result, trade deals allowing UK exporters access to the EU and worldwide markets will have been negotiated which protect domestic producers where this is regarded as in the national interest. These deals will have started to work effectively by the end of the 2020s. Despite opposition from the farming industry and parts of what was left of British manufacturing, trade barriers will have been kept to a minimum.

The shrinking of UK car manufacturing will have stopped short of all production ending. Assistance to the sector by the government, freed to some extent from EU state aid rules, along with technological advances in the automotive industry, and converging wage rates in Europe – will have helped persuade some car manufacturers to invest again in the UK so as to be close to market.

Immigration policy will allow businesses and the public sector to have the labour supply it needs but it will have taken labour shortages to almost crisis level in the mid-2020s. The reality of trade negotiations will have made it clear that mutually managed migration is an important element of trade deals with other countries, including within the EU.

An excellent digital and physical infrastructure will have been created and will be essential in underpinning sustainable economic growth. This will include the building of high-speed rail and other state-of-the-art public transport alternatives to highly regulated private car ownership. Physical infrastructure development will have given a boost to domestic tourism as well as to the sustainability of inward tourism.

As the economy began to grow again in the early 2030s, any tendency for sterling to strengthen will have been dampened by modest interest rate cuts by the Bank of England after the increases in the late 2020s as the government sought to encourage overseas investment.

The government will have made substantial investment in electric car charging points at motorway service stations and will have entered partnerships with service station providers to install points at every parking bay. A number of additional service stations, roughly 50 miles apart – the range of the latest electric cars – will also have been built and the work involved will have given a major economic boost to the construction industry.

Publicly owned and run high-speed broadband will have been extended not only to all major towns and cities but also to most rural areas. The free-to-use digital network will have been accepted as making sound economic sense, contributing to government policy on environmental sustainability. This will have stimulated the creation of businesses in the service sector and in green tourism, which will have enjoyed fairly steady growth in the late 2020s and 2030s.

A key priority for the government will have been investment in research. The main beneficiaries will have been higher education. The government will have made a significant and sustained investment in university research both by directly funding research institutions and by the strategic distribution of public funds through research councils. This will have been focused, in part, but not entirely, on applied research with a particular emphasis on technologies supporting the drive for a sustainably growing, net zero carbon economy. Blue sky research will not have been neglected and through a series of tax incentives there will have been successful commercialisation of the results of medical research into age-related conditions and the profiling of serious illnesses.

Alongside support for higher education, a new priority will have been given to vocational training, with additional funding for technical and further education. Financial incentives for colleges, employers and other economic partners will have encouraged an increase in modern apprenticeships. This will have addressed the shortages of skilled workers resulting from both strict immigration controls on entry to the UK as well as the returning migrant workers to their home country in the face of the cheap pound and improving living standards throughout the EU.

Legislation will have been introduced to increase the tax take from multinational corporations, balanced by incentives for those corporations to work with UK higher education institutions on research and development.

The seismic shift in the political landscape in the early 2020s after Brexit will have resulted in a new generation of politicians of all shades of opinion, keen to learn the lessons of 2016–2020 and committed to less adversarial politics and deeper participation by citizens and communities. The Fixed Term Parliament Act will have been amended to extend the lifespan of a parliament from five to ten years. This will enable governments to take a longer-term view and be able to take what might be regarded as some of the "brave" decisions to invest heavily in infrastructure and research and development, which began to pay off in the 2030s.

All of these decisions and actions to develop the country's economic infrastructure were guided by the need to integrate local and regional plans, priorities, investments and services into a comprehensive national planning framework.

SOME "BRAVE" DECISIONS

Among the courageous decisions will have been those that resulted in a substantial tax increase to pay for government spending. This will have affected all taxpayers above a certain minimum amount to protect socially and economically vulnerable citizens. The top rate of income tax will have increased and while this will have seen the departure offshore of some highly remunerated individuals and entrepreneurs, the numbers involved will have been lower than feared – the pull of our well-run cities has not been underestimated.

The world's top earners want to live in civilised places, where their homes and cars are secure, good restaurants are on hand and great entertainment from football to ballet is available. The introduction of a significant tax surcharge on earnings in excess of £1 million per annum will have boosted tax returns, and tax breaks for early stage new business start-ups will have encouraged the emergence of a new generation of young entrepreneurs, taking full advantage of superfast broadband. People registered as domiciled overseas but spending time here will be taxed accordingly.

A review will have been made of competition rules and ministers will be allowed to intervene, taking due care of possible retaliatory action, to stop UK businesses from being sold to foreign buyers where there were social, economic and security considerations to be taken into account.

Decisions will have been taken to accelerate investment in renewable energy sources and in safe alternative energy generation to ensure an appropriate mix of generation capacity, reducing reliance on imported energy.

Legislation will have been passed requiring a long-term perspective to be taken by financial and commercial enterprises. For example, banks and other financial institutions will be required to work constructively with businesses to agree on financial support based on long-term investment rather than quick returns. This will encourage a new spirit of enterprise among young people and helps businesses to grow and have meaningful long-term plans for a secure future. Further, financial and equity bonuses for CEOs and other senior corporate executives will be required to take account of their enterprise performance over five years rather than simply focusing on short-term returns to shareholders. This will have caused the exodus of some senior people to the United States and other countries in the 2020s, but it will have been discovered that there are plenty of talented individuals waiting in the wings, and the payback in terms of business survival and sustainable growth began to be evident in the mid-2030s.

Partnership investment in researching and developing alternative packaging technologies will have allowed the government to legislate against the use of plastics and other harmful, unacceptable pollutants.

Equality and human rights will have been preserved and strengthened through enhancing earlier legislation and supporting compliant practice. The development of a more humane and responsive approach to asylum and immigration will have been built on this approach. Funds will have been allocated to ensure we have a fit-for-purpose immigration system with secure technology and identity confirmation systems that protect personal data while treating people with respect and care.

A top priority in the short and medium term will have been to create robust and comprehensive plans for designing and resourcing public services across the country which meet citizens' needs and involve them in their design. In parallel with this, a common framework was introduced for the performance assessment, review and development of all public services.

Two key services highlighted by the Delphi Panel for attention were health and caring services, and social housing services.

HEALTH AND CARING SERVICES

One of the first significant citizen juries will have considered how the focus of health services can be moved from illness treatment to illness prevention and health protection. The jury will have recognised that this was a long-term agenda since prevention requires radical and fundamental shifts in public attitudes in the focus for *all* public services and the allocation of resources. The main conclusion was that there should be a major national government programme prioritising illness prevention alongside its twin priority of the treatment of people who are ill, injured or in poor health. Political parties, governments and key decision-makers have accepted that this shift from treatment to prevention is essential if public health and social care are to be sustainable. They will also accept that government thinking has to go beyond the traditional four- or five-year parliamentary cycle if it is to be successful in reducing the financial and social burden of treating ill health.

The jury will have had various recommendations for actions which were implemented over time by government.

The NHS Boards/Trusts and government departments will be committed to the identification and monitoring of a range of national health prevention outcomes. This will be implemented along the lines of the existing Scottish Government's National Performance Framework, which was in place in 2020.

To support the fundamental shift in health service philosophy and practice, a delivery strategy will be implemented which guides and coordinates the five-year change process and ensures adequate research, finance and human resource transfer to be enabled. This will be supported by an early allocation of kick-start funds for prevention work – acknowledging that front-loading is required as the results in some service areas may take time. Effective transition arrangements will be developed to enable that shift to take place smoothly.

New multidisciplinary "healthy living" teams will have been created, led by local authorities in partnership with other government and non-government organisations in their area. These teams will draw on new and existing resources across agencies and stakeholders. Recognising the long-term nature of the transition, the initial focus of the teams will be on three specific target age groups, namely, children and their parents, teenagers and young adults (20–30). The teams will operate through and with the full range of community groups as well as public and private leisure, recreation, sport and cultural amenities.

It will have been recognised that health issues are multidimensional and so decisions will be taken to embed health in all government departments and agencies, with appropriate cross-cutting protocols and collaboration and community engagement arrangements. The rules and assessment of all public procurement will be extended beyond the "price" and "quality" considerations to include "health and social impacts" and "community benefits". Regular reports on prevention actions and health outcomes will be provided as a matter of course, with an aggregate review conducted at an annual "health summit" of key health and community stakeholders.

A "healthy living" public marketing and promotion campaign will be implemented. A supporting in-service training programme will be designed to ensure everyone involved in the service changes and ongoing delivery of health outcomes is fully informed, encouraged and engaged in all aspects of the prevention campaign.

A commitment and allocation of resources will be injected to increase the pace of change in the integration of health and social care. This will be built on a fundamental review and repurposing of the social care system to one based on the needs of the individual. At its core will be dignity and respect and, with effective training invested in the workforce, a game-changing shift will have been made in the culture and status of social and care work.

In line with general practice of performance assessment of public services, priority will be given to the assessment and reporting of health outcomes and measurements of progress in people's well-being, experience, health, dignity and care. The reporting and analysis of the allocation of resources, inputs and processes in public health services will continue to ensure service economy and efficiency. These will be used both to understand past performance and inform future resource and service design change decisions. These will be incorporated into national economic planning as a major dimension of the nation's economy.

HOUSING SERVICES

A strategic review and analysis of the various types of housing tenure, their capacities and future demands will have resulted in the government having a better understanding of the scale and complexity of the financial and social issues involved. Following extensive consultation, the ten-year "Homes for All" transition began in 2020.

Government will have achieved a party-political consensus to provide a range of viable and affordable housing tenure options for families and individuals suited to their needs across the country. This will be achieved by investing resources in building new homes and reducing the amount of public money going directly to subsidise rents and home ownership with their resulting inflationary effects. Additional priority and focus, as well as resources, will have been invested in improving community coherence by eliminating homelessness and reversing the creation of social housing "ghettos" in some areas.

An extensive national programme of house-building will have provided additional social housing, and this will have redressed the imbalance in social tenancies, private tenancies and home ownership. The government will actively partner with local authorities, providers of commercial homes for sale or rent and social housing associations to offer people a genuine choice among affordable tenure options in existing communities. Revenues to local authorities from the sale of housing assets will be able to be invested in building more homes.

An annual review will be undertaken with key stakeholders and communities engaging to consider progress and to update the ten-year house-building strategy on a rolling basis.

The changing mix of housing tenure will be supported by rebalancing the financial support given to individuals, communities and businesses. This will have encouraged growth in private as well as public tenancies and in a variety of forms of home ownership. Resource support will also be available from government for private housebuilders, local authorities, housing associations and other social landlords to acquire land for housing development. New developments that are subject to planning permission will, however, be subject to enhanced rights of communities to input into the planning system to balance those of developers.

The government, along with key stakeholder housing agencies and communities, had convened a national taskforce to implement a "One Roof" action plan. This taskforce was tasked with eliminating homelessness and helping people into sustainable accommodation and independent living, adequately supported by social, welfare and other public services.

The government will have legislated for a national policy of price "controls" on housing rentals and sales and people's access to mortgages will be enhanced through legislation to end insecure employment contracts.

Conclusions

The future doesn't stop in 2040, and while the eight purposes identified by the Delphi Panel will probably still be as relevant in the future as they are now, there is a myriad of possible contexts which might emerge over the coming period. Whatever these futures might be, there will be significant demands made on all of the stakeholders in government.

There will be a need for governments to develop strategy, capacity and a willingness to engage with citizens in understanding which change issues cause them most concern. Governments *do* listen to citizens now – often following rather than leading public opinion on some of the most difficult issues – and this may be extended in future, moving towards a more participative democracy, facilitated by communications technology with appropriate data safeguards. Opinion polling on issues will continue to be conducted, although arguably on issues that will less obviously have an influence on citizens' voting intentions at the next election.

The synthesised feedback from Delphi Panel members indicates a number of challenges for government actors and politicians as well as public servants and services:

- There will need to be shifts from short-term thinking and planning to more long-term, strategic decision-making, actions and appropriate alignment of resources. Supporting this more strategic approach with an extended fixed-length parliamentary term (to say ten years) will bring significant PESTEL[1]-type challenges and impacts, especially when simultaneously encouraging mass participation and engagement in government decision-making.
- Increased inter-agency collaboration and cooperation will increasingly be required to "join up" public services. Developments in information and communications technology may make this much easier than before – although major risks, for example, in data protection, system cyber-attacks and system compatibility, will need to be identified and actively managed.
- Differences in organisational cultures, governance and accountability arrangements between collaborating public service agencies will also have to be successfully addressed.
- Systems that allow meaningful public engagement will need to be developed, and welcomed, by government as central, not only in meeting citizens' needs, to ensuring effective decision-making and the appropriate allocation of public funds. Decisions on these systems will have to strike an acceptable balance between individual privacy/liberties and any increase in the involvement/interference of the state in people's everyday lives.
- There will be a pressing need for governments to engage cooperatively and act collaboratively with partners to tackle national and global challenges such as the climate crisis, health epidemics, national catastrophes and international terrorism and crime.
- Clear lines of accountability and responsibilities will need to be defined since leadership and accountabilities will be distributed across local, regional and national responsibilities as well as within government and its agencies. Indeed, it is arguable that a consensus on community interest, with genuine partnerships working to deliver this, can ever be reached – and, if it is, how "minority" interests might be weighed against majority "community" interests.
- Governments will also most likely need to create "Futures" units with considerable research capacity. Their research and analytic findings, although perhaps conducted privately and able to "think the unthinkable" to challenge difficult policy choices, must ultimately be in the public domain.

So, the world of 2040 presents big challenges not just for those with power in government, it will place demands on us all – as individuals, as businesses, as organisations, as public services, as a third sector and, not least, for the academic community.

Although the focus of this study has been the government of the UK (and Scotland), there may be lessons as well as questions that governments across the world might take from it.

Post(Covid-19)script

The Delphi Panel research study reported here was completed before the declaration by the WHO of Covid-19 as a pandemic on 12 February 2020. Most of the challenges cited earlier were encountered during the pandemic in the UK. The compliant public response to government decisions placing severe restrictions on individuals' freedom of movement and social contact was unexpected by some commentators. Perhaps this life-threatening experience provides limited evidential support and weight for the Delphi Group's findings around public engagement with, and participation in, government decision-making. If nothing else, the Covid-19 pandemic has underlined the importance of national/regional coordination and international collaboration in tackling global challenges. It also highlighted the need for rigorous research across a range of academic and practical disciplines to support difficult government decision-making. All of these capacities and capabilities, and more, will be required for a successful transition to an acceptable "new normal" nationally and internationally. A repeat study when, if ever, the Covid-19 pandemic is over might shed more light and build on the 2018–2019 Delphi Panel findings reported here.

Note

1 PESTEL - Political, Economic, Social, Technological, Environmental, Legal.

7 The Future Corporation as a utility

Greg Trainor

Introduction

In 2040, utilities will have completed the evolution from asset-rich behemoths to networked customer-centric systems. Similarly, traditional utility retailers, such as electricity, gas, water, and telecommunications (telco), will no longer exist. The Future Corporation as a utility service provider will be organisations such as Google, Facebook, Amazon, Tencent, Tesla and others that have intimate, customer-dependent relationships where the company provides a consistent, comprehensive and all-encompassing suite of home services. What started in the early 2020s has fully matured into the commoditisation of all "utility type" activities.

This has resulted in the exit of direct suppliers in the sector of commodities that can be packaged and delivered as easy-to-access and use services. This was followed by the emergence of a parallel system that operates at the global level and also at some national levels. Countries more technologically and cyber security capable leveraged the broad and extensive advantages of a global supply network for these services. In some countries, the government has restricted the provision of these services to national networks. This occurs either via local players or global players deploying franchise models subject to government regulations.

These changes have had far-reaching implications not only for customers but also for the following:

- Governments at national, state and local – community – levels
- Industry regulators
- Suppliers at the energy generation side (what is left of it from the 20th-century mega asset infrastructure)
- Networked (systematised) suppliers

They have resulted in the proliferation of personal service brokers and the blurring of boundaries regarding these products and services. Customer demand has driven this change, facilitated by:

- massive advances in technology, especially personal, mobile computing (handheld, voice-activated devices) – linked to artificial intelligence (AI) enabled service provision;

DOI: 10.4324/9781003183679-7

- the acceleration of climate change that resulted in the public, communities and countries taking the matter into their own hands, creating;
    - unprecedented change in growth in distributed energy resource management, the rise of virtual power plants across households, apartment complexes and whole countries; and
    - the arrival of broader, consumer demand for cleaner, more efficient and economic energy sources where most advanced economies in 2040 almost completely rely on renewable energy sources alone. Examples include solar, wind, hydrogen and hydro.

Customers in this industry now determine;

- What they want and how they want to be supplied;
- What it should cost them, if anything, given the commoditised nature of the sector;
- Who is the most likely organisation or network best placed to satisfy their primary buying persona? Alternatives are family vs individual, house dweller vs apartment, city vs regional, itinerant worker vs office-bound employee. Their personas may change over time, they may even change and change back frequently depending on their needs and situation/s in life.

Customers no longer identify individual utility and individual service providers and have come to expect these "global hubs" to provide "everything" a consumer needs in and around the home. This is especially true for city dwellers and suburban households. This lifestyle choice of inner-city living is characterised by an "always-on" availability of services, food, entertainment, travel and immediate, consistent and efficient access at any time. This includes such products and services as electricity, gas, water, telco, entertainment and broadband packages, food and transport.

Whether it be from a mobile phone, a home management system or some other ubiquitous but customisable device, inner-city dwellers especially will be able to access, order and consume whatever they want, when they want at a simple command. Getting there was not without its pitfalls and seismic shifts in industries that have had more than 100 years of evolution – from the industrial age, through monopolisation and domination as bedrocks of developing countries in the early 20th century. They were then challenged and transformed through the digital and AI age that accelerated through 2020–2030.

The fall out in the late 2020s resembled previous "crashes" such as the dot-com boom in the late 1990s – early 2000s – but was less catastrophic as advanced technologies, globally allowed and facilitated new but experienced players to come in and shape "new service provision platforms" for customers. The casualties were the traditional utility corporations stuck in infrastructure paralysis.

The winners were the networked platform organisations, light on people, heavy on customer centricity and advanced in accessible technology. Technology now satisfies all consumers' basic product and service provision needs.

As organisations with billions of subscribers, these global hubs have effectively become key infrastructure players, possessing the buying power across multiple countries and therefore able to influence pricing and conditions across the entire supply chain for these communities. While many countries continue to maintain and protect their sovereignty, the global marketplace, and the technology it runs on, has broken down. Many if not most of the country-specific markets supply a range of basic services which, as referenced here, are being made universally available through these hubs. This infrastructure mostly originated from renewable sources; across advanced technologies and platforms harnessing solar, wind, hydro and hydrogen power. Accessible to the hubs in commoditised, productised forms, with many similarities and price parity (where possible), these service many regions and countries across the globe.

The key characteristics of the corporations that deliver these levels and breadth of service to customers include:

- Strong visionary leadership. From the design of what is possible and accessible to customers, to the highly networked delivery capabilities that remain profitable as they become ever-expanding entities with a global footprint. It is this visionary leadership combined with seamless technological capabilities that "lead" consumers to want to adopt and adapt this range of services to suit themselves from a convenience, affordability, reliability and loyalty perspective.
- Technology rich platform/s are the main feature, whether that be connecting and/or leveraging asset platforms (e.g. renewable energy networks at the customer and industrial scale) through to detailed and flexible customer buying, usage and management preferences. The "technology knows the customer" and exceeds their needs. This requires advanced levels of interactive, AI and predictable technologies.
- Analytics rich. Teams of data scientists networked across service platforms and geographies help to "design" what trends are telling them will be the next service need and how to meet it.
- Customer advocate. Highly qualified and engaged customer specialists that have learnt to define and ensure delivery of a "customer utopia" for full, integrated, seamless and economic services.

Method

The findings in this chapter were based on data collected through surveys and interviews of senior executives conducted by the author. An "expert review process" was adopted for this research, which has been widely used for forecasting industry technological changes (Jones, 1978). The selection of appropriate industry experts for the interviews was critical to gaining useful insights into the future of the utility sector and the implications of change in the sector in the next two decades. To provide the best representative perspective possible, a diverse group of energy utility industry experts from many countries and sectors of the industry were selected to participate in the study – providing a wealth of insights and information from which to develop the research themes (Jones, 1978). The data sources utilised included:

- Industry knowledge, practice and experimentation results research
- Utility industry actors, including utility senior executives, energy and utilities related government department senior executives, industry institutions, market suppliers and customers in Australia and overseas
- Energy and utility industry researchers

The demographics of the industry expert participants are provided in Table 7.1. The data was collected as part of a large Australian government-funded research project investigating distributed energy resource management. The data from the interviews were thematically analysed to identify a range of themes that explain the customer expectations of utility services in the future and how this will lead to different organisational configurations of the Future Corporation. The data were coded as part of the thematic analysis to create a backcast view of the path that led to the service features of the Future Corporation (Miles and Huberman, 1984). This coding included:

i) Affixing codes to a fieldnotes drawn from the expert review interviews
ii) Identifying similar themes, relationships between variables and topics, patterns, distinct differences/outliers and common sequences
iii) Elaborating the generalisations that covered the consistencies in the data
iv) Converging those generalisations with a formalised body of knowledge to construct theories

The conditions that will create the Future Corporation have been identified from the literature and assembled using the backcasting approach, described in the first chapter of this book. The opening section of this chapter describes the Future Corporation and the following sections of this chapter explain the evolution process and major external factors and industry conditions that create the impetus for the evolution of the Future Corporation.

The evolution of the Future Corporation

Jian Wei, Suzanna Sanborn and Andrew Slaughter (2019) have provided a useful assessment of where utilities saw their future prospects and the roadmaps needed to get there. Their opinions were based on the dynamics of the evolving occurrences of market demographics, digitalisation, climate change and advances in technology.

The power and utilities sector morphed into an increasingly attractive, high-tech magnet for a multitude of new players. From large conglomerates in technology, retail and oil to asset managers and hot new tech start-ups, the sector has been reshaped from rising costs and changing load patterns to newly viable technologies, regulatory change and the growing call to decarbonise (Diamandis and Kotler, 2020).

Table 7.1 Demographic description of survey participants

Company type	*Individual interviewed*	*Location*	*Business type*
Public utility	Senior energy adviser	Paris, France	Digital energy and renewables business
Public utility	Senior digital technology leader	Paris, France	Digital energy solutions and infrastructure
Private utility	CEO	Melbourne, Australia	Energy retail business
Private utility	Senior technology leader	Melbourne, Australia	Energy networks business
Private business	Chairman	UK	Renewables software start-up
Private business	Founder and CEO	Melbourne, Australia	Renewables software start-up
Private business	Founder and CEO	Melbourne, Australia	DERMS Software business
Private business	Chairman	Melbourne, Australia	Utility sector advisory
Private business	CEO	Melbourne, Australia	Utility sector advisory
Public company	Global leader digital energy	Boston, USA	Global software business leader – energy sector
Public company	Regional leader digital energy – APAC	Christchurch, New Zealand	Regional software business leader – energy sector
Public company	Global technology leader digital energy	California, USA	Global software business leader – energy sector
Public company	Global energy strategy leader	California, USA	Renewables manufacturing, EVs, battery storage and solar
Public company	Regional energy sector leader – Australia and New Zealand	Sydney, Australia	Renewables manufacturing, EVs, battery storage and solar
Government – energy dept: federal	Senior adviser – projects funding	Canberra, Australia	Renewable energy projects
Government – energy dept: state	Energy ministerial adviser	South Australia	Renewable energy infrastructure and projects
Government – energy dept: federal	Senior leader – energy market operator	Melbourne, Australia	Renewable energy projects and energy market operation
Academic institution	Professor – energy sector	Sydney, Australia	Renewable energy sector
Academic institution	Professor – energy sector	Melbourne, Australia	Renewable energy sector

The proliferation of technologies such as AI, Internet of Things (IoT), cloud computing and blockchain have delivered new business models that completely disrupted the utilities sector overturning the monopolies in many countries. These will now be considered.

New digital technologies which transform industries

Execution and the compounding realisation of efficiencies, reach and customer satisfaction through simplification have been the hallmark of advancing digital technologies over the past 20 years (Fontaine et al., 2019). This was especially true in the total disruption brought about by the utility-to-consumer relationship. It no longer exists in 2040 and has been superseded by new players – highly evolved companies managing digital platforms of services for consumers.

Strategic perspectives

Technology has removed all barriers to entry for utility-type services to customers. Organisations such as Amazon, Apple, Google and Facebook have long been selling and providing "home service bundles" to customers (subscribers) that are initiated by the free of charge provision of an always-on connection device (mobile phone, tablet, home management system). These services offer and deliver a menu of tick box services that customers can take up with their Amazon or Apple subscription. Not only does this include entertainment streaming, movies, TV, search and music but electricity, gas, water, broadband, waste management and a range of what are in 2040 "out of mind" needs. In contrast, traditionally, utilities have been consistent with being a monopoly such as stalwarts of electricity and water, telco and gas which represent the staples or essential type services every household, apartment or business need on a daily basis (Parker et al., 2016; Galloway, 2017).

Interviews with Australian utility managers conducted by the author in earlier research (Trainor, 2001), Kelly (2016) and Diamandis and Kotler (2020) indicated that, as service provision becomes increasingly more automated and ubiquitous, the utility landscape can be expected to expand into a broad array of services that various individuals, families and households can leverage. This can cover such essentials as the following but is not limited to these only.

- Electricity (via their own installed renewable resources)
- Water (via individual and localised water treatment recycling)
- Gas
- Telecommunications (including broadband), entertainment – streamed, interactive and customised
- Food selection and delivery – preparation and disposal
- Home essentials selection and delivery – almost making it unnecessary for consumers to ever visit supermarkets

- Waste disposal
- Transport via electric vehicles (EVs), which will be shared and communal
- Work "spaces" shared and the technology and infrastructure to support this
- Ongoing education, learning and development
- Home or apartment
  - Cleaning
  - Maintenance and support across a range of areas also including IT, hot water, air conditioning, plumbing, carpentry and electricians
  - Personal physical fitness

New workplace practices

New twists on design, processes and ways of doing business accelerate industry disruption and amplify opportunities for start-ups and break-away businesses. Diamandis and Kotler (2020) suggest that these new workplace features include:

- Human-centred design
- Agile and adaptive business practices
- Ever-evolving features shaping the way we work
- Crowdsourcing
- The sharing and subscription economy
- Mega-platform ecosystems

Digital technology and the transformation that follows it across industries bring the dynamics of disruption and enablement in not only the utility industry but in most industries worldwide.

On the one hand, disruption challenges the very structure of industries, the infrastructure and business models deployed to operate them. It breaks down barriers. In many countries, utilities which have been regarded as long-term monopolies are proving to be easily disrupted by privatisation and deregulation, especially in the UK, Australia, New Zealand and parts of the United States (Rifkin, 2013). This disruption is typically fired by the rapid expansion, speed and coverage of advanced technology and fragmented industries, introducing many more suppliers and increasing price-based competition. This disruption and fragmentation will be particularly significant in the utility sector.

In particular, digital technologies act as catalysts to enable incumbents and new entrants to develop new business and operating models, for example, advanced analytics enabling the segmentation of customers and targeting of customer groups for new services. Disruptors that open the door to new market entrants – such as technology platforms that aggregate output from distributed energy resource (DER) owners – are set to change the nature of utility markets. Enablers, such as automated systems which inspect and correct issues in infrastructure, reduce maintenance time and costs and are likely to enter the industry with new market entrants (Kelly, 2016).

Industry developments shaping the Future Corporation

In the future, customers will no longer be interested in the extra burden of dealing with single service providers. This has already occurred in sectors where the "bundling of services" has become common because of customer preferences and the value they place on their time (Kelly, 2016). Technology such as AI, IoT, touch, voice recognition, face recognition and activation, and the commercial leverage of cryptocurrencies, makes this possible.

Developments in technology (especially AI, IoT, blockchain and personalisation/customisation) provide convenience and time and money saving to "buy" customers precious time they would otherwise be spending organising these services, monitoring and managing them to their satisfaction and switching and changing. In practice – their preferences will be constantly responded to by "smart technology" – it is the platform that is meeting their needs with invisible service providers managing a web of service lines and support in a highly connected and responsive network.

While technology enables ease of use and understanding of what services and products are being supplied and at what grade of quality, cost and continuity, it also means that customers have unencumbered choice (fewer contracts), problems solved and utilities covering many services and products over many communities and geographies – seamlessly.

Increases in living standards across the board (especially the rapid and vast expansion of the middle class in mega populations such as China and India) have driven and increased the development of technology. In 2020, on a per capita basis, there was at least one smartphone per person, by 2040, customers will have a "smart life" fully enabled by technology, ubiquitous networks and platforms delivering products and services.

These factors encourage more advanced, customer-oriented business designs in the Future Corporation. They can be categorised by tough design, functional strategies, platforms and customer focus.

Industry focus

Commercial teams that are equally skilled and focused and producing and maintaining the best buying and sustainability options for consumers ensure loyalty, while at the same time ensuring optimum, repeatable and sustainable profitability for the host business. This includes close attention to the cost/cost benefit for consumers. Other important factors include:

- Experience – specific units, capabilities and expertise, and where needed, partnerships for designing products, users, services and supply together with business and commercial model design
- Solutions – designing the bringing together of products, services and solutions on the supply and demand end of the customer life cycle
- Customer focus – the integration of the consumer development lifecycle and loyalty and affiliation

Environmental management is also important for the evolution of the industry. Governments have committed to increasingly comprehensive, realistic and sustainable energy solutions worldwide. Gameau (2019) points out that aside from the focus on renewables, consumers are interested in finding a different way for us to interact with our energy. Community energy projects (including many microgrids) are springing up all over the world. From India to Scotland to Brooklyn to Daylesford in Victoria, people are not waiting for their state or federal governments and are taking energy democracy into their own hands.

Customers have moved to experiencing the "output" rather than the service across a whole range of utilities such as heat, water, search, entertainment and transport. They no longer look for "the service" and have little to no regard for "the service provider" – there is NO visible need for traditional "one" service/product providers (Kelly, 2016). While there will be a need for a continuation of some form of physical network infrastructure, these will continue to be invisible to customers.

As a result, there is an increasing tendency to pick a utility provider by choice and shopping around for convenience, commercially desirable and bundled and leveraged "output and outcomes". The consumer-oriented "content creative" part of the business needs to address customer needs and buying and usage patterns to develop and customise content and ensure it is synchronised across mediums and physical environments – home, work and travel will become increasingly important.

According to Diamandis and Kotler (2020), developing areas in the industry include:

- Educating customers about energy use
- Creating sharing communities
- Content on affiliation and loyalty programmes
- Early (young children) and family engagement
- Real-time ability to access and respond to utility trend marketing for offer take-up – deliberately or in an automated scenario

Industry platforms

The establishment and development of infrastructure that supports platforms are now both internally and externally oriented, with the following characteristics:

- For the consumer – integrated and responsive
- Bi-directional – consumers operate as producers and buyers/takers of products and services, for example, renewable energy captured in their home energy management system
- Aggregators in the market, brokers capturing benefits for consumers
- Providing either scale or speciality

Dominant organisations

According to Galloway (2017), a number of large companies outside the utilities sector are beginning to shape the future of utilities, including:

- Google – internet, search, telco, services. Massive reach internationally with consumers as the number one search engine on the planet
- Tesla – cool products, energy focused, cars, battery storage, solar tiles. The vanguard new energy company
- Telcos through to entertainment – cable TV, subscription entertainment services
- Apple – extension of the smartphone, tablets, streaming platforms, the connected home, connected car and connected life. Major industry disruptor and the change in how people adopted mobile technologies and responded to "designed services and solutions"
- Disney – focus on the "entertained life" through to anything else you want bundled with that focus. Platforms across entertainment and family engagement
- Banks – financial management, support, subscription payment against a bundled array of products and services
- Property managers (apartments)/developers – take all this on not only providing the physical building but all the lifestyle expectations that come with "living" in a house, gated community or apartment complex. This could happen through concierge management of "all homeowners need – full menu service" via a home management team (read AI/software/IoT platforms)

These suppliers are responding to a continuing and highly politicised shift to renewable energy development and use at both industrial and domestic scales. There has been a constant drive from government, driven by the community, for renewable energy targets and drastic climate change reform. Energy companies have had to fall into line, and in many instances, have fallen by the wayside to companies that have conservation and environmentalism in their DNA.

Technology

Fully automated customer service is fast approaching, utilising technologies that enable AI, internet development platforms and vast processing power and data storage. This has caused the migration of established parts of traditional utilities to non-traditional suppliers in the energy market. These are the service hub management organisations and service brokers that we have spoken of earlier – taking over vast portions of the utilities, energy and services supply chain.

This is requiring companies of the future to break down organisational and cultural barriers that stand in the way of new technology. In addition, new, innovative, technology-rich organisations are finding opportunities in these markets by offering fully integrated, easily accessible ubiquitous services (Fontaine et al., 2019).

Features of the Future Corporation

In response to these factors, the Future Corporation that is the catalyst of an aggregated array of utilities and services to customers in the future will be ubiquitous and automated service providers that interact with customers online, via mobile devices, and advanced AI will interpret and predict customers basic living needs.

These can be expected to have a major effect because of the increase and proliferation of advanced technologies that have given the power to consumers to shape, chose and design what products and services they want and when and where they want them at the price they are prepared to pay (Schmidt and Cohen, 2013; Fontaine et al., 2019). There will be no need for shop fronts and stores as these utilities and services are so ubiquitous and interchangeable that they can be bundled into a large variety of services.

Many features of these organisations will have evolved from the leasing, rental and subscription industries. As the home solar energy generating trend has demonstrated, energy can go back into the system for other products and services through these multidimensional suppliers.

While the corporation/s that sit behind this service provision appear to be "faceless and nameless", the talent and technology that will support them in data analytics, predictive modelling, advanced AI and neuro linguistic programming (NLP) will be significant. These technologies can be expected to create a personalised, secure and trusted interface between customer "voice" and company service provision that is highly qualified and valuable (Fontaine et al., 2019).

Key issues for customers will be seamless operation and the ability to effortlessly transition between product and service selection and provision. The customers will have pre-programmed preferences that will enable a corporation's "hub technology" to constantly seek out and secure the best deals. Future customers may never know who their real utility provider is – they just know they have a constant and consistent service delivered at the best price possible. The service company will have to be able to accommodate customer requirements while continuing to ensure reliability, security and transaction transparency.

Learning algorithms interfacing between the customer and supplier will provide constant data and analytics regarding customer behaviours, to which organisations will leverage and respond (Fontaine et al., 2019).

New forms of organisational design

Post-2010, successful corporations (Apple, Google, GE, Tesla) relied heavily on bringing design to the forefront (Galloway, 2017; Diamandis and Kotler, 2020). These organisations focused on a large range of design factors, ranging from product design to business model design, right through to the detailed and curated design of working environments to make work experience more creative, innovative and enjoyable. Organisational design became the driving force in these key areas (Brown 2009) and key features were as follows:

- Customer experience (CX) – designing the customer experience. Regardless of the device, the customer was engaging with the service provider on, whether that be face to face via phone or mobile phone, tablets and specific apps, kiosks or via other mediums such as TVs, what is the most desirable, easy, efficient, economic and satisfying experience for the consumer and how does that carry across consistently regardless of which way they interact with the supplier?

- Product – making product design extremely important. Mobile phones – especially the introduction and ongoing development of the iPhone – vehicles, fashion and holidays experience product development and all benefit from a healthy new indulgence in design as the underpinning driver of setting "product" apart from competitors – before consumers even think about price.
- Service – designing the "least" possible touchpoints in an interaction, building in scale, redundancy and easy replication should that be the consumer's desire.
- Package bundling – bringing parts together through design that disrupts the status quo and creates new and greater opportunities. A prime example is the iPhone and the iTunes store tearing apart the music industry.

Technology effects

Technology has become synonymous with the way consumers interact with suppliers and service providers. On both the buy and sell side it is all-consuming, while at the same time, almost appearing to be seamless and simple. Kelly (2016) and Trainor (2001) suggest that this interaction will be achieved through the following:

- Infrastructure leverage – building scale and then using it across selling platforms, customer service, supply chain and delivery as examples. Moving away from proprietary builds and deploying advanced systems and infrastructure customised to the company's needs.
- Analytics – taking full advantage on both the suppliers' behalf and the personal benefit to the consumers in deploying analytics across all aspects of selling and servicing based on the vast, continuous data available.
- CX – deployment of customer experience technologies that not only serve what consumers want and when they want it, but at the same time, observe, study, model and propose what they might require in the future.
- Artificial intelligence – advancing CX and analytics through machine learning and IoT, where permissible and this is now almost universal in 2040, to predict, anticipate and deliver consumers every conceivable need and service based on their history, affordability and profiled agreed (with service provider) needs.
- Mobility – both in the context of access to service and solutions via multiple devices but also more specifically at any time anywhere not restricted to previous generation "store opening times" and/or only available in certain geographies.

- Cyber security – covering the critical and essential: consumer privacy and financial, technology and security requirements. Making secure of consumers' environment, needs, platforms and finances.

Global partnerships

Partnerships are required to achieve the resources and coordination necessary for successful global-scale operations. Some of the key areas for global partnerships supporting this evolution in utilities include:

- Technical – platforms, infrastructure, Interfaces and scale
- Commercial – business models, commercial platforms
- Support – 24/7 global support: automated, operator and VIP support levels
- Advanced technology development – looking to smaller, nimble and focused organisations to bring and develop new technologies to the partnership
- Service provisions – additional products and services and variations at different levels such as national and local
- Product supply – consistency in quality, cost, application and support

Under these conditions, consumer demand is likely to force these organisations to provide instant access to utility products at a constant and economic price and only suppliers with scale and localised access will be able to meet this demand. This will inevitably lead to outsourcing global trading for utility services as global commodities.

Many different organisational designs may evolve to meet these conditions. The Hub Provider could be comprised of 20 high-level specialists in their respective fields, or anywhere from 200 to 200,000 employees, depending on the level of outsourcing and internal development required for their customer segment.

The CEO will become an important factor in these organisational relationships, facilitating multilevel negotiations with suppliers, partnerships with other comparable organisations and new structural designs.

Constructing the Future Corporation

In response to these factors, the Future Corporation will possess new decision-making processes, relationships with customers and an increased scope of operations. Fontaine et al. (2019) suggest that, while cutting-edge technology and talent are important, a company's culture, structure and support for broad AI and advanced technology adoption are key in the Future Corporation. The Future Corporation will make three main shifts from its current format.

- *From siloed work to interdisciplinary collaboration.* AI has the biggest impact when it is developed by cross-functional teams with a mix of skills and perspectives.

- *From experience-based, leader-driven decision-making to data-driven decision-making at the front line.* When AI is adopted broadly, employees up and down the hierarchy will augment their own judgement and intuition with algorithm recommendations to arrive at better answers than either humans or machines could reach on their own.
  - Experienced human planners then apply their expertise to make final decisions supported by the data without the need to get input from their leaders. The planners adopted the tool readily, trusting its output because they'd help set its parameters and constraints and knew that they themselves would make the final call.
- *From rigid and risk-averse to agile, experimental and adaptable.* Organisations must shed the mindset that an idea needs to be fully baked or a business tool must have every bell and whistle before its deployed on the first iteration. The fundamental shift to agile, testing and learning, rapid development and deployment did not come easy.
  - Leaders had to prepare, motivate and equip the workforce to make the change.
  - Leaders must first be prepared themselves to lead, design and execute the change and transformation to service-oriented organisations as opposed to asset management organisations. They must become highly developed in understanding AI, its benefits, challenges and adaption and leverage.

Customer influence

Customers are interested in energy conservation, sustainability and climate change. They are champions of discontinuing the misuse of damaging energy production and the sustainable outcomes made possible through new technologies. Energy supply will operate within a network of integrated production and delivery platforms of similar products and services such as electricity, gas, water, telecommunications and transport. These networks will encourage localised communities which act as customer groups, such as the following:

a) Small towns – producing, using, bartering and maintaining sustainability
b) Apartment complexes – buying, using, saving – sharing as one integrated unit
c) We work where we live users – users of services and products at home, requiring more personal utilities to satisfy both home and work needs
d) Regional, country and community groups – reflecting consumer preferences, the availability and access to technology and the commoditisation of the services available to consumers (Figueres and Rivett-Carnac, 2020; Anderson, 2013)

Increased scope of operations

Corporations have launched initiatives and projects that have led to a suite of essential products and services available through an integrated service model. Level playing fields have been established for products and services across the world. The increasing take-up of products and services worldwide has also brought about negative impacts such as the effects of climate change through increased pollution from energy production and consumption. Global, national and community-based organisations will be working to satisfy consumer requirements, playing a more engaged role in sustainability across the planet and encouraging measured consumption as countries, communities and individuals.

There will be a consolidation of the means of energy production and the delivery of "solutions" with the key characteristics of:

- Heavily, if not fully renewable energy oriented
- Seamless supply chains
- Multilevel in-house and third-party platforms
- Customers are involved in the supply side, where waste minimisation is also a factor of the optimisation model
- Economical bundling packages of products and services for optimum consumer satisfaction, while at the same time minimising environmental impact (Kelly, 2016)

Key features of the Future Corporation

The Future Corporation set up internal digital foundries, which act as hubs or accelerators of digital projects. Many of these skillsets involved new ways of thinking for the power sector such as agile and design thinking. The foundry enables these utilities to create more flexible, collaborative, self-organising and fast-changing capabilities. The Future Corporation has also become more outcome-focused, continuously innovating and iterating at a fast pace. Adopting these agile business practices has been a significant departure from the slow-moving culture for which most utilities are known. A key challenge was adopting these changes across the entire enterprise.

Future utility services are delivered through fully integrated and interoperable "Hub and Spoke" organisational arrangements. The services will be generated and supplied through "Hubs". These services have become so commoditised and advanced in their use of "cheap" renewable sources that large consolidated, global corporations are the only structures with the scale sufficient to invest, replicate and deploy these at very low cost worldwide. These organisations manage technology-rich, interfaced and integrated platforms for customers, however, all inputs, content, product and service delivery come from either a branded or non-branded third party.

Suppliers have developed life cycle service provision that includes the recycling, repurposing and/or reuse of products and services as consumers use and/or discontinue using them (Gameau, 2019). The ubiquitous "utility service package" will evolve into an ever-increasing and dynamic selection of services the customers adjust, depending on needs, availability and location.

It is accessible while travelling and in variable quantities based on customer whereabouts. Blockchain and similar technologies enable customers to access utility services with ease.

Conclusion

Some of the largest energy and telco sector corporations in the world such as Tepco, Engie, Centrica, Enel, EON and PG&E will disappear or fade into the background in the next ten to Twenty years. Corporations such as Google, Facebook, Amazon, Apple, Disney, Comcast and Netflix are, by comparison, successful in creating interfaces between customers and their daily needs on which they are dependent. Customers maintain a continuous, almost constant conversation (awareness) with major platforms (e.g. Apple) that increasingly provide and anticipate what customers need. Basic but critical services such as electricity, gas, water, broadband, entertainment and transport are increasingly bundled and provided through these organisations. These corporations have billions of customers and are accessible 24/7 through amazingly advanced technology activated by customers' speech, touch, sight and even "thoughts" across thousands of products and services. They will form the backbone of highly integrated and needs-oriented utility service provision in 2040.

References

Anderson, C. *Makers – The New Industrial Revolution*, Random House Business Books, New York, 2013.

Brown, T. *Change by Design*, HarperCollins, New York, 2009.

Diamandis, P.H. and Kotler, S. *The Future is Faster than You Think*, Simon and Schuster, Sweden, 2020.

Figueres, C. and Rivett-Carnac, T. *The Future We Choose – Surviving the Climate Crisis*, Manilla Press, Sweden, 2020.

Fontaine, T., McCarthy, B. and Saleh, T. *Building the AI-Powered Organisation*, Harvard Business Review - July–August, Cambridge, MA, 2019.

Galloway, S. *The Four – The Hidden DNA of Amazon, Apple, Facebook and Google*, Penguin Random House, New York, 2017.

Gameau, D. *2040 – A Handbook for Regeneration – Based on the Documentary*, Macmillan, Sydney, 2019.

Jones, H. and Twiss, B.C. *Forecasting Technology for Planning Decisions*, Macmillan, London, 1978.

Kelly, K. *The Inevitable – Understanding the 12 Technological Forces That Will Shape our Future*, Viking, New York, 2016.

Miles, M.B. and Huberman, J. *Qualitative Data Analysis*, Sage Publications, New York, 1984.

Parker, G.G, Van Alstyne, M.W and Choudhary, S.P. *Platform Revolution – How Networked Markets are Transforming the Economy and How to Make Them Work for You*, W.W. Norton & Co. Inc, New York, 2016.

Rifkin, J. *The Third Industrial Revolution – How Lateral Power is Transforming Energy, the Economy and the World*, Palgrave Macmillan, St. Martin's Griffin, New York, 2013.

Schmidt, E. and Cohen, J. *The New Digital Age – Shaping the Future of People, Nations and Business*, John Murray (Publishers), London, 2013.

Trainor, G.A. 'A Strategic Approach to Creating Value for the Utility Customer of the Future'. Doctoral thesis, RMIT, Melbourne, 2001.

Wei, J, Sanborn, S and Slaughter, A. *Digital Innovation – Creating the Utility of the Future*, Deloitte, 2019. https://www2.deloitte.com/us/en/insights/industry/power-and-utilities/digital-transformation-utility-of-the-future.html. Accessed 11 April 2022.

8 Backcasting of the electricity industry from 2040

Tim Mactaggart

Introduction

The electricity industry has been going through an extended period of technological change. Promoted by concerns about climate change and sustainability, technologies that have remained latent for almost 40 years (notably solar and wind energy) are starting to have an impact on electricity generation around the world. These technologies are replacing incumbent fossil fuel-powered generation as advanced economies look to address the issue of climate change. As a result, clean energy technologies, or "cleantech", are being adopted at an ever-increasing pace to decarbonise the power sector. The subsequent reconfiguration of electricity networks is transforming the technical landscape of power generation, but the rate of change being achieved is falling well short of what is needed to reduce the impact of electricity supply on global warming. If the world is to decarbonise electricity generation quickly, a new approach is required. The prominence of power generation and its often-visible emissions means that technological substitution in the sector has been receiving the most attention. However, electrical technologies form part of broader and well-established socio-technical systems. These systems are defined by identifiable configurations of social structures as well as technologies that evolve together over long periods of time. This "co-evolution" creates a dominant design which constrains the direction of future development by directing the thought processes of system participants towards incrementally improved technological innovations, rather than radical ones. The dominant design is reinforced through the development of a technological trajectory that determines future system design. Also called technological lock-in, the resulting socio-technical system becomes highly resistant to radical change.

One process that presents a promising option for breaking well-established socio-technical systems out of their locked-in state is disruptive innovation. This type of innovation has been shown to be capable of inducing rapid and widespread technological change. In models of disruptive innovation, low-performance radical innovations find a home in socio-technical niches, before experiencing rapid performance improvement and emergence into the mainstream. Tied to sunk investments in incumbent technologies, dominant technology vendors are rapidly displaced, along with the technological basis of the industry they inhabit. This process has been shown to occur in industries as diverse as computer hard drives,

DOI: 10.4324/9781003183679-8

hydraulic excavators and steel making, and the same process may be underway in the electricity industry. Prior research indicates that the normative processes of change established for disruptive innovation may not be as effective in the electricity industry. Instead, rapid technological change is likely to be mitigated by the actions of strong socio-technical systems that are reinforced by the highly interlinked nature of electrical technologies within power networks. The resulting technological transition is therefore likely to experience an extended period of "hybridisation" where radical innovations complement the incumbent ones, addressing shortcomings in those technologies (environmental impact) until a more lasting transition can occur.

The complex, evolutionary and interconnected nature of electricity systems means that many approaches to examining technological change are ineffective. As a result, a systems perspective is used here as it accommodates the evolutionary constraints that exist within socio-technical systems while providing a framework for understanding processes of non-evolutionary change as electricity systems transition from fossil fuel-based technologies to more sustainable ones. In addition to using a system perspective, it is necessary to employ forward-looking tools to understand what future socio-technical configurations might look like. Several suitable techniques have been developed in the past which can be broadly divided into three categories:

- Tools that use scenarios to focus on what *will* happen in the future and use quantitative methods to extrapolate trends. These approaches tend to generate business-as-usual scenarios that consider major trends.
- Tools that use scenarios to focus on what *could* happen in the future to create a range of alternative outcomes that reflect uncertainty and a range of differing perspectives.
- Tools that are more directed towards *desirable* futures and that focus on what should happen, or what future is collectively being targeted. This approach is called backcasting, or transition management.

While all three methods can be applied to examine socio-technical change within electricity systems, the first two are likely only to extrapolate on trends already occurring, all of which are proving inadequate in addressing climate change. When looking at what the electricity system might look like in 2040, backcasting is likely to be a more effective tool. This is because, despite the more recent acceleration of change, approaches that build off the current configuration are likely simply to extend or extrapolate the existing technological trajectory that dominates the electricity sector. In contrast, backcasting offers the opportunity to formulate radically different futures and work backwards to determine the incremental steps required to achieve these futures. For example, backcasting has been defined as a way to generate a targeted future, then look backwards from that in order to determine how it could be achieved (Vergragt and Quist 2011), or a way to formulate a desired future state and determine the steps required to bring that future state about (Quist and Vergragt 2006). The application of backcasting to the future of the electricity systems is therefore more likely to identify a pathway that can overcome the strong constraints of technological trajectories within the electricity sector.

The application of this approach to electricity systems has precedence within the field of sustainable innovation (Quist 2013). This includes application to climate policy (van de Kerkhof, Hisschemoller et al. 2002), sustainable system innovation (Vergragt and L. Jansen 1993; Weaver, Jansen et al. 2000) and energy more generally (Anderson, Mander et al. 2008; Gomi, Ochi et al. 2011). Where this chapter diverges from these approaches is in explicitly accommodating the co-evolutionary nature of electricity systems as socio-technical systems (and the associated processes of trajectory development and socio-technical lock-in) while considering the impact of disruptive innovation processes. Following this, the process used here partially follows that outlined by Quist (2013), which includes five steps as follows:

1. *Strategic problem orientation* in order to explore the problem from a systemic point of view to frame the problem and identify unsustainability, opportunities and possible solutions.
2. *Developing future visions* to construct sustainable futures that incorporate solutions to the identified problems associated in the present.
3. *Backcasting analysis* aims to identify the changes necessary to enable a future vision to become true.
4. *Elaboration of future options and the creation of a follow-up agenda* to elaborate on general scenarios through quantification of the vision and translation into follow-on actions.
5. Embedding of results and agendas and the stimulation of follow-up and implementation activities.

This chapter applies the process described by Quist, but as a standalone undertaking lacks the collaborative element anticipated by the technique used to define a follow-up agenda that can be used to embed results and stimulate further actions to progress towards the envisioned future state. Consequently, this chapter can be considered as a preliminary step towards a full backcasting exercise to be conducted by others, providing pointers as to a possible future scenario which accommodates the unique elements of modern electricity systems. As a result, the first four steps of the backcasting process are completed here, with the fifth step omitted due to the non-collaborative nature of the exercise. Instead, observations on some possible improvements in the backcasting technique are made for application in the context of widespread socio-technical change, including within large socio-technical systems such as the electricity sector.

Step 1: Strategic problem orientation

The importance of electricity to modern economies

Electrical power is used every day for a range of applications, from lighting to heating, cooling and refrigeration, and for operating appliances such as electrical machinery, transportation infrastructure or data centres. It underpins critical industrial systems including the internet, air transportation and public health, “keeping the lights on” for consumers in a growing range of applications. Electricity sits at the centre of modern industrial economies and the lives of billions of people around the world. Research into the role of electricity in the economy has established a connection between the quantity and quality of electricity consumed and economic growth (Cleveland, Costanza et al. 1984; Ayres and Warr 2005). In addition to underpinning economic activity, electricity also plays a crucial role in poverty alleviation and the improvement of living standards. The importance of electricity to economic development has been underlined by the United Nations, which has set access to affordable and clean energy as one of its 17 Sustainable Development Goals (UN General Assembly 2015).

The importance of electricity to the effective operation of national economies will only increase with time. The electrification of the transport sector via the adoption of electric vehicles will help drive the global share of electricity in total final use from 20% today to nearly 50% by 2050 (IRENA 2018). In addition, other industrial processes that currently use gas, oil or coal for energy are likely to transition to electricity as well. As a result, global electricity demand is forecast to increase by 57% by 2050 (Bloomberg New Energy Finance 2019b). The systems that generate and distribute electricity to consumers will therefore remain critical infrastructure into the foreseeable future.

Trends driving change in the electricity industry

Despite this criticality, the electricity industry is facing several trends which are putting pressure on the technologies within the system, and the overall structure of the system itself. First among these is a push towards decarbonisation of the economy. Electricity is one of the largest producers of carbon emissions, with most of the energy used in the production of electricity coming from fossil fuels. For example, coal, crude oil and natural gas together provided over 90% of primary energy consumed in 2017 (Smil 2017), with a marked increase in total volume since the 1950s. The dominance of fossil fuels used in energy supply means that the electricity sector was responsible for 25% of the annual global greenhouse gas emissions in 2017, a proportion forecast to rise to 30% by 2050 (Harvey, Orvis et al. 2018). Based on the need to reduce carbon emissions by 25% to 55% to maintain global warming below 2°C, the electricity sector needs to undergo significant change (Harvey, Orvis et al. 2018).

A second trend affecting the electricity sector is digitisation, which enables the widespread adoption of digital technologies to collect huge volumes of data to support better decision-making (IBM 2018). Many of the functions of electric grids can be optimised through the application of digital sensors and switches. This includes the application of advanced control technologies to automate feeder switching to monitor voltages and manage outages within networks, for example (US Department of Energy 2016). Digital technologies also enable two-way communication between electric utilities and customers. This can be applied via smart meters, sensors and other communication-enabled devices to provide real-time data that support demand response and distributed generation. Artificial intelligence (AI) is also poised to drive change in electricity networks. As markets, networks and assets increase in complexity, AI can help electricity networks better predict user behaviour, balance supply and demand in real time and improve customer experience (Moniz and Yergin 2019).

A third trend starting to affect the electricity industry is the electrification of the transport sector. Electric vehicles are forecast to form 57% of passenger vehicle sales by 2040 (Bloomberg New Energy Finance 2019), up from only 0.6% in 2018 (International Energy Agency 2019). Charging electric vehicles presents both risks and opportunities for electricity grids. On the one hand, these mobile batteries could help reduce peak demand on electricity networks if they can feed energy to the grid during periods of increased demand. In contrast, it has been estimated that when local electric vehicle penetration hits 25% of the vehicle fleet, peak load on electrical networks could grow by up to 30% when vehicles charge in a coordinated fashion (Engel, Hensley et al. 2018). This places strain on both the current set of technologies that make up the grid and the way in which they combine to deliver power to consumers.

A final, significant trend affecting electricity systems is the rising adoption of distributed generation technologies and energy storage. The grid has historically been built on large-scale, centralised power-generating facilities and the one-way transmission of electricity to consumers (Hughes 1983). This paradigm grew out of economies of scale that accompanied large power station construction through the 20th century, and the need to site these generating facilities near the fuel supply rather than the point of consumption. Technological innovation has more recently broken the connection between technology deployment and economies of scale, with photovoltaic systems becoming cost-effective at almost any scale (International Renewable Energy Agency 2016). When combined with the rising adoption of energy storage, this has enabled power generation to take place in any location. The resulting change in power flows, combined with localised network constraints, is posing significant challenges for traditional electricity grids. In addition, changes in consumer perceptions and expectations for grid performance – on the back of becoming active participants in electricity markets via distributed technologies – are also challenging traditional views about the role of electricity networks in society.

Decarbonisation and technological change

Of all these trends, the push towards the decarbonisation of the electricity system has received the most attention. This is largely because changing the set of generation technologies appears relatively easy, and they are the largest single source of carbon emissions. This focus is supported by a range of options which exist to facilitate the decarbonisation of electricity generation. These include fuel switching (from high to low carbon fuels), energy efficiency in the transportation of electricity, carbon capture and storage and the deployment of zero greenhouse emission technologies, including both renewable and nuclear energy options

(Bruckner, Bashmakov et al. 2014). The validity of this approach is borne out by research work that indicates that the technologies required to effectively reduce the carbon intensity of the electricity sector have been available for some time. For example, a 2004 paper on addressing climate change proposed a series of "stabilisation wedges" that applied the cumulative impact of a range of commercial technologies to reduce carbon emissions enough to prevent significant global warming (Pacala and Sololow 2004). These technologies included wind, solar, hydro, geothermal and nuclear, all of which can generate electricity without creating the carbon emissions associated with the use of fossil fuels such as coal and natural gas. The need for action on climate change and the availability of these technologies have spurred the development of energy policies that have supported an explosive growth in the deployment of renewable energy capacity. Since 2001, investment in renewable energy has grown from around 15% of all new generation capacity to over 60% in 2017 (IRENA 2019). In the same year, while investment in conventional fossil fuels and nuclear power generation amounted to US$144 billion, global investment in renewables was over double that at US$333 billion. This represents a 14.5% increase over 2017 investment levels, and as a result, clean energy has been forecast to make up almost 50% of installed capacity by 2040 (Jackson 2018).

Despite the increasing use of renewable technologies, the mix of fuels present in global power systems has remained relatively unchanged, with coal producing almost as much electricity in 2017 as it did in 1997 (38% of total generation). Not only that, but carbon emissions from the power sector increased by approximately 2.7% in 2018, accounting for around half of all growth in global carbon emissions. This outcome has occurred despite accelerated technological development (Johnstone, Haščič et al. 2010) and a proliferation of policy measures designed to support renewable energy technologies (BP 2011; REN21 2011; IEA 2012). As a result, despite significant efforts around the world, the electricity sector is not transitioning to clean technologies at the rate required to avoid dangerous levels of global warming.

Constraints to change

Part of the problem is that the electricity industry has a poor history of innovation adoption (Martin 1996), suggesting that the transition to low carbon electricity generation faces a number of challenges. Part of the issue facing the transition to a sustainable electricity system is that the generation technologies responsible for carbon emissions sit within a tightly interconnected system of complementary technologies. For electricity to make its way from the generation plant to the point of consumption, it needs to transit high- and low-voltage power transmission systems. These systems are made up of a multitude of technologies ranging from transformers to switchgear, all of which have evolved to support the geographic distribution and technical idiosyncrasies of fossil-fuelled power generation technologies. These technologies are also supported by well-developed technical standards and operating principles that have evolved hand in glove with the technology over time. As a natural monopoly, electricity systems are also heavily regulated and overseen by political processes at the state and national levels. All of these, from technologies to institutions, knowledge and ways of working have evolved together since the emergence of power networks in the late 19th century to become tightly interlinked, meaning that changing one element – in this case, power generation technologies – has unavoidable impacts on other elements of the system. As a result, change in the electricity sector is not a simple case of swapping one type of technology for another.

The strong interlinking of social and technological structures that exists within electricity systems is characteristic of a dominant design. Dominant designs evolve over time to reflect a standardised view of what a system should look like, including its constituent technologies. The emergence of a dominant design acts to limit the development of alternative technologies, or combinations of technologies, which can develop in the future (Nelson and Winter 1977; Dosi 1982). These constraints have also been referred to as technological regimes, referring to the rules that both enable and constrain activities in relation to particular technologies. In the case of the electricity industry, the dominant design is based on centralised power generation using fossil fuels (Hughes 1987). The constraining effect of this dominant design has been referred to as "carbon lock in" (Unruh 2000), reflecting socio-technological constraints which present ongoing impediments to the adoption of new energy technologies, particularly those that avoid the generation of carbon emissions (Unruh 2002; Foxon 2003). In practical terms, the barriers that the dominant design presents manifest themselves in several ways. For example, the intermittent nature of the energy resource (for example, the sun, wave or wind) creates issues for supply security, reliability and network efficiency (McCarthy, Ogden et al. 2007; NREL 2008a, 2008b; Molina C, Martinez A et al. 2010) and the physical distribution of renewable resources when compared to existing electricity grids also creates problems for existing networks (Vittal 2010), requiring the construction of expensive complementary network infrastructure (Østergaard 2003; Hammons 2008). The introduction of renewable energy technologies into existing electricity systems therefore faces a range of barriers which are grounded in the configuration of existing electricity networks.

Dominant designs are also highly static in nature, pointing to factors that prevent the adoption of innovations. However, electricity systems have evolved over time, if slowly, and this evolution requires the generation, adoption and use of a range of novel new technologies. The process whereby this evolution occurs is through a collection of actors, networks and institutions which work together, but also moderate and constrain each other in the diffusion of technological innovations (Fleck 1992). This combination of actors, networks and institutions forms a "technological system" which exerts a strong influence over the types of technologies that are successfully adopted (Nelson and Nelson 2002; Anderson 2005; McKelvey 2005). In the case of the electricity sector, the boundary of the technological system encompasses the generation, distribution and consumption of electrical energy (Hughes 1987). Actors within it include manufacturing firms, electrical utility companies, industrial energy users and households, distribution network operators, national and state governments and regulators (Hughes 1987; Foxon, Hammond et al. 2010); institutions include regulatory structures, market rules and national policies (Foxon, Hammond et al. 2010) as well as the rules and norms which regulate social behaviour within the system (Edquist and Johnson 1997); and networks include the relationships between actors, such as user-supplier relations, production chains and knowledge networks (Stankiewicz and Carlsson 1991). These networks, actors and institutions work together to develop, diffuse and utilise technological innovations (Stankiewicz and Carlsson 1991) but also moderate and constrain each other in the diffusion of those innovations (Fleck 1992). The existing configuration of a technological system, therefore, exerts a strong influence over the types of technologies that are successfully adopted over time (Nelson and Nelson 2002; Anderson 2005; McKelvey 2005). The electricity sector – in the form of a technological system – should therefore be capable of supporting the development, adoption and use of renewable energy technologies. However, these technologies display several characteristics which present challenges for diffusion processes and widespread technological change within these systems.

Barriers to renewable energy adoption

First, renewable energy technologies will rapidly displace fossil fuel-based technologies if a range of national policy objectives are fulfilled (Pacala and Socolow 2004; Held, Ragwitz et al. 2009). However, technological systems are based on evolutionary principles of socio-technical development (Stankiewicz 1995; Edquist 1997), which means that they are poorly suited to accommodating rapid technological change (Rip and Kemp 1998). Instead, technological systems evolve through the generation, selection and retention of a range of technologies (Nelson and Nelson 2002), the majority of which are incremental in nature. As a result, the system evolves at a steady pace in response to the diffusion of incrementally improved technologies (Dosi 1982; David 1988; Oinas and Malecki 2002; Markard and Truffer 2008). This cannot be the case with renewable energy technologies if decarbonisation is to occur in the short to medium term.

Second, the diffusion of renewable energy technologies has the potential to disrupt the electricity system. A type of innovation identified by Clayton Christensen in the mid-1990s, disruptive innovation has been identified as a source of rapid change in industries from computer hard disk drives to taxi cabs and financial services. The disruption predicted by Christensen takes the form of a rapid displacement of incumbent technologies and an associated reconfiguration of existing industry structures (Christensen 1997; Christensen, Anthony et al. 2004). These industry structures are represented by firms utilising the technologies and the relationships that exist between them. When diffusion takes place within a technological system, this disruption affects existing actors as economic agents are displaced (including existing firms). Networks are also affected as the links that exist in user-supplier relationships, supply chains and knowledge networks break down in response to actor change (Stankiewicz and Carlsson 1991; Malerba 2002). As a result, when diffusion takes place within technological systems, the effects of disruption extend to the system as actors and networks are displaced through the diffusion process.

In addition to inducing changes to actors and networks, the diffusion of disruptive technology alters institutions. Technologies embody both a technological artefact and the knowledge required to design, build and utilise them (Dobrov 1979; Hughes 1987; Pinch and Bijker 1987). In addition, technology includes socially defined rules that determine how it is used in practice (Dobrov 1979). These separate elements combine to create overall working systems, or "socio-technical configurations" (Rip and Kemp 1998) which are both social and technical in nature. As a result, the diffusion of a technological innovation includes the diffusion of new institutions. Taking this holistic view of technological innovations is critical to understanding how they are adopted over time, and it is even more important when looking at broad-scale technological change. The diffusion of technological innovations requires the adoption of new institutions as much as new technological artefacts (McKelvey 2005). The tight interlinking of established systems with a set of technologies is one of the reasons why technological change has proven to be so problematic in the electricity industry. The enduring need for a *set* of technologies and the supporting actors, networks and institutions that constitute the system means that changing out one technology for another is highly problematic, particularly where an innovation is highly radical in nature. Whether it is the social elements of the existing system that influence innovation adoption, or the necessity for co-evolved institutions that support an individual technology, the social elements of technological innovation are as important to their adoption as the technical ones.

Technological transitions as a model for change

The challenges that the need for supportive social institutions presents to highly novel technological innovations within technological systems are extensive. As a system, the electricity sector has evolved through processes of slow, evolutionary change; in contrast, the rapid change required to address climate change needs renewable energy to behave more like a disruptive innovation than an incremental one. However, the system presents barriers to adoption as it relies on a much broader set of interconnected technologies, as well as the actors, networks and institutions that are needed to diffuse innovations. Despite this, history suggests that there is a way forward for the transformation of the electricity sector, in the form of a "technological transition". Technological transitions rely on several mechanisms to transition a system from one dominant form of technology to another. Where technological regimes, dominant designs and technological systems highlight the stability of existing systems, technological transitions highlight the dynamic processes that lead to a major shift in how society transitions from one type of technology to another. Technological transitions provide a pathway, or roadmap, for understanding how change can occur when regimes have been established. Unlike processes of technological change in technological systems – which are grounded in an ongoing renewal and continuation of a technological trajectory – technological transitions anticipate change by looking at these systems in a different way. Rather than presuming continuity, technological transitions consider existing regimes to be only one of three "levels" that influence the development and adoption of new technologies. In addition to the regime, there are technological "niches" and a "socio-technical landscape", or "socio-technical environment" (see Figure 8.1).

As the name implies, niches are isolated pockets within socio-technical regimes which provide a protected environment for the development of technological innovations. In effect, these niches act as incubators for the development of radical technologies. These innovations need protection from the broader regime because of their inconsistency with the institutions that govern the regime. The inconsistency can be technical in nature, for example, the problem posed by the intermittency of renewable energy sources in grids which are premised on controllable energy generation. However, radical innovations bring radical socio-technical configurations of their own with them and the inconsistency is much broader than the technical. Niches provide an environment where the influences of the socio-technical regimes are weak, and the radical socio-technical configurations can gain some traction. For example, early niches for photovoltaic technologies have often been in remote or isolated locations, where prohibitive costs have prevented established electrical grids from supplying power. As a result, this environment rendered the low technical performance and the high cost of early systems less relevant to adoption. Once established, these niches provided an environment for learning processes to occur, providing space for supporting social networks to develop which support innovation, for example, supply chains and user–supplier relationships.

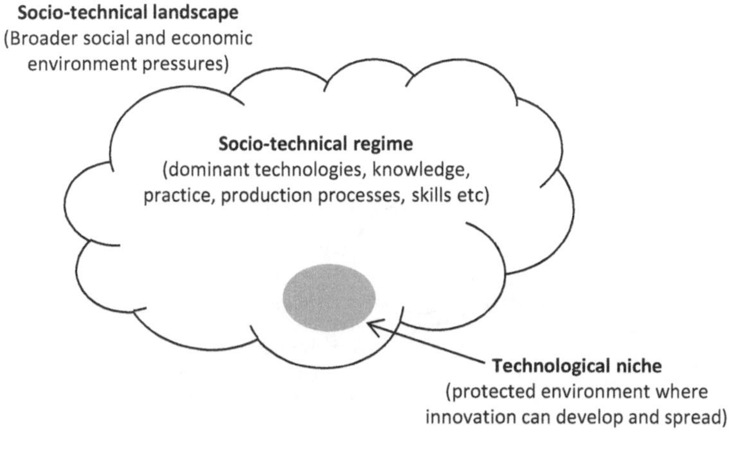

Figure 8.1 Key elements of technological transitions.

The third element of technological transitions is the broader socio-technical environment. In contrast to regimes which refer to rules that both enable and constrain activities in relation to particular technologies, the socio-technical environment refers to factors that are external to those technologies. The socio-technical environment is a "macro" level phenomenon that contains slow-changing external factors which help to shape the direction of development of technological trajectories within regimes. These changes occur as trends in the socio-technical environment put pressure on the regime, creating openings for new technologies. The oil crises of the early 1970s are an example of this type of pressure as they created an opening for the development of many alternative energy technologies such as solar photovoltaics. While those pressures passed with a return to normal levels of global oil production, similar forces have arisen through the issue of climate change. Once again this has created openings for the development and adoption of new technologies, such as wave, wind, geothermal and a range of other innovative generation technologies. The emergence of these pressures is a necessary, but not sufficient condition for radical innovations to break through and create widespread technological change. They contribute by loosening up the links that exist within a regime, but they must be accompanied by change at the other levels to effect overall regime change. Pressure from the socio-technical environment provides a mechanism for the loosening of regimes, opening niches for early stage technology development and adoption. These niches shelter these innovations and provide time for supportive socio-technical configurations to develop. As these configurations grow in strength, they can enter the main system, compete with incumbent technologies and drive socio-technical change. When change at the three levels of the system aligns, technological transitions provide a pathway for widespread technological change to occur (Figure 8.2).

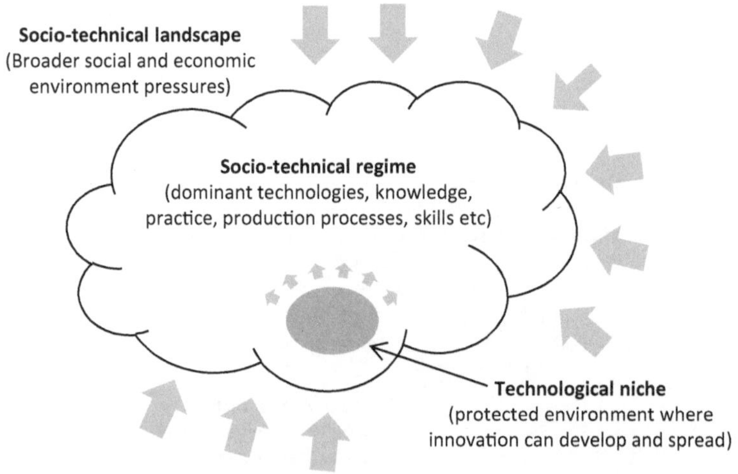

Figure 8.2 Technological systems showing niche and environmental influences.

Technological transitions also progress when newly developed technologies work together with established ones, often to overcome bottlenecks. The two technologies do not immediately compete directly but function in a form of symbiosis (Raven 2007). This process has occurred in the electricity industry at a minor level in the past, with the introduction of gas turbines, which were initially applied to the improvement of steam turbine performance in combined cycle power stations. As gas turbine technology improved, these roles were swapped, with the gas turbine providing primary generation, and the steam turbine becoming an auxiliary generator (Raven 2007). During technological transitions, major transformations result in the replacement of collections of technologies, not one specific technology or group of closely related technologies such as power generation. In a prior case of steam ships, a transition occurred from timber-hulled, wind-powered ships to steel-hulled, steam-powered vessels using screw propulsion systems for sea transportation. A full transition occurred when several innovations linked together, providing a much more compelling and competitive set of technologies. Prior to this point, steam power alone tended to be used as a complement to sail, rather than a replacement.

Technological transitions also involve change at a broader level than technological artefacts. Technology involves production skills, supporting infrastructure and distribution networks, codified and informal designs and manufacturing and operational knowledge, as well as financial and regulatory frameworks (Rip and Kemp 1998). All these system elements need to evolve to support the new technological artefacts and make them successful. In the case of the electricity system, this requires the changing of human as well as technological infrastructure. Further, technological transitions involve stepwise evolution, where a change in one part of the system leads to changes in other parts, and the development and diffusion of supporting innovations take time to occur. In the case of technological transition in the electricity sector, technological innovation (such as small-scale solar) has at times preceded institutional change – notably the development of climate policy – and at other times the sequence has been reversed. The size and complexity of the new system mean that the reconfiguration process can be time-consuming and difficult to predict. However, it is important to note that transitions occur as a cumulative result of many smaller changes, and not because of a predetermined attempt to force technological change.

All the constraints and change pathways discussed so far demonstrate the challenges that exist in trying to transition an established technological system from one set of technologies to another in a relatively brief period of time. These systems are technologically complex and have evolved over a period of decades to support the development, diffusion and utilisation of novel technologies that are mainly incremental in nature. In the context of climate change, the pace of possible change needs to accelerate, and change efforts to date demonstrate that this is not occurring. It is within this context that backcasting may provide scenarios and pathways that can shift the electricity system onto a sustainable pathway between now and the year 2040.

Step 2: Scenario analysis

The second step in the backcasting method is to develop envisioned futures that incorporate solutions to any unsustainabilities that have been identified. As noted earlier, the history and stability of electricity systems form a backdrop for any scenario development. The evolution of electricity systems over an extended period has resulted in the dominant use of large-scale power generation based on fossil fuels, combined with the one-way transmission of electricity to consumers. As the embodiment of a dominant design, the physical infrastructure presents a logical starting point for defining the current nature of electricity systems which acts in turn as a baseline for considering where they may go in the future.

The starting point: Electricity systems as they are today

As discussed in the prior section, the technologies and the architecture of electricity systems did not evolve in isolation. Instead, a wide range of complementary systems evolved with them at the same time. In addition to generation, transmission and distribution hardware, the system evolved manufacturing firms, electrical utility companies, industrial energy users and households, distribution network operators, national and state governments and regulators. It also came to encompass regulatory structures, market rules and national policies, and the rules and norms which regulate social behaviour within the system. In turn, each of these became interconnected by the relationships that existed between actors, such as user-supplier relations, production chains and knowledge networks. A high-level map of these system elements is shown in Figure 8.3.

The development of the electricity industry in the future will build on this socio-technical configuration as a starting point, forced into change by the trends discussed earlier. For clarity, those trends are as follows:

- A push to decarbonise the sector led by efforts to change high carbon intensity generation technologies for low ones.
- The digitisation of electricity, which is allowing for a more nuanced control of electrical power, and the creation of two-way communication with previously passive consumers of electricity.
- The electrification of transportation presents challenges and opportunities for managing peak load on electrical networks.
- A trend towards the deployment of generation and storage technologies at all scales across networks, challenging the existing architecture of one-way transmission of power to consumers.

There are three broad scenarios that may result from these trends, being:

1. A system that looks significantly like the system that exists today, with the integration of a range of renewable energy technologies at a scale similar to today's power generators.

Figure 8.3 Components of the electrical supply technological system.

2. A system that retains some elements of the existing system based on a continuation of the existing architecture of large, centralised generation technologies but also including a sizeable portion of decentralised generation based on scalable and sustainable local technologies.
3. A system that is a highly decentralised collection of isolated, self-sustaining "microgrids" with an associated retirement of most of the physical and institutional structures that accompany today's grid.

These scenarios are not equally likely to occur as the established nature of electricity systems as large, socially based technological systems provide a strong tendency for the future to look much like the present. The progressive development and integration of new technologies into an existing socio-technical structure is the fundamental purpose of technological systems. This means that in the absence of rapid and unexpected change, the first or second scenarios described above are also more likely to occur. Conversely, a system that is no longer interconnected in a physical sense (isolated "microgrids"), would be based on radically different technologies than we have today, and would operate without the oversight of existing monolithic institutional infrastructures, representing a definitive break from the technological trajectory of the past century. This type of change requires discontinuous social and technological developments that are difficult to predict ex-ante, the very challenge presented by disruptive innovations. For this reason, the third scenario is most suited to the backcasting process, as it provides an opportunity to develop lessons learned that are not directly interpretable from current events. Despite that, each of the scenarios is explored here, and referenced against the current situation as a starting point. In addition, the common principle used in the development of each scenario is a need to decarbonise the electricity sector, as described previously. Each of the three scenarios is presented below.

Scenario 1: Continuation of the current trajectory

The evolution of the electricity sector has produced a powerful system for the incremental development of the industry. However, as noted earlier, the system has evolved over time and more recently has been adapting to the replacement of an increasing proportion of system generating capacity with large-scale renewable plants. The integration of these plants requires changes to the technologies and institutions that exist within the system, but the changes are relatively small in nature or occur over a period that enables the existing system to adapt. This scenario embodies the current system trajectory but presents several challenges. Primary among these is the challenge of integrating substantial amounts of intermittent energy supply into a grid that requires real-time balancing of supply and demand across the entire network. Electricity systems will likely deal with this through the use of fossil fuel-based generators that can be "turned up" or "turned down" as required, much like the engine of a car. Intermittent generation will create issues in that a sudden loss of power (the wind stops blowing or clouds pass over a solar farm) needs to be accommodated by a traditional plant that is less well suited to quick changes of output. Electricity networks will continue to deal with this by using "fast start" gas-fired power plants, which allow renewables to enter the grid, but still use fossil fuels as a moderating power source.

The use of renewables will also drive a change to actors, networks and institutions. For example, the manufacturers of wind turbines have not been the manufacturers of traditional generation plants. With a few exceptions, this means that a new set of actors will enter the system. Similarly, the rules, regulations and engineering principles that enable intermittent energy sources to be integrated into the grid have been developing incrementally as networks experiment with large wind and solar farms. For example, South Australia experienced a significant network blackout when a set of cascading faults rippled through their network in response to localised storm damage to transmission lines. Inappropriate settings in the turbines caused several wind farms to "trip out" of the network (i.e. suddenly stop generating power), which caused further farms to stop putting electricity into the grid. Despite the care taken in the design of the system, it was only through learned experience that the design principles and network management processes could be sufficiently developed to consistently manage the new technology at scale. This type of co-evolved learning process is typical of system evolution in a relatively steady state environment.

While this scenario would see a decarbonisation of the electricity sector, it would require the adoption of new technologies, the entry of new actors to the system and modifications to institutions to support the successful transition to a sustainable electricity system. Despite that, the current system of actors, networks and institutions would largely be able to accommodate the change through a process of gradual adaptation and change.

Scenario 2: A centralised/decentralised hybrid system

In the second scenario, the configuration of the electricity system would be forced away from its current development trajectory, creating a system that has a grounding in the current configuration but also departs from it in more significant ways than in Scenario 1. Starting again with the physical architecture of the system, in this scenario, large-scale, centralised generation would still be required to provide power to large load sources, such as city central business districts, industrial processes and major transportation networks, such as electric trains. This would necessitate the retention of an electricity grid, as it would be required to carry power between the locations of supply and demand. Bulk supply of electricity would transition to carbon neutral technologies, including solar, nuclear, wind, wave and potentially fossil fuel generators with carbon capture and storage, particularly as the marginal cost of abatement through intermittent technologies rises sharply at higher renewable energy penetration rates.

In this scenario, the trend towards distributed generation and storage would also advance to the point where less dense energy demands (in this case, outside of the areas noted above) would be supplied locally. This would include almost all low-rise residential areas, outer urban industrial facilities and all locations outside of major cities. Within these areas, the grid would become more localised and may not be interconnected to high voltage networks for backup. The application of artificial intelligence would balance out variations in supply and demand from individual sites through intelligent localised energy trading. By optimising asset utilisation, the need to connect to a larger grid as a form of backup supply would become unnecessary. Institutions would also depart from their current structure and function, potentially being divided into institutions with one of two distinct functions. One function would be to manage the current form of bulk power supply, including rules and regulations like those that exist now. This would include the retention of wholesale and retail electricity markets, engineering design principles, financial regulations and operational principles that govern electricity networks now. The second function would be to govern the operation of electricity supply and consumption in the small-scale consumer sector, where energy would become locally generated, traded and consumed. This would require a change in technologies as well as institutions. For example, the creation of the "microgrids" incorporated in this scenario would generate new ownership options. Rather than being owned by utilities, grids covering a city block or suburb may be owned collectively by the users. This would require a new set of formal and informal institutional structures that support collective – rather than centralised – ownership and management of an electricity grid. For example, it would require the creation of formal rules relating to the economic and technical operation of the asset, in some respects being similar to how body corporates operate in multi-tenanted buildings but applied to a distributed asset (opening up similar needs for managing investment decisions, technology selection, operational and dispute resolution mechanisms, etc.). Consumer expectations around energy would also change, with all consumers becoming active participants in their local networks.

This scenario departs from the existing system because it involves the creation of two distinct electricity systems, one based on large-scale generation and consumption, and one based on localised, small-scale generation and consumption. The creation of such a system relies less on the development of new technologies – such as small-scale solar energy or grid control technologies – and more on the development of new institutional arrangements such as ownership structures and ways of working. This is likely to face barriers due to the resistance within the established socio-technical regime, which would need to cede control of part of existing power networks to new stakeholders (i.e. modification of existing institutions), and within the new stakeholder groups as they negotiate new understandings of their roles in the newly independent small-scale power systems. The social/institutional basis of such an arrangement is a long way from being in place.

Scenario 3: Fully decentralised and sustainable

The most different future – resulting from disruptive change – represents a significant break with the historical development of the electricity sector at both the technological and socio-technical levels. In this scenario, generation technologies become completely distributed and all energy generation would occur locally, with any location needing energy generating it on-site. In the most fully realised scenario, there would be no grid at all, with each customer capable of generating all their own energy. In this system, the demand for local generation would drive technology costs down to the point where electricity becomes so cheap, that there is no economic incentive to trade it with others. This, in turn, would obviate the need for an electricity grid as a mechanism for electricity trading or a form of backup supply. This future scenario may be enabled by the development of truly disruptive technological innovations that rapidly displace existing technologies and the system that surrounds them. For example, the creation of scalable hydrogen generation and storage linked to high-efficiency micro-wind or solar could combine to produce unlimited, clean, on-demand and localised energy production. These innovations would negate the need for any form of electricity "system", including regulation, system interconnection or other features of the current system architecture. Alternatively, this scenario could be driven by disruptive social developments. For example, the occurrence of a catastrophic environmental event (for example, the widespread bushfires in Australia in early 2020) could create a "tipping point", leading customers to conclusively reject the system as it now exists. This could lead to massively reduced energy consumption as environmental concerns drive changes in consumer behaviour and a push towards localised, sustainable energy systems that reject "big energy" driven by its economies of scale. These sorts of movements have occurred in the past (for example, the Appropriate Technology Movement that followed the oil crises of the early 1970s) but lacked the enduring social pressures and viable technologies to ensure a sustainable transition to new energy systems. Radical technological innovation combined with a sudden, sustained shift in social attitudes to energy could radically remake electricity systems in a brief period of time.

Regardless of the drivers of change, this scenario would be disruptive because it would make almost all the technologies, actors, networks and institutions that currently make up established electricity systems redundant. For example, large-scale generation technologies would no longer be needed when "on-demand" power is available everywhere. Similarly, there would be little need (if any) for the poles and wires that currently distribute centrally generated power, and the use of sustainable technologies means that carbon emissions would be eliminated from the sector. In addition, the role played by actors that are currently part of the electricity system would be significantly reduced. With locally generated and controlled power production and consumption, the natural monopoly of electricity supply would no longer exist, removing the need for regulators. Similarly, without large-scale generators or a grid, there would be no wholesale trading markets to aggregate and dispatch supply, no system operators to balance supply and demand and no electrical utilities to build and manage transmission and distribution networks. Many of the manufacturers of large-scale power equipment would need to transition to the production of new technologies or face a significantly reduced demand for their traditional technologies. In contrast to the existing system, the dominant actors in the new system would be the firms that install the on-site power solution and the consumers of electricity, who are currently on the fringe of the existing system.

The institutional frameworks underpinning electricity supply would also be disrupted. At the level of formal institutions, the rules and regulations that govern large-scale electricity supply would no longer be needed. This includes rules that govern how, when and where electricity can be inserted into the grid by generators, the rules that govern the natural monopolies of transmission and distribution networks, the rules that control energy trading markets and retail sales and the rules that govern the state-based organisations (e.g. regulators). In short, almost all the formal institutions that exist now would be superseded by institutions relevant to local power generation and consumption. Informal institutions would also change, with any recognised best practice, expectations about technology performance or configuration, operational expectations and all the tacit expectations about the grid being significantly transformed. In the place of current institutions aligned to large-scale generation and power distribution, new institutions based on the technologies that support localised, sustainable on-site power generation would need to evolve. For example, expectations about having a power company assure supply reliability would transition to a model of self-reliance. This would place consumer expectations about power at the centre of the system, complimented by informal institutions needed within the companies that supply, install and maintain the on-site power systems. In this scenario, the electricity system would be less physically interconnected than today and would rely on a significantly changed network of actors and institutions and technological artefacts to function.

Step 3: Backcasting

Subsequent analysis of the backcasting scenario requires looking backwards from the targeted future state and asking questions such as what changes are needed to bring about the desired future, how those changes can be implemented and who should be involved in the transition, and what will their roles be? (Quist 2013). This analysis is applied to the third scenario, which anticipates a transition to a fully decentralised electricity supply based on sustainable (i.e. low/no carbon) technologies. As a socio-technical transition, this requires a change to the technologies used to generate and use electricity, as well as the social systems that surround individual technologies (socio-technical configurations) and the broader socio-technical system. The constraints imposed by that system (discussed earlier) can be overcome through a technological transition, with the technical and social changes required to bring about the envisioned state requiring the presence of technological niches, sustained technological landscape pressures and the gradual transition of the regime itself. This process is best examined along the dimensions of social and technological change as executed through processes of niche accumulation in the context of technological landscape pressures. To give clarity to this, the progression towards the future state will be broken down into three phases, namely:

- Phase 1 – the grid to 2025: this phase represents development towards the new systems and largely reflects the socio-technical systems as it is today, but one that is preparing for accelerated change in Phase 2.
- Phase 2 – 2025 to 2030: in this phase, socio-technical change accelerates but the old and new systems operate in concert, with new socio-technical configurations addressing the deficiencies of the old ones.
- Phase 2 – 2030 to 2040: this phase represents a period where the existing socio-technical system is replaced in its entirety and any remnant socio-technical configurations are removed.

Phase 1: The grid to 2025

Looking at the required technological changes, the first phase of the transition to a clean and decentralised energy system is likely to see an accelerated adoption of technologies that are already available. Within the five-year timeframe, the architecture of the grid (large-scale generation and one-way transmission of power) is unlikely to change significantly as existing, long-lived assets continue to operate economically, even in the face of technological innovation. Instead, current technologies – notably photovoltaics – are likely to be adopted in an increasing range of applications, fostering the niche accumulation effects that are required to allow later large-scale change to occur. Energy storage technologies, currently at the early stage of adoption, are also likely to continue to find wider applications as costs come down and long-term reliability increases. An increasing level of electric vehicle adoption will contribute to this, as vehicle-to-grid technologies allow cars to act as mobile batteries. At the level of the networks, the increasing adoption of distributed generation and storage is likely to force changes to how these networks are managed, with two-way power flows increasing over time. This will require modifications to distribution network technologies, as control and protection systems, transformers and network switches are modified to accommodate these new power flows. Similarly, power and voltage management systems will need to change to allow networks to carry higher average loads, as more consumers seek to exploit opportunities to sell power back to the grid, rather than self-consuming their on-site generation. More intelligence will need to be built into power networks to allow them to be self-managing, self-repairing and capable of rerouting power depending on local generation and demand conditions.

In terms of institutional developments, this phase of the transition will require an increasing level of trust and confidence to develop distributed generation and storage technologies within their niches. This includes both the domestic and commercial scales, and even for grid-connected large-scale renewable wind and solar farms. Learning how to integrate large volumes of intermittent generation into the grid will need to continue as models for network design and control advance in tandem with technology adoption. Similarly, new technologies that support two-way power flows at the distribution level will need to be trialled and understood, particularly in situations where the grid is stressed, such as during peak demand events or natural disasters. The electrical workforce will need to learn the new skills required to operate and maintain innovative technologies to ensure the electricity supply continues to meet historical reliability standards. Institutional changes at the level of regulation and market design will also need to change to allow many more points of connection and to prepare for the participation of much smaller generators in energy trading markets.

These changes will require the participation of all the current actors in the electricity system, as well as new actors in the form of the owners of distributed generation capacity. The major challenge in this phase will be gaining acceptance from incumbent actors (notably generators, utilities, regulators and industry associations) given the emerging threat that widely distributed power generation poses to their status and power. Whereas electricity systems have evolved to be managed by technocratic organisations overseeing natural monopolies (with the associated power structures), distributed generation will create greater influence for a multitude of new asset owners. Ongoing pressure at the technological landscape level (e.g. environmental political movements such as Extinction Rebellion) will place persistent pressure on institutional arrangements with the existing system. The primary mechanism for change will be the political process which feeds into industry design and policy setting, such as renewable energy targets. While political actors are as likely to be influenced by incumbent actors as they are by new actors, the increasingly widespread adoption of distributed generation technologies will make the new actors – with their new expectations and understanding of electricity supply – increasingly influential. At the same time, owners of distributed generation technologies will need to start developing an understanding that they may eventually lose the lifeline of the existing grid; for some this will be a concern, and for others, a liberation. The resulting understandings and expectations about the nature and performance of electricity supply will influence the development of new institutional arrangements such as safety and reliability standards for distributed generation technologies. Forward-thinking network regulators can play a role at this stage, pushing the development of regulations that support the opportunity for technology adoption in a wider range of applications such as large-scale grid-connected storage. Pushing these institutional boundaries will support an even wider adoption of new technologies. Similarly, establishing rules that allow for smaller generators to participate in energy trading (wholesale markets or peer-to-peer energy trading) will help move towards institutions that support future stages of the grid transition. The creation of "sandpit" environments that allow for the trial of novel technologies and novel institutional arrangements will help to demonstrate the viability – and desirability – of the new socio-technical arrangements to all actors in the system, thereby helping to break down ongoing resistance to institutional change.

Phase 2: The grid to 2030

Technological changes moving towards 2030 will include the further advancement of distributed generation systems, which will allow premises to disconnect from the grid on a permanent basis. Whereas in Phase 1 the technologies required to do this (PV, wind and energy storage) were available, their price – particularly energy storage – would be likely to make permanent disconnection uneconomic in most situations. The ongoing technical development and cost reductions flowing from manufacturing economies scales built on widespread adoption are likely to reverse this situation, with locations that cannot economically disconnect being in the minority. The emergence of economically viable fuel cell technologies in this phase will also support the transition of the transport sector to clean energy technologies, with demand for "green hydrogen" making hydrogen a viable alternative to batteries for long-term/seasonal energy storage in many locations. These technological advancements will place additional pressure on any remaining carbon-intensive generation technologies, providing them with decreasing markets in which they can compete economically. As a result, the grid is likely to start being dismantled, as high voltage transmission is no longer required to carry generation to load centres, other than perhaps large industrial processes, or city CBDs. This will necessitate the development of technologies that support devolved management and control of grids as sustaining fully integrated national or transnational power networks becomes increasingly uneconomic in the face of decreased demand from the number of connected users. Similarly, network monitoring technologies will need to advance to allow increasingly smaller utility organisations to minimise network maintenance costs as the grid starts to fragment and decrease in size.

The transition of the grid to a more fragmented set of mini or microgrids accompanied by the increased adoption of distributed generation will require the development of institutional arrangements that support a wider range of power supply systems than was previously the case. A dismantling of the traditional grid will require two broad sets of institutions: one that supports the remaining high voltage transmission network and its connected utility-scale generators, and one that supports distributed grid systems based on smaller scale technologies and a wider range of system participants. In terms of the former, the institutional arrangements are likely to be similar to what they were in the earlier period, with centralised network control and planning, and strict rules around power dispatch, but with a reduced role for wholesale energy markets as power sales shift towards direct power purchase agreements for large energy users. The historical regulatory and organisational structures that supported this model will be able to persist, although they will be much smaller in scope and scale. In terms of the latter, ten years of transition will have allowed for the co-evolution of technologies and their supporting institutions at the niche level; for example, the use of distributed photovoltaics combined with batteries, early stage fuel cells and electric vehicles to provide reliable power will be well understood. The challenge in this phase will be to establish institutional arrangements that support widespread disconnection from the grid and sustainable business models to maintain the remaining grid which will continue to be used by late adopters, or those seeking to sell power to other users. The traditional model of rewarding utilities for energy throughput or the size of their asset base will no longer be sustainable. Shifting this more strongly to reliability standards will encourage these utilities to serve both connected and disconnected customers rather than focusing only on those connected to their networks. Politicians and regulators will play a significant role in this design process, as shared visions of the future will influence whether new rules protect the remnants of traditional utilities or direct them towards the emerging future grid. Overall, however, ten years of transition will have made it clear that electricity systems are shifting onto a new socio-technical pathway, and active resistance by incumbent actors should have decreased. The more forward-looking of these will be trying to understand what role they can play in a fully decentralised grid – for example, as technology or maintenance service providers, or as the owner/operators of emerging micro grids – rather than the increasingly irrelevant custodians of legacy electrical infrastructure.

Phase 3: The grid to 2040

The final phase of the transition to a clean, distributed electricity grid is likely to see the development of more sophisticated technologies for managing the flow and consumption of power on single premises and within microgrids. Building off institutional changes that occur in Phase 2, local communities are likely to want to utilise the old distribution grids to trade power locally, optimising the use of their own technologies, while being able to draw on third-party capacity when local generation or storage capacity is insufficient to meet demand. This would require less in the form of new electrical technologies – although the adoption of distributed generation and storage technologies, including electric vehicles will advance towards 100% – and more on the development of artificial intelligence that could manage generation and demand in many locations at once. Therefore, while rural and outer urban areas may have adequate space to install enough generation capacity to remain disconnected from any other source of electricity generation, denser urban areas would benefit from sharing capacity via the old distribution networks. These networks would need to be more robust than in the past, as each self-contained microgrid will need to fund the maintenance of its local network lines. The increased adoption of cost-effective fuel cells will provide a further avenue to restock power supplies, with the existing network of gas stations potentially being repurposed to hydrogen refuelling stations, particularly for the refuelling of domestic energy storage systems and long-haul transportation vehicles. The resulting range of technologies would provide several options for remaining independent of power systems or participating in microgrids to both buy and sell power into local communities.

Institutional arrangements would need to evolve to support the move to microgrids. This would include the development of energy trading mechanisms, which are likely to be managed through artificial intelligence, rather than actors wielding more manual systems. The range of microgrid size and complexity would necessitate the use of adaptive systems as designing control systems for every situation will be uneconomic. The application of artificial intelligence to the technical and commercial operation of these microgrids would require confidence within user communities that they are managing power networks in their best interests. It would also require the development of regulatory oversight to ensure that autonomous management systems are similarly acting in users' best interests. The possible emergence of hydrogen as an energy carrier would also require the development of suitable institutional arrangements, although the systems and processes that supported petroleum supply chains may provide a suitable model as a starting point. Even if this is the case, much like new electrical technologies, distributed hydrogen technologies would need to go through a process of trials to develop socio-technical configurations that integrate with society's needs and the newly emerged distributed electricity systems. This stage of grid evolution is also likely to see the retirement of the last vestiges of the old system, including any remaining large-scale power generators and their associated transmission networks. The associated commercial and regulatory structures would also be phased out, as hydrogen supplants grid supply for energy-intensive processes. This final phase is also likely to see the emergence of strong community-based models for power supply. The microgrid infrastructure could be owned and managed by community organisations which contract technologies and services as required, or they could be owned by a newly evolved version of energy retailers or smaller utility-style organisations that transitioned to owning and maintaining microgrid infrastructure. One issue to be dealt with would be how people or organisations that rent their premises rather than own them access electricity supply. Where microgrids exist, this may occur under contracting arrangements, but institutional arrangements that impose mandatory generation installation at all consumer locations may emerge to address the problem (for example, as a part of updated building standards). In the absence of this, late adopters – particularly the poor – would need to have an assurance of secure and affordable electricity supply.

A summary of each phase and key changes that need to take place to enable the transition to a decentralised and sustainable electricity system is shown in Figure 8.4.

The transition envisioned by this process is made up of developments that represent varying degrees of change across the four dimensions of technology, structure and industry and consumer institutions, and as a result, presents varying challenges in moving from the current system to a new one. In relation to technological developments, innovation in the sector is ongoing, and this is adding to the stock of zero-carbon technologies that have been available for several decades. While technical challenges exist to the integration of these technologies into the future grid, these are largely engineering and financial in nature and can be solved relatively easily. In contrast, the most intransigent element of the socio-technical transition to clean energy systems has been in the institutional acceptance of new technologies and the system they will inhabit, and as a result, the institutional changes required will be the most disruptive of the changes necessary

	To 2020	To 2030	To 2040
	Current Grid	*Transitionary Grid*	*Energy Independence*
Technological	• Ongoing evolution small scale photovoltaics • Emergence of cost effective of energy storage	• Emergence & adoption of integrated small scale systems that enable permanent grid disconnection • Initial adoption of fuel cell technologies	• AI controlled power management and asset optimisation • Full power independence via on site including fuel cells, PV & storage Conversion of renewable energy sources to high energy density liquid fuels (hydrogen)
Structural	• Grid engineering to support two way power flows • Re-engineering of utility business models to support new grid architecture	• Disaggregation of large national electricity networks based on local supply & demand	• Flexible, self managed & self healing localised power systems • Automated asset optimisation (operations & maintenance)
Institutional ('Industry' based)	• Liberalisation of energy trading rules • Explicit acknowledgement & accommodation of 'prosumer' customers	• Consumer participation in regulation setting via aggregated technology choice and intentions • Devolution of network control to more localised, AI supported micro-grids	• Flexible regulatory frameworks that respond to rapid consumer driven innovation and cooperative local power systems • Enablement of flexible local power system aggregation & dispatch as required
Institutional (Consumer based)	• Broad acceptance of the future role of the individual in the provision of power • Acceptance of 'self reliance' over 'the grid'	• Emergence of energy independence expectations and communities • Consumer engagement in technology development and road mapping	• Deep involvement of consumers in shaping future technology development through usage in practice • Expectation of power independence and ability to profit from on site generation

Figure 8.4 Transition summary.

to transition to the envisioned future state. This is one reason why a backcasting process is useful for mapping a pathway to a radically different future, as the development of a shared vision enables social changes to occur at the same time as the accompanying technological change. That is, it anticipates and supports the socio-technical changes required to enable a successful transition to occur.

Elaboration of future alternatives and defining the follow-up agenda

The fourth stage in the backcasting process is to expand on future alternatives and create detailed next steps. The main thrust of the potential future scenario developed above is the transition from a complex and large-scale electricity supply system based on carbon-intensive centralised power generation plant to a simpler, highly distributed system based on small-scale, local power generation and usage. This transition is likely to eliminate many of the technologies, actors, networks and institutions that co-evolved over a century to produce the system that exists today. In its place will be a new range of technologies, actors and institutional arrangements that overcome the primary limitation of today's system – the production of large amounts of greenhouse gases that lead to global warming. The transition pathway has been outlined in some detail in the previous section and is not developed further here. However, the beginning and end states can be summarised (Table 8.1 and Figure 8.5).

The second element of Step 4 is to define follow-up activities that enable the realisation of the targeted future state in the longer term. In leveraging the technological transitions concept, any follow-up agenda needs to be built around the identified socio-technical niches and processes of niche accumulation in tandem with technological landscape pressures, both of which are critical to inducing broader change within the established system. A key element of the follow-up agenda will therefore need to focus on the creation of a wider range of technological niches, and the broader adoption of technological innovations with those niches. This will include encouraging the ongoing adoption of scalable clean energy technologies (solar, wind and batteries) in commercial and residential installations, but also in emerging applications such as large, grid-connected energy storage, vehicle-to-grid and microgrid applications. It will also require the encouragement of innovations that can control the use and possible export of energy in preparation for local energy trading opportunities that are likely to arise in later stages of the transition. Information sharing on the trial and development of these technologies – and combinations of technologies – will be important to building functional socio-technical configurations that can operate in the mainstream system. Work at the technological landscape level will include ensuring that pressure for change continues to open opportunities for innovations within the established socio-technical system. Maintaining international agreements (e.g. UNFCCC Paris Agreement and its successors) and supporting political movements calling for change will remain important. Even though the focus of both is typically on technological change, the resulting impact is

Table 8.1 Current and future system elements

	Current system	*Possible future system*
Technical architecture	• Large-scale, fossil fuel-dominated power generation • One transmission of electrical power	• Distributed power generation based on sustainable energy technologies • Localised generation and power trading
Institutional architecture	• Centralised planning and control • Wholesale electricity markets • Regulated natural monopolies (transmission and distribution) • Formally documented market rules and standards • Formally documented design, construction and maintenance principles • Expectations that future networks will look like the networks of today • Passive consumers of electricity • Electricity networks stop "at the meter"	• Decentralised, emergent network architecture based on distributed intelligence • Local, peer-to-peer electricity markets • Lightly regulated competitive markets • Locally negotiated and dynamic market rules and standards • Design, construction and maintenance principles based on specific needs • Expectations that electricity networks will be dynamic and evolutionary • Consumers active as participants in electricity markets • Electricity networks include consumer premises and equipment as well as active consumer participation in network operation
Actors and networks	• Generators, utilities and retailers, plus regulators at the centre of the system • Traditional equipment manufacturers, constructors, engineers and financial institutions • A continuation of the networks that exist between traditional system actors	• Reduced/eliminated role for generators, utilities and retailers • A dynamic variety of equipment manufacturers, constructors, engineers and financial institutions • The formation of new, fluid networks as electricity systems and actors evolve over time

a general shift in expectations about what electricity systems should look like in the future. They will also act as a counterforce to likely resistance to change arising from established actors within the system. Policy design that encourages socio-technical change (for example, efforts that seek to shift how utilities are rewarded) will also be required, both as a direct input into socio-technical

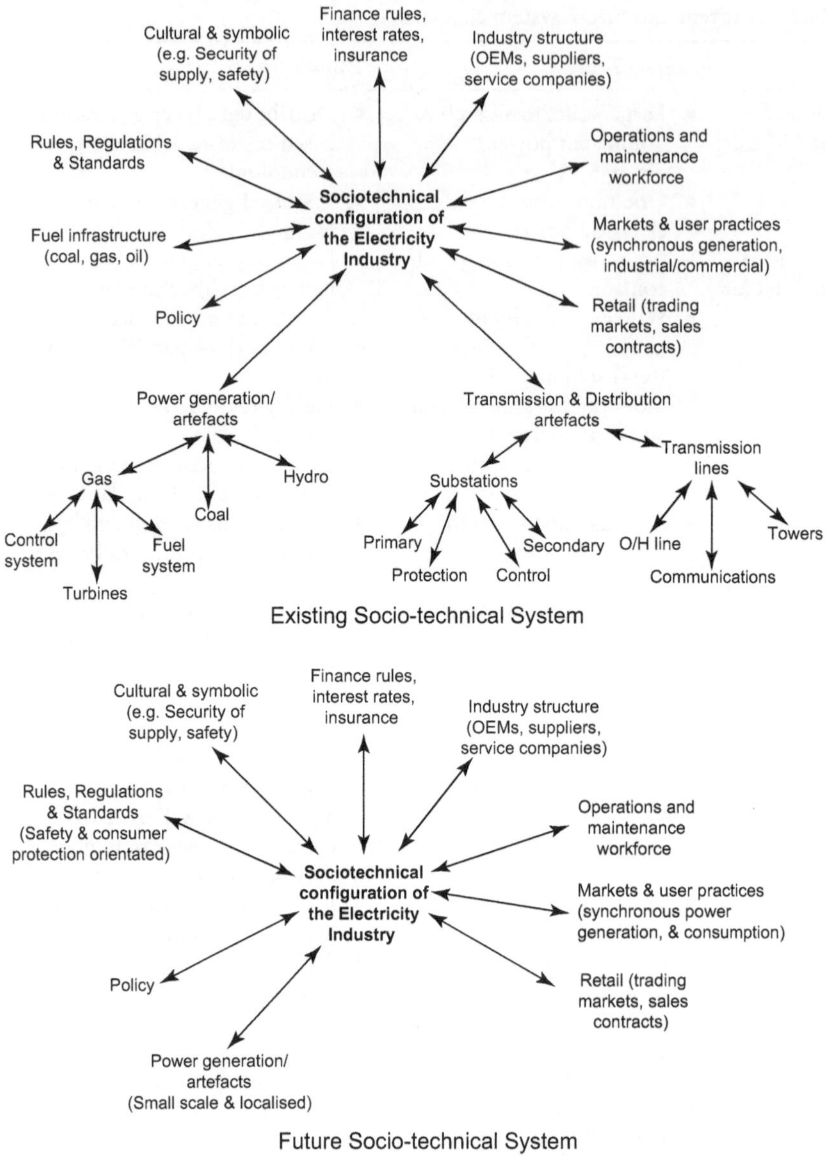

Figure 8.5 Current and future socio-technical systems.

change and as a signal to all actors that the system is being shifted towards a new socio-technical configuration. Ongoing financial support for emerging technologies will also remain important as new technologies lack economies of scale in production or deployment that can make them competitive as they emerge into mainstream markets.

Comments in relation to backcasting and socio-technical change

Backcasting applied to the technological systems

Technological systems present a challenging scenario for rapid and large-scale change. This is demonstrated by the persistence of a dominant design in the electricity sector that evolved over a century to become the primary guiding mechanism for ongoing technological innovation in the industry. The network of actors and institutions that underpin the system has worked to constrain the direction of development, as seen in the negligible impact that renewable energy technologies have had on power generation worldwide. Other industries embody similarly enduring technological systems, for example, transportation as centred on the internal combustion engine, personal computers on IBM/Windows architecture and mobile telecommunications based on CDMA/GSM. Each of these industries is facing periods of radical innovation while remaining grounded in a dominant socio-technical design that will constrain the rate and direction of development. In these circumstances, the backcasting method is well suited to mapping out alternative pathways as it accommodates an interactive development process that includes both social and technical elements in considering future development trajectories. It aligns with the co-evolutionary development that underpins technological systems meaning that a stepwise pathway towards a different design can be envisioned and progressively implemented. Backcasting is particularly well suited to the task, as the development of shared visions should avoid the persistence of institutional barriers to change as it applies a consensual process of envisioning the future state and the steps required to get there. Rather than allowing the social elements of socio-technological change to lag the introduction of innovative new technologies, backcasting can be used to link the social and institutional elements of change more tightly to progressive technological substitution.

The method is less well suited to situations of disruptive innovation, as the discontinuous change predicted by disruptive innovation theory is difficult to forecast in advance. This is a key reason this type of innovation is so disruptive, as it catches incumbents by surprise. This creates obvious challenges for backcasting, as it makes the development of possible future states highly uncertain. The technique can be used to develop a range of future states and development pathways, but in doing so it will alert incumbent actors to the threat of disruption and enable them to act strategically to defend their dominant positions (and technologies). However, Christensen has demonstrated that incumbent actors are often aware of the emerging technologies and the threats that they pose but fail to act due to their investment in the established regime. So, while backcasting may provide insight into imminent disruption, that disruption may continue to be ignored by incumbents. Backcasting may then be used to identify the socio-technical conditions that support disruption (e.g. accommodative technological niches) and to enable the required social changes in advance of the necessary technological innovations. In the case of the electricity system, the application of this approach would have brought forward many of the actions that we now see being used to address climate change. For example, rather than national and transnational bodies developing CO_2 targets well after the necessary technologies became available, these could have been developed prior to, or at least contemporaneously with those innovations. Application of the backcasting technique could have been used to accelerate the co-evolutionary processes of socio-technical change thereby anticipating possible barriers and developing ways to overcome them. Therefore, while the inherent uncertainty present in processes of disruptive innovation makes the application of backcasting more difficult (or at least, more uncertain) the technique has merit, particularly if the contingent nature of any follow-up agenda is clearly recognised and the backcasting method is regularly revisited as disruptive change unfolds.

The role of actors and institutions in socio-technical change

An important takeaway from the backcasting exercise conducted here is that actors and institutions play a far more significant role in processes of technological change than is normally acknowledged, but the backcasting method is well structured to account for this. Actors are the primary movers of technological change, and institutions guide their behaviour in the development and use of technological innovations. As noted previously, when technologies are embedded in complex networks of technological and social structures, this is a co-evolutionary and iterative process that occurs over extended periods of time. As a result, the most prominent signs of socio-technical change are modifications to the technological basis of an industry. The resulting tendency to focus on technological artefacts is compounded by modern experiences of rapid technological change in consumer technologies, such as mobile telephones, TVs or personal computers, where a device is updated by innovation, with little other attendant change. This experience directs attention away from the critical role that actors and institutions play in large-scale technological change and de-emphasises the fact that it is actors that select technologies, and institutions that enable their use in practice. In this respect, rather than focusing on technological change, the backcasting method is useful in explicitly including actors and institutions in working towards an anticipated future. The technique engages actors by putting those actors – rather than technological innovations – at the centre of the change process. The creation of an envisioned future state can then accommodate current technologies and technological trends, while simultaneously calling for the development of highly divergent future states that may include technologies not yet available, or even anticipated. This avoids any tendency to veer towards technological determinism, where the dominant technology determines the development of the associated social structure and cultural values. Putting actors at the centre of the process also emphasises institutions, particularly the development of expectations about the future. Shared beliefs and meanings in relation to the existing system are one of the most powerful conditioning mechanisms for determining choices in relation to future technology selection and use. In contrast to the institutions that need to evolve in support of individual technologies, system-related institutions can determine the opportunities for technology adoption within the system itself. The backcasting method ensures that these are considered through the development of shared vision and follow-up agendas. Therefore, while the role of actors and institutions in widespread technological change is often underemphasised or even ignored, the backcasting method ensures they receive equal attention to technological artefacts in facilitating a desired future state.

Backcasting and socio-technical change

The backcasting method used here has been applied to the clean energy transition in several cases as can be seen from the discussions earlier and is well suited to large-scale technological change. This suitability is mainly grounded in the use of a consensus approach to future scenario building, which enables the development of shared visions and expectations and understandings of the future with key institutions involved in socio-technical change. The effectiveness of this approach will rely heavily on the range of stakeholders involved in the backcasting exercise. Like many change management processes, the buy-in of these stakeholders is critical to achieving the formulated outcome. Where radical socio-technical change is being targeted, however, it can be difficult to involve all the likely stakeholders in the process. The co-evolutionary nature of socio-technical change means that the system can evolve in unexpected directions, particularly as disruptive technological innovation unfolds. This means that the backcasting process needs to be conducted as an ongoing process, as new actors enter the system, innovations are developed and adopted and new socio-technical configurations evolve to replace those that exist already. The backcasting technique could be improved when applied to large-scale socio-technical change by explicitly accommodating the co-evolutionary process into the method and by acknowledging the widened range of uncertainty in scenarios as they move further from the present. This can be done by incorporating actor-institutional evolution in the transition pathway alongside technological change. As these develop in a stepwise manner – with actor-institutional leading technology development at some times, and the sequence being reversed at others – the process is iterative, both within the short, action-orientated periods and in the longer-term progression towards the future state.

Explicitly incorporating the co-evolutionary nature of technological systems into the backcasting method would strengthen the technique by accounting for the process of socio-technical evolution that underpins large and complex technological systems such as the electricity sector. While this change has been examined here in the context of electricity systems, the dominance of complex established technological systems in society means the suggested modifications have broad applicability. Other major socio-technical systems that underpin modern economies, such as transportation, genetic engineering, the internet and social media, are all undergoing rapid and ongoing socio-technical change and arguably need to be managed to produce desirable outcomes for society. The modification of the backcasting method to cater for the persistent stability of co-evolved socio-technical systems will enable the application to these and other sectors facing technology-driven disruptive innovation. In doing so, the method will enable the development of more specific action plans that avoid some of the barriers to transformative technologies in well-established systems – barriers that have been apparent in the electricity sector over the past 20 years. It will also reinforce backcasting's emphasis on combined social and technological change in creating improvement in systems "with a factor [of] ten or a factor [of] twenty" as anticipated by Quist. Despite this, the co-evolutionary basis of socio-technical development means that long-term outcomes will remain difficult to predict. Any given development trajectory can be changed by the emergence of disruptive innovations (social or technological), which can create acute changes in the institutions and actors within a system. As a result, it may also be worth indicating a widening range of possible outcomes that may emerge as the time element moves towards the future vision. Making this change would also emphasise the contingent nature of any action plans developed through the application of the backcasting method.

References

Anderson, E. S. (2005). "Innovation systems: Evolutionary perspectives." In C. Edquist (Ed.), *Systems of innovation: Technologies, institutions and organisations.* Abingdon, Oxon: Routledge, 174–179.

Anderson, K. L., et al. (2008). "The Tyndall decarbonisation scenarios - Part II: scenarios for a 60% CO_2 reduction in the US." *Energy Policy* 36: 3764–3773.

Ayres, R. U. and B. Warr (2005). "Accounting for growth: The role of physical work." *Structural Change and Economic Dynamics* 16(2): 181–209.

Bloomberg New Energy Finance. (2019a). "Electric vehicle outlook 2019." Retrieved 23 May, 2019, from https://about.bnef.com/electric-vehicle-outlook/.

Bloomberg New Energy Finance. (2019b). "New energy outlook 2019." Retrieved 17 July, 2019, from https://about.bnef.com/new-energy-outlook/.

BP. (2011). *BP statistical review of world energy.* London: BP.

Bruckner, T., et al. (2014). Energy systems. Climate change 2014: Mitigation of climate change. In O. Edenhofer, R. Pichs-Madruga, E. F. Y. Sokona et al. (Eds.), *Contribution of working group III to the fifth assessment report of the intergovernmental panel on climate chan.* Cambridge and New York: Cambridge University Press, 511–597.

Christensen, C. M. (1997). *The innovator's dilemma: When new technologies cause great firms to fail.* Boston, MA: Harvard Business School Press.

Christensen, C. M., et al. (2004). *Seeing what's next.* Boston, MA: Harvard Business School Press.

Cleveland, C. J., et al. (1984). "Energy and the U.S. Economy: A biophysical perspective." *Science* 225(4665): 890–897.

David, P. A. (1988). "Path dependency; putting the past into the future." *Economic Series*, Stanford University, Institute for Mathematical Studies in Social Sciences.

Dobrov, G. (1979). "The strategy for organized technology in the light of hard-, soft- and org-ware interaction." *Long Range Planning* 12(4): 79–91.

Dosi, G. (1982). "Technological paradigms and technological trajectories: A suggested interpretation of the determinants and directions of technical change." *Research Policy* 11(3): 147–162.

Edquist, C. (1997). "Systems of innovation approaches - their emergence and characteristics." In C. Edquist (Ed.), *Systems of innovation - technologies, institutions and organizations.* Abingdon, Oxon: Routledge, 1–35.

Edquist, C. and B. Johnson (1997). "Institutions and organizations in systems of innovation." In C. Edquist (Ed.), *Systems of innovation - technologies, institutions and organizations.* Abingdon, Oxon: Routledge, 41–63.

Engel, H., et al. (2018, 23 March 2019). "The potential impact of electric vehicles on global energy systems." https://www.mckinsey.com/industries/automotive-and-assembly/our-insights/the-potential-impact-of-electric-vehicles-on-global-energy-systems.

Fleck, J. (1992). *Innovation during implementation configuration and CAPM.* Edinburgh: Edinburgh University, 21.

Foxon, T. (2003). "Inducing innovation for a low-carbon future: Drivers, barriers and policies." Retrieved 28 October, 2007, from www.thecarbontrust.co.uk/Publications/publicationdetail.htm?productid=CT-2003-07.

Foxon, T. J., et al. (2010). "Developing transition pathways for a low carbon electricity system in the UK." *Technological Forecasting & Social Change* 77(8): 1203–1213.

Gomi, K., et al. (2011). "A systematic quantitative backcasting on low-carbon policy in case of Kyoto city." *Technological Forecasting and Social Change* 78(5): 852–871.

Hammons, T. J. (2008). "Integrating renewable energy sources into European grids." *International Journal of Electrical Power & Energy Systems* 30(8): 462–475.

Harvey, H., et al. (2018). *Designing climate solutions: A policy guide for low-carbon energy.* Washington, DC: Island Press.

Held, A., et al. (2009). "On the success of policy strategies for the promotion of electricity from renewable energy sources in the EU." *Energy & Environment* 17(6): 849–868.

Hughes, T. (1983). *Networks of power: Electrification in western society.* Baltimore, MD: John Hopkins Press.

Hughes, T. P. (1987). "The evolution of large technological systems: The social construction of technological systems." In W. Bijker, T. Hughes and T. Pinch (Eds.), *New directions in the sociology and history of technology.* Cambridge, MA: MIT Press, 51–82.

IBM. (2018). "Big data analytics." Retrieved 16 June, 2019, from https://www.ibm.com/analytics/us/en/technology/hadoop/big-data-analytics.

IEA. (2012). *Policies and measures database.* I. E. Agency. Paris: International Energy Agency.

International Energy Agency. (2019). "Electric vehicles - tracking clean energy progress." Retrieved 23 May, 2019 from https://www.iea.org/reports/electric-vehicles.

International Renewable Energy Agency. (2016). "The power to change: Solar and wind cost reduction potential to 2025, international renewable energy agency." Retrieved 17 July, 2019 from https://www.irena.org/DocumentDownloads/Publications/IRENA_Power_to_Change_2016.pdf.

IRENA. (2018). "Global energy transformation: A roadmap to 2050, international renewable energy agency." Retrieved 19 December, 2018, from www.irena.org/publications/2018/Apr/Global-Energy-Transition-A-Roadmap-to-2050.

IRENA. (2019). *Renewable capacity statistics 2019.* Abu Dhabi: International Renewable Energy Agency (IRENA).

Jackson, F. (2018). "Renewables investment nudges out fossil fuel and nuclear." Retrieved 21 May 2019 from https://www.forbes.com/sites/feliciajackson/2018/05/15/renewables-investment-nudges-out-fossil-fuel-and-nuclear/?sh=11124aa03752.

Johnstone, N., et al. (2010). "Renewable energy policies and technological innovation: Evidence based on patent counts." *Environmental and Resource Economics* 45(1): 133–155.

Malerba, F. (2002). "Sectoral systems of innovation and production." *Research Policy* 31(2): 247–264.

Markard, J. and B. Truffer (2008). "Technological innovation systems and the multi-level perspective: Towards an integrated framework." *Research Policy* 37(4): 596–615.

Martin, J. (1996). "Energy technologies: Systemic aspects, technological trajectories, and institutional frameworks." *Technological Forecasting and Social Change* 53(1): 81–95.

McCarthy, R., et al. (2007). "Assessing reliability in energy supply systems." *Energy Policy* 35(4): 2151–2162.

McKelvey, M. (2005). "Using evolutionary theory to define systems of innovation." In C. Edquist (Ed.), *Systems of innovation: Technologies, institutions and organisations.* Abingdon, Oxon: Routledge, 200–222.

Molina, C. J. D., et al. (2010). "Technological impact of non-conventional renewable energy in the Chilean electricity system IEEE-ICIT 2010 International Conference on Industrial Technology Viña del Mar, Chile." Institute of Electrical and Electronics Engineers.

Moniz, E. J. and D. Yergin (2019). *Advancing the landscape of clean energy innovation. Online, breakthrough energy.* https://www.belfercenter.org/sites/default/files/files/publication/Full%20Report%20-%20Advancing%20the%20Landscape%20of%20Clean%20Energy%20Innovation.pdf

Nelson, R. and K. Nelson (2002). "Technology, institutions, and innovation systems." *Research Policy* 31(2): 265–272.

Nelson, R. R. and S. G. Winter (1977). "In search of useful theory of innovation." *Research Policy* 6(1): 36–76.

NREL. (2008a). *Impacts of large amounts of wind power on design and operation of power systems; Results of IEA collaboration.* Golden, CO: N. R. E. Laboratory, National Renewable Energy Laboratory.

NREL. (2008b). *Renewable systems interconnection: Executive summary. N. R. E. Laboratory.* Golden, CO: National Renewable Energy Laboratory.

Oinas, P. and E. Malecki (2002). "The evolution of technologies in time and space: From national and regional to spatial innovation systems." *International Regional Science Review* 25(1): 102–131.

Østergaard, P. (2003). "Transmission-grid requirements with scattered and fluctuating renewable electricity-sources." *Applied Energy* 76(1–3): 247–255.

Pacala, S. and R. Socolow (2004). "Stabilization wedges: Solving the climate problem for the next 50 years with current technologies." *Science* 305(5686): 968–972.

Pinch, T. and W. Bijker (1987). "The social construction of facts and artifacts: Of how the sociology of science and technology might benefit from each other." In W. Bijker, T. Hughes and T. Pinch (Eds.), *New directions in the sociology and history of technology.* Cambridge, MA: MIT Press, 17–50.

Quist, J. (2013). "Backcasting and scenarios for sustainable technology development." In J. Kauffman and K.M. Lee (Eds.), *Handbook of sustainable engineering*. Dordrecht, Netherlands: Springer, 143–165.

Quist, J. and P. J. Vergragt (2006). "Past and future of backcasting: The shift to stakeholder participation and a proposal for a methodological framework." *Futures* 38(9): 18.

REN21. (2011). *Renewables 2011 global status report*. L. Mastny. Paris: Renewable Energy Policy Network for the 21st Century.

Raven, R. (2007). "Niche accumulation and hybridisation strategies in transition processes towards a sustainable energy system: An assessment of differences and pitfalls." *Energy Policy* 35(4): 2390–2400.

Rip, A. and R. Kemp (1998). "Technological change." In S. Reynor and L. Malone (Eds.), *Human choice and climate change*. Washington, DC: Batelle Press, 2: 327–399.

Smil, V. (2017). *Energy transitions: Global and national perspectives*. Santa Barbara, CA: Praeger.

Stankiewicz, R. (1995). "The role of the science and technology infrastructure in the development and diffusion of industrial automation in Sweden." In B. Carlsson (Ed.), *Technological systems and economic performance: The case of factory automation*. Dordrecht: Kluwer Academic Publishers, 165–210.

Stankiewicz, R. and B. Carlsson (1991). "On the nature, function and composition of technological systems." *Journal of Evolutionary Economics* 1(2): 93.

United Nations General Assembly. (2015). *Transforming our world: The 2030 agenda for sustainable development*. New York: UN Publishing.

Unruh, G. C. (2000). "Understanding carbon lock-in." *Energy Policy* 28(12): 817–830.

Unruh, G. C. (2002). "Escaping carbon lock-in." *Energy Policy* 30(4): 317–325.

US Department of Energy. (2016). *Distribution automation: Results from the smart grid investment grant program*. Washington, DC: Office of Electricity Delivery and Energy Reliability.

van de Kerkhof, M., et al. (2002). "Shaping diversity in participatory foresight studies: Experiences with interactive backcasting in a stakeholder assessment on long-term climate policy in the Netherlands." *Greener Management International* Spring 2002, 85–99.

Vergragt, P. J. and L. Jansen (1993). "Sustainable technological development: The making of a long-term oriented technology programme." *Project Appraisal* 8: 34–140.

Vergragt, P. J. and J. Quist (2011). "Backcasting for sustainability: Introduction to the special issue." *Technological Forecasting and Social Change* 78(5): 8.

Vittal, V. (2010). "The impact of renewable resources on the performance and reliability of the electricity grid." *The Bridge* 40(1): 5–12.

Weaver, P., et al. (2000). *Sustainable technology development*. Sheffield: Greenleaf Publishers.

9 Entrepreneurship in the Future Corporation

Robert Cagnoli

The longevity economy and the ageing worker

> Oldness: a special construct at odds with reality that constrains how we live after middle age and stifles business thinking on how to best serve a group of consumers, workers and innovators that is growing larger and wealthier by the day.
>
> (Coughlin, 2017)

It was clear as early as 2017 that by 2040 there was a new demographic kid on the block – the over 60s who would go on to shake up long-held socio-economic norms in business, government and society, all of whom were ill prepared for the coming change. Populations were getting older, and institutions were continuing to act as though they would deal with it in the future.

According to the Economist Intelligence Unit, for example, it was apparent that only 31% of companies were considering this cohort in their sales and marketing plans. For the first time in European history, the percentage of working-age people fell as a percentage of the population in 2012, with this trend forecast to continue through to 2060 (Economist Intelligence Unit, 2014). In the United States, the 50+ age group was already contributing US$8.3 trillion in 2018 and is forecast to grow to over US$28 trillion in 2050 (Economist Intelligence Unit, 2019).

In the early 2000s, a growing realisation was beginning to dawn on policymakers, how could a smaller working population support a growing number of pensioners who were also becoming longer lived? Not only were many workers forced to deal with challenging home affordability issues and salary growth being outstripped by cost-of-living increases, and to add insult to injury, they would also be required to contribute to 20 years of pension support for three pensioners, a heavy burden indeed. What solutions could there be? The most obvious solution was to keep the skilled and capable in productive roles, this was not only redesigning workplaces but also social mechanisms to enable the capable to continue to contribute. This is a non-trivial exercise for a society to balance the needs of a smaller number of younger workers and a largely untapped cohort of older skilled workers deemed to have outlived their usefulness to corporate life.

DOI: 10.4324/9781003183679-9

Across three vectors of life, work and financial power, the 60+ age group is and will continue to be a powerful force to be reckoned with across all socio-economic-political dimensions. These changes have over time changed the perception of age and the actual and potential contribution of this growing cohort. The trend of longer active lives in association with high wealth has contributed to a growing, but insufficient, workforce participation for older workers to offset the reduction in the traditional working-age population.

Longevity increases over the past century have dramatically impacted population ratios, leading to a cascading impact on intergenerational contracts, government policy and relevant products and services that appeal to a growing population of older active healthy consumers. The increasing longevity is changing the market for what these consumers want and need as they continue to stay in the workplace longer. As the Gen X cohort was entering pensionable age, their desires for products and services were very different from the baby boomers, being more aspirational lifestyle products and services and wanting to enjoy life for as long as possible. This shift also shaped housing solutions, health and wellness products. Supply in terms of this cohort is wanting to work longer and on the demand side these older adults differ from past generations – they are driving changes in sectors ranging from financial services, housing and health to entertainment, travel and retail goods.

If younger generations do not capture these opportunities, it will be left to the seniorpreneurs (those over 50 years of age) looking to capture the opportunities in this changing marketplace. A market opportunity that is all too often invisible to younger cohorts but more visible to the seniorpreneurs, who identify products and services that they themselves identify. Although some may be slowed down by the effects of ageing, others will continue to enjoy the lifestyle to which they have been accustomed and leverage opportunities for many years to come.

By the early 2010s, a trend was set in motion that continues to this day as older workers make way for younger workers either voluntarily or not. As this cohort of older workers left work through rapid technological change, the financial crisis of 2008 and subsequently exogenous shocks like the Covid-19 pandemic, they began to outperform younger generations in launching new businesses (Economics O, October 2013). This was due in part to the difficulty of older workers adapting to rapidly changing workplaces – a trend that was accelerated during the early 2020s when Covid-19 forced workplaces to adapt to forced isolation and adoption of technology.

How can corporates accommodate this powerful and growing group? For the workplace to become a more welcoming place, perceptions of "oldness" need to be modified. This change would enable greater workplace participation just as happened for other groups in society.

It is evident that a common definition of when old age begins does not exist with large variations across cultures. These different perceptions have a significant impact on social attitudes, government policies including pension age, pension reform, labour market investment and corporate attitudes. The importance of these different perceptions also impacts how they then translate into hiring, promotion and separation decisions within companies.

There are many myths surrounding the differences across different age groups in the workplace, the urban legends that do not stand up to the rigour of analysis. When workplace attitudes are tested (Economist Intelligence Unit, 2014), two clear findings consistently emerge regarding older workers:

1. They are not perceived as being less productive
2. They have greater skills than younger workers

We will touch on the productivity issue later in this chapter, but it is clear that if older workers are productive and have "better" skills, then the rise of the seniorpreneur is a logical consequence of highly skilled and productive workers not finding a role in a large company and translating those skills to realise long-held dreams or driven by financial need, in either case, increasing life expectancies and healthier active lives meant more of these people started their own business once out of the corporate world.

So far, we have touched on the trends indicating that a new older and more resourceful demographic was becoming important and yet institutions for the most part were ill-prepared for this epochal change. To cater for this change, talent recruitment, talent retention, compensation and benefits, workplace design and flexible work conditions would need to be adapted to the needs of this cohort. With some notable exceptions, very little was done.

Japan was and still is a leader in accommodating the use of older workers. Notwithstanding the valiant efforts of Japan to turn the over 65s into active workforce participants, the drop off in workforce participation is still above 50%, and in 2020, Japan introduced legislation to oblige employers to "make efforts" to secure job opportunities for employees that want to continue working. Despite these efforts, there is still a 50% point drop in labour force participation.

To capture the opportunity provided by the need to work beyond retirement, a company in Japan, Mystra staffing agency, specialises in recruitment and placement for the 60+ age cohort and follows the same example for its employees. This trend, although slow to catch on in the West, has been gaining traction, with some examples listed as follows:

- The CVS "Snowbird" programme (US pharmacy) allowing older employees more flexibility
- Home Depot recruiting retired construction workers to leverage their expertise for the benefit of customers
- Bunnings (Australia) hiring retired tradesmen to provide expertise to buyers
- Brooks Brothers (USA, clothing/retail) engages and elicits feedback from older workers to ensure that the workplace also caters to their needs
- Kagome (Japan, food): workers over 60 are supported in the transition to part-time work

- Takashima (Japan, retail): workers over 60 are supported in the transition to part-time work
- Astellas (Japan): workers 55+ do not undertake shift work
- Achmea (NL): workers over 57.5 years are offered flexible contracts to avoid losing highly skilled workers, and if there is no work, these workers still receive 75% of their pay

Japan was the canary in the mine and a precursor to many of the elements we now view as normal. The hyper-ageing population and economic situation forced Japan to make a coordinated effort across government policy, central bank actions and industry to deal with the issue of demographic change:

- Ageing population
- Persistent high levels of government debt
- Pension coverage shortfalls

We will only touch on some of the key issues related to how the hyper-ageing Japanese economy adjusted and the lessons drawn from the Japanese experience. The ageing population has large economy-wide impacts but what emerged in the 2000s was the ability to manage an economy with large levels of government debt – a factor in the Japanese economy from the 1990s that slowly but surely was adopted by many other developed economies, in particular after the Covid-19 pandemic that saw a dramatic rise in unemployment – the ILO (International Labour Organisation, 2020) estimated the loss of the equivalent to 400 million full-time jobs in Q2, 2020, government debt and more reliance on the state than ever before. After the failure of the EU to deal with the economic crisis of 2008, a radically different approach was taken during the Covid-19 pandemic to ensure the economy was able to bounce back quickly, at the cost of large debt loads. The pressure on health systems and pension liabilities with a smaller relative tax taken through fewer workers put significant pressure on government accounts and Japan was a leader in showing the world how to live with a high debt burden.

What was once thought of as impossible became acceptable, in part, due to Japan, where consistently high debt levels above 200% of GDP did not end in disaster. Daan Struyven and David Mericle, economists at Goldman Sachs, said the example of Japan could prove instructive as the world's third-largest economy has not suffered a debt crisis, even though it arguably has the most public debt as a share of GDP in the world (Mauldin, 2019).

One major contributor to the high levels of government debt is pension funding. In ten years (2050), Japan is estimated to have over a US$25 trillion gap in funding its pension liabilities, and although Japan has taught us the ability to maintain high levels of government debt, one way to limit this growth is to maintain and incentivise continued workforce participation.

We are merely highlighting this issue as it is a potential issue hampering aged workers' re-employment due to company pension liabilities and to highlight the pressure on governments to tighten pension payments, further encouraging the

60+ age group to remain in the workforce. Although it could be argued that Japan's ability to function and living with consistently high debt to GDP levels of 200% also functioned as a potential damper, many of the dire predictions made by economists did not eventuate.

In 2017, the World Economic Forum published a white paper asking how we can afford to live to 100. Already forecasters were estimating an unfunded retirement savings gap of over US$400 trillion in eight economies by 2050. If governments and private savings are insufficient to prepare to support the wave of older people, it became clear that retirement ages must inevitably rise. The creation of opportunities and incentives to retain active older workers longer became an urgent need both for governments in terms of budget repair and for individuals.

Today in 2040 we live comfortably into our 80s and beyond, and we have the flexibility in the workplace to work if our productivity levels remain high. The over 60s have become a powerful force as consumers and political movers in developed economies and companies recognise the upside of an intergenerational workforce. Research (Siliverstovs, 2011) has suggested that structural transformation of economies is taking place as the effects of the ageing population take hold through changing consumption patterns towards a different product/service mix such as energy, home care, health and leisure activities.

Some of the changes were already taking shape as far back as 2014, and across Japan and the United States, some macro trends were evident such as increased medical expenses, although cultural differences also appear, for example, recreation spending increasing in Japan and decreasing in the United States. It is evident that although we must be aware of broad economic trends and shifting market and workforce opportunities that are visible across sectors such as health services, education and leisure activities, cultural differences must always be considered. Of note is that we should be aware that just as the perception of when old age starts is country specific, so are the trends impacting how older adults spend their time and money. Some prefer to age in place while others prefer a retirement village or a nursing home, regardless, many of the opportunities in how time and money are spent will be captured by the seniorpreneurs that understand the opportunity and specific market needs.

In 2020, the Covid-19 pandemic acted as an accelerator for the transformation of the economy by forcing the entire service sector workforce of many countries to work from home. Cultural and technological barriers to flexible work arrangements crumbled under the barrage of forced closures and from that pandemic the current flexible work arrangements supported by seamless communications technology have enabled older workers to thrive. Age-related issues that may have held a worker back in the past such as poor mobility or the need for more flexible arrangements were no longer a hindrance when working from home.

The workplace is now a more welcoming place for older workers through improved workplace design, increased flexibility for work-life balance and reinforced legal protection, but changing perceptions and stereotypes continue to be a challenge.

If the perception is that you are old at a certain age, the implications for the workforce are many. This age will then become a de facto cut-off point not related to the official pension age. Although people often say 50 is the new 30, the reality is walking into a meeting there are very few "white hairs".

Extending the time people can provide a meaningful contribution to the workplace and society was and still is the solution to tackling the consequences of the low participation rate for older workers.

Demographics: Increased longevity and declining birth rates

So far, we have spoken of demographic trends but how much do we really need to be concerned about demographic changes? What are the numbers?

Today in 2040 (Kyle J Foreman, 2018), Singapore, Spain and Switzerland all have an average life expectancy above 85 years of age and a further 59 countries including China have life expectancies above 80 years of age.

The challenge Europe is experiencing is evident in the population bulge for the 50+ age cohort. Fertility rates have remained low despite government incentives or the removal of disincentives such as the one-child policy in China. Policies regarding immigration have also failed to halt the impacts of low fertility rates across Europe.

It is estimated that in just ten years by 2050, there will be the same number of old (60 and over) as young (under 15) in the world, with each group accounting for 21% (approx. 2 bn) of the world population and the situation as highlighted by the population pyramids is even more accentuated.

In Europe, what we have is not so much a population pyramid as a population bulge in the 50+ category as years of low fertility rates and lower mortality combined to create the bulge – reducing the size of the available workforce.

These demographic changes have conspired to create high dependency ratios we live with today. This is a global phenomenon with a dependency ratio of over 60 in the major economies. In 2012, Europe reached an inevitable tipping point. That year, the working-age population peaked at 304 million (Economist Intelligence Unit, 2014), from that point, the long decline began a trend that is not expected to reverse until 2050 at the earliest. To counter this effect, it is inevitable that a smaller workforce will need to work until later in life (in addition to increasing productivity). As the dependency ratio has increased, the pressure on state-funded pensions and universal income programmes have also come under pressure as the pool of tax receipts has shrunk with fewer workers supporting more non-workers. This has created a situation where intergenerational pacts from the time of the baby boomers no longer hold true.

Workforce participation rates

Across the OECD, we find confirmation of a typical drop of 40% in workforce participation after age 65 as workers arrive at the mandated pension ages. Today (in

2040), the mandatory retirement age has been abolished to allow those able and willing to continue working. The ability to continue working has to some extent offset the dire predictions of the few working to support the many but the ability to continue working has been driven minimally by large corporations harnessing experience and more by the experienced leaving large businesses to become "seniorpreneurs" – starting their own activities either as sole owners or as a partnership of people over 50.

Fiscal impacts

In Figure 9.1, we highlight the three typical sources of retirement savings. With retirement age at 65, and life expectancies over 80 years of age, savings must go a long way to maintain lifestyles, which even today is not the reality. In ten years (2050), the World Economic Forum estimated that the retirement savings would be ~US$400 trillion, compared with a mere US$70 trillion in 2015. This means an additional US$28 billion of deficit each day ((Rachel Wheeler, 2017)). How can this be?

Each pillar covers the three major economic pillars of society: government, employers and individuals. The impacts on these three groups are a derivative of individual country policies but the overall trends are clear and the benefits we see today are the results of policies enacted in the 2020s across the major developed countries and with various degrees of success.

Government pensions. Pension means testing, basic universal income trials, pension age, unemployment benefits prior to pension eligibility and so on.
Corporate. Company-funded pension schemes, schemes to keep employees longer.
Individual. Self-funded pension schemes, greater use of equity release products and top-up self-funded pension schemes.

Policy impacts

Some policy choices allowed the harnessing of mature age workers, knowledge and skills but also allowed the synergic coexistent of multigenerational workforces. The position we find ourselves in today is the result of some enlightened

Pillar 1	Pillar 2	Pillar 3
State Pension	Occupational Retirement Planning	Private Retirement Savings
Government schemes	Work related pension schemes	Individual pension products
Safeguarding of basic income and secures individual subsistence needs	Continuation of accustomed standard of living and secures an appropriate standard of living	Additional needs

Figure 9.1 The three pension pillars.

reviews in the early 2000s and the action of corporates as opposed to government. The corporates were required to change due to the inevitable and irresistible force of demographics.

Today, it is difficult to imagine the scale of age discrimination and yet in the United States alone there were more than 24,000 age discrimination complaints filed in 2008, but ten years later, the number was still stubbornly high at over 18,000. Progress was made in eliminating discrimination in the workplace across every group except for mature age workers. Discriminatory age-related practices are challenging in that ultimately even the discriminators grew old so the incentives to eliminate these practices were high, but far off in the future.

Some of the results of these policies include:

- Older workers being protected against age discrimination and supported through wage subsidies and/or targeted reductions in social security contributions
- Removal of mandatory retirement age across all sectors – retirement is a choice based on performance, capacity and sustainability
- Increasing participation suiting the needs of the employer and employee
- Redefinition of mature as longevity and health awareness and access improved quality of life and mature age performance
- Lower cost of healthcare to alleviate the burden of health care costs on an individual and societal level

However, perceptions of growing mental and physical frailty associated with age and when this decline begins are more difficult to change, and in 2040, we are still working against these biases.

The changing workplace

As we have previously noted, Japan was the canary in the mine in terms of a hyper-ageing society and the implications to be drawn from the experience in increasing workforce flexibility and growing participation of mature age workers.

People want to be age-agnostic; corporations want age markers (Lynda Gratton, 2017). As we age, people want to be treated as individuals and corporations (HR and Legal) find comfort in the ability to segment by age. A well-defined and legislated retirement age offers an easy route to separation; the position is clear from the corporate point of view, but often individual circumstances and capabilities are not taken into consideration. How many companies would benefit from a transition phase allowing intergenerational knowledge transfer and workers benefiting from continued income and paying taxes? Some examples of these early leaders in this field, in addition to those already cited, include the following:

- BMW (*Today for Tomorrow programme*) and Porsche redesigned their factories for a more mature workforce
- In the UK, Aviva (insurance) began a "midlife MOT" – a review of finances, career and well-being for those over 45

The physical and mental Impacts of ageing

The journey towards old age is being better understood on a daily basis by the scientific community, from the impacts at a cellular level to cognitive and physical impacts. Although everyone follows a similar journey, each ageing journey is an individual built on a lifetime of genetics and lifestyle choices and other environmental factors. Biological age is of limited value as an indicator of health, cognitive ability and ability to contribute productively.

Improved health care access and knowledge have led not just to improvements in longevity with businesses such as Altos Labs in Silicon Valley working to reverse cellular age with US$3bn in funding, making it the best-funded start-up in the early 2020s. As affluence has increased so have improvements in health and this has led to mature age people being physically active and capable for longer than previous generations.

This extended active life functions as an opportunity for seniorpreneurs to tackle the creation of a new business into their 50s as they see a long active life ahead of them, a significant difference compared with previous generations.

Mature age employment expectations

Although data is scarce, some surveys such as those conducted by Pew Research highlight that over 50% of 65+ workers work because they want to and are not driven by financial need. Of course, this may also be driven by the fact that people do not want to admit to working for need as opposed to desire. But the interesting finding is how satisfied older workers are compared with younger cohorts, this also highlights the desire of older workers to work as it also provides social interactions that may wane as people age.

This has been borne out in US data highlighting the increased mortality rate among US males above 62 years of age as this was the entry age for social security benefits. As men (it is mostly a male issue) leave the workplace to access social security, the mortality rate appears to rise. Numerous studies have shown the risk of retirement and the increased death rate upon retiring, there may be a correlation, but the issue becomes one of causation, an issue not for this chapter, but staying productive and working is surely important.

The policy implications (Moore, 2016) of the findings are:

- There may be an increase in mortality risks when people stop work.
- More research may shed light on the reasons for this and the ways these elevated risks could be reduced.
- Initiatives and policies that assist people through the transition to retirement may have health benefits.

Mature age employees as a competitive advantage

A quick literature scan of the early 2000s highlights how mature age employees were not seen as a competitive advantage as we see them now. The opportunities to mentor and support younger workers and remain productive were not available.

Examples of some article headlines:

- "Demographic time bomb"
- "Are older workers harmful to firm productivity?"
- "Over 65s flooding the job market – and finding they're not so employable"

Few companies were farsighted enough to see the opportunity, now mature age employees are seen as an asset because, contrary to what was a prevailing view at the time, this cohort has:

- Proven leadership skills
- Clarity of purpose and higher levels of job satisfaction
- Strong networks
- Higher levels of loyalty than younger workers

Many large corporates drive for improved efficiency through the better use of technological and human capital, which led in many cases to separation with older workers that were more expensive than younger employees. This separation did not always coincide with the desire, capabilities and continued potential to contribute of the employee, so with many years of productive working life ahead of them and with experience, contacts and capital, the seniorpreneur was born.

The rise of the seniorpreneur

The thriving seniorpreneur – not preparing to go quietly into the sunset but to actively participate and thrive in the economy. Today (2040), we see the over 50s actively starting new businesses as never before across the OECD.

Age discrimination or bias does not exist when you are your own boss, a commonly heard refrain from the 2020s. As youth unemployment was high (across the EU) and over 50s found it increasingly difficult to find work, self-employment became an ever more popular solution to the challenges of finding work. With the help of better education, forms of universal basic income and more flexible arrangements to access pension savings, the over 50s' entrepreneurial spirit was unleashed as never before.

The post-baby boomers, generations X and Y (otherwise known as millennials), with the Gen X cohort having already established their companies and the millennials in full entrepreneurial flight.

Investors, policymakers and entrepreneurs found that age is a predictor of success. In the 2010s, the focus was on disruption and youth, but it became evident youth and disruption were poor predictors of success. If you wanted to increase the likelihood of a positive return on investment, back a seniorpreneur. The pendulum of age-related skills is as follows:

- Human capital
- Financial capital
- Social capital

This offsets the perceived energy of youth.

In 2017, across the OECD, 7% of seniors were starting entrepreneurial endeavours. The rate has continued to rise as technology and demographics conspired to create a perfect alignment of forces, incentivising older workers to go out on their own.

Although Canada and the United States have vastly different social structures, the entrepreneurial mindset is very similar. Neither country offered direct subsidies to start a business, yet in both countries, the entrepreneurial drive is strong as evidenced by the high start-up rate relative to other countries.

This again reinforces the issue of culture and mindset and how each culture varies in its approach to ageing and risk appetite. In Europe, there is a great emphasis on government intervention, whereas there may be more need to begin to develop future entrepreneurial mindsets early to create a risk-taking culture of dynamic entrepreneurial dynamism.

After the battles for workplaces to be representative of the composition of society, age discrimination is much less evident than in the past, but as the attention on many groups in society forced change, the older workers were slower to coalesce and make themselves heard. With up to 50% of society over 50 and opportunities for career enhancement and mobility decreasing for this age group, intergenerational tensions in the workplace continue to be evident today. As companies have accepted the changed demographic profile of the workforce and consumers, the experience of older workers is crucial. The skills of this age group are better leveraged to support the growth of younger groups, and retaining skills and networks, if not used internally, are being used externally to create new businesses.

Linked to an increase in longevity, the over 50s (silvers) have either through need or desire continued to create and build new businesses and have been remarkably successful. Over 70% of ventures started by silvers are still in operation after five years of operation compared with only 28% started by younger entrepreneurs (Age UK, 2012). These high success rates have been consistent over the decades.

As mentioned, several factors have led to the rise of the seniorpreneur but the motivations for starting a business broadly fall into three categories:

1. *The constrained entrepreneur.* Always had a desire to start a business but for constraints that could be economic, family or both did not embark on an entrepreneurial adventure in younger years.
2. *The rational entrepreneur.* A natural career progression and utilising the experience and skills built up in the workplace moves to enhance and grow personal wealth.
3. *The reluctant entrepreneur.* Forced to become an entrepreneur through redundancy and lack of alternatives tied to insufficient wealth.

Technology has changed the nature of work itself, allowing greater flexibility and improved access to expertise and resources, but it has also changed how work is approached. An often-heard phrase is that technology does not replace jobs but rather tasks and this very remodulation of jobs has opened opportunities for silvers to leverage their skills and experience. Freelance work offers an opportunity to either work with companies by providing services or to service the senior market – now one of the largest consumer markets and the richest.

In terms of business success, younger entrepreneurs tend to be less successful in terms of business longevity with many failures in the first three years, this holds true across different geographies (Age UK, 2012; Amelia M. Biehl, 2014).

So which sectors have attracted the most interest of the seniorpreneur? The three key areas of self-employment in the EU in 2016 were:

1. Agriculture
2. Professional services
3. Construction

The industries where more mature workers participate through the application of their skills, knowledge and business acumen today are no longer as they were in 2016, as technology has evolved, markets have been shaped that are well suited to the skills of more mature workers but also the flexibility older workers may desire/require as they ease into lower workloads. Today, in 2040, over 25% of seniors are self-employed compared with 18.2% of working seniors in 2016, and in the OECD, we have a vibrant entrepreneurial market with people over 55 creating new businesses at the same rate as younger cohorts. However, they tend to last longer and are more profitable, the younger entrepreneurs may be better at creating the unicorn but on average the seniorpreneurs are more successful.

The largest and most complex area of self-employment has been in professional services where large numbers of professionals were displaced. For lawyers it began in distant 2018 when the AI system LawGeex, an AI contract review platform, outperformed 20 top US-trained lawyers with decades of experience, being both faster and more accurate in analysing and reviewing non-disclosure agreements. This was the start and now in 2040 no lawyer/attorney/barrister would trust a person over an AI platform to review a contract, but the nature of the work has changed, and the advice and relationship offered by lawyers with many years of experience continue to see them branching out independently.

Management consulting has been transformed with AI able to gather and analyse data in more depth and breadth than any consultant, and over the last 15 years, the recommendations made by AI are also updated in real time as fresh competitor data is analysed, thus improving both long- and short-term recommendations. Where consultants have come to provide a valuable service and have continued to provide service is in implementing and humanising change.

As the population has grown and aged, there has been an exponential growth in the need for care as the increase in longevity has often meant an increase in unhealthy years. While the traditional view was for retirement homes, there has been a dramatic increase in home ageing, again Japan was a precursor with the increase in spending of people 75+ on home maintenance. The increase of in-home care has resulted in greater remote monitoring of older people (health, safety, falls, etc.) and in-home support, for example, cleaning, cooking, pre-prepared meals, pain management, etc. creating many new jobs.

Covid-19 was a great accelerator in the move to ageing in place technological solutions, allowing both independence for older people and peace of mind for family members. The opportunities provided by increased longevity have been many and more mature workers have been better able and more willing to service this market through affinity and the comfort of older customers, although more research is required in this field.

How did we get to this thriving senior entrepreneurial market?

Although demographics were perhaps the single largest factor that drove the increase in older entrepreneurs, this is not enough to explain what happened. The increase in the number of over 50s has coincided with the exponential increase in the use of technology and the widespread adoption of artificial intelligence, robots and technology replacing both professionals and manual labour. Climate change has transformed industries from construction to agriculture in addition to major changes in economic flows as new industries have developed while others have declined.

The transition to greater self-employment and entrepreneurial activity really kicked into gear in the 2020s but the seeds were sown in the 2010s. During the 2010s, this period was conditioned by rising markets, historically low-interest rates and quantitative easing following the great recession triggered in 2008, a cycle then repeated on a grander scale in the post-Covid-19 pandemic recovery.

The 2020s saw many changes, the single largest was the realignment of growth expectations to lower growth rates across the OECD compared with the growth experienced by the baby boomers and millennials. The big economic reset of the 2020s was even more challenging than the previous economic shock. Printing money and the classic Keynesian pump-priming approach was limited by the extremely high levels of debt that triggered the crisis and the already discussed normalisation of high debt based on the Japanese model. The Covid-19 pandemic accelerated the extraordinary rise in public debt with central banks also taking extreme measures and leveraging their balance sheet to prime the economy.

There were various spot fires around the globe from greater tension between hegemonic powers China and the United States to Brexit. As the UK left the European Union, many multinationals reconsidered the costs of being based in the UK in the context of their global supply chain, even with the recognition of a highly skilled work base, supply chains were realigned to the new reality, this was also reinforced by the view of the over-reliance on Chinese manufacturing capability post-Covid-19. New bilateral free trade agreements took years to renegotiate in an environment of ever-escalating tension between China and the United States as they continued to battle for global economic hegemony. Although financial services in London were impacted by some moves to other

European financial centres, for example, Frankfurt, Amsterdam or Dublin, the largest impacts were felt across businesses such as manufacturing, for example, the automotive industry where closures across the sector and associated supply chain led to the closure of all Japanese auto manufacturers. As the decade wore on, over 300,000 people were left without work across the large manufacturers and smaller suppliers.

In the United States between 880,000 and 1.5 million people were laid off annually from 2000 to 2008 with a peak of 2.1 million during the height of the great recession in 2009. Globally, data from the International Labour Organization shows that unemployment rose by 34 million from 2007 to 2010 (Sandra J. Sucher, 2018). In April 2020, there was a jump in unemployed of 15 million people as measures to curtail the Covid-19 pandemic were enforced.

Who bore the brunt of this restructuring? Many older workers never recovered, with many over 50s having difficulty re-entering the traditional workforce, a trend repeated in the EU. As this was happening in the United States, major restructuring in large companies also continued in Europe, where each economic shock took longer than in the United States due to more rigid labour markets. Each major restructuring led on average to many over 50s losing their jobs because of the layoffs. The older the workers, the more difficult it was to find work in a tightening environment. This trend accelerated through the 2020s with restructuring efforts getting larger in scale.

In the late 2010s and early 2020s, policies to favour younger workers and minorities were implemented across the OECD, while simultaneously delaying access to pensions. Then in the 2020s, governments became aware of the political power of this powerhouse voting block and the wealthiest group in society. As the dependency ratio moved in the wrong direction, government pension liabilities mounted, health care payments continued to levitate and the wealthiest cohort in society looked like an easy target to tax. But with the power of older households, often multigenerational with up to three generations sharing a home, this could not go on and society acted.

Governments recognised that entrepreneurship was one route back into work and dignity for people who were displaced because of large firm restructuring or those that had decided it was time to make the move to follow a dream. They also recognised the negative impacts of long-term unemployment on the individual but also their family's prospects. Not all people made redundant will become entrepreneurs, and not all will be re-employed. The EU and OECD identified a set of conditions related to business type and competency/skillset that would predict the ability of laid-off employees to find new employment opportunities.

An example of this is the case of Siemens (OECD/European Union, 2017a), where these differences are highlighted by the entrepreneurial success across two sites of workers with different skillsets:

- 8% of software developers in Munich
- 1% of general administrative staff in Bocholt and Kamp-Lintfort

It became evident that not all redundant workers could be treated in the same way and the support mechanisms would need to take this into consideration, so a series of different approaches slowly emerged and evolved.

In the 2010s, the EU provided two instruments:

- The European Globalisation Adjustment Fund (EGF). The EGF fund had a budget for the period 2014–2020 of €1.05 billion and a further €1.6 billion to 2027. The EU Member States applied for help from the Fund when job losses were due to changing global trade patterns – automation, digitalisation or the transition to a low-carbon economy or the consequences of the financial or economic crisis.
- The EGF was also supported by another fund, the European Social Fund (ESF), with extremely broad aims including investing in its people: in their education and training, skills and employability, as well as their potential to innovate with a budget of approximately €100 billion for the period between 2021 and 2027. One of the destinations for the funds is for entrepreneurship training, coaching and mentoring.

The results of these initiatives were of interest but follow-up results highlighted the challenges for people to be re-employed with almost 50% not finding work, of these, only 4% dropped out of the workforce and another 4% retired, with the remaining 42% seeking work, upskilling or others, which we can assume referred to working towards self-employment" (European Commission, 2016).

These financial investments at the EU level were often not matched at a country level as labour market investment in selected countries was reduced with few exceptions just as the need was greatest. Today (2040), all EU countries have over 40% of the population above 50 years of age and the investment in the labour market and ongoing education is critical to the ongoing productive employability of this cohort, unfortunately very little investment was directed to labour markets in the early part of this century.

The future looked bleak for the over 50s, which in some cases were 50% of the population, with automation being forecast by McKinsey to result in 400 million people being displaced, many of these over 50s would be out of a job. In the United States, of 39 million displaced workers, only 14 million will find new work. Faced with a potential disaster for the largest and most powerful voting bloc in history, government and industry moved in unison to avert this disaster. This pressure on government and industry was reinforced by the "silvers" beginning to use their financial and political power.

In this context, the government had strong incentives to ensure continued labour force participation of the over 50s, both as a direct contribution to GDP and lowering pension/social benefit contributions. To incentivise self-employment, governments have utilised three levers to spur and incentivise over 50s to continue to use their talents, skills, experience and passions while remaining in the workforce as active participants, either as employees or self-employed.

A three-pronged approach was developed to help the displaced and those individuals interested and motivated in moving into self-employment and entrepreneurial activities to not only become self-sustaining but also to grow and provide employment for others.

1. Government policy
   - Providing transition and income support
     - Unemployment insurance
     - The long-term negative impacts of unemployment
     - Forms of universal basic income
   - Actively supporting workers in job transitions
     - Job matching
     - Retraining and skills development
   - Pension reform and access

Pension reform sits across government policy and access to capital. With dire projections on government funding liabilities, reform of the pension system, both to safeguard national budgets but also free the over 50s entrepreneurial spirit, became a top agenda item for all governments. Pension reform was an evolution that is to this day a work in progress.

Across the OECD, the three major forms of government pensions are earnings-related (Germany, France, Italy), means-tested (Australia) or flat rate (Ireland), these different systems make comparisons challenging but the major trend across the OECD is to delay pensions as longevity increases.

2. Access to capital
   - Government-sponsored access to funding
     - This began in the EU to stimulate younger workers, particularly in areas of southern Europe with chronically high youth unemployment. These policies, although appealing to the electorate, did not bring the expected gains in employment for the inverse reasons as to why older entrepreneurs are successful. In the areas of high youth unemployment, the unemployed, although supported by incentives, lacked the experience, business network and "skin in the game". Therefore, although these schemes continued, new schemes were developed to incentivise the older 50% of the population.
     - The Europe 2020 strategy recognised entrepreneurship and self-employment as key to achieving future-oriented growth and innovation. Harnessing the innovative potential would drive growth without additional debt (of course, this was a pre-Covid-19 vision). Mature age workers being within the definition of vulnerable groups incentivised by the European Commission were a priority destination of these funds.

A seminal work (Pierre Azoulay, 2018) identified how age bias within venture capitalist (VC) funds was leading to venture capitalists betting on relatively young founders, resulting in lower fund returns, as investors became aware of the bias, and the resultant lower returns, pressure mounted on the VC funds to rebalance their portfolios. The sweet spot for starting a new business appears to be from 45 onwards when the combination of skills, experience, finance and human capital come together to make for a more successful new venture. The seniorpreneur makes economic sense – their businesses have more chance of success and are more profitable, yet they still struggled for funding.

For those that saw ageism as an issue for over 60s, the truth was that ageism in the tech industries was already rearing its ugly head by the age of 36 (stateofstart-ups, 2018). Multiple reports including Jane VC's survey of early stage founders all came to the same conclusion: founders and investors were less likely to invest in innovative start-ups when the founders were over 45. This bias in part can be explained by the unicorns that were created by young entrepreneurs.

In 2040, age bias has somewhat diminished but not gone. There is positive action through:

- Improved access to angel investors and the finance community who have come to appreciate the success rate (better ROI) of "silver" start-ups. This success rate has remained consistently high, thus reducing the bias towards investment in younger entrepreneurs.
- Access to capital for more mature entrepreneurs is much easier today (2040) than in the past, spurred on by the crop of "young" entrepreneurs that shaped the earlier part of the century as they are all over 55 years of age, for example, Elon Musk 69, Jeff Bezos 76, Larry Page 67, Sergei Brin 67, Mark Zuckerberg 56, and as they have aged, their predisposition to invest in mature age entrepreneurs (even those over 45) has improved.

Funding for seniorpreneurs is now much more accessible than in the past, enabling the continued rise of this dynamic economic actor.

3. Industry collaboration

In large restructuring efforts, collaboration between enterprises and governments is common in working to provide employment opportunities and creating new businesses for outplaced workers, particularly for larger restructuring efforts but companies have also taken a proactive approach in easing the transition out.

Industry also played its part in recognising the need to minimise the blowback from a powerful customer group – an example of this was the Nokia Bridge programme designed to provide viable alternatives for employees and spending €2,800 per employee (Sandra J. Sucher, 2018). One of the paths was the opportunity and support to start a new business with financial support of up to €25,000 as a sunk cost in the business.

This is but one example with many more available companies supporting the outplacement of employees through different support mechanisms towards self-employment, including support in new businesses or contracting opportunities back to the employer.

Retirement income

Today, in 2040, we have both a retirement income and other forms of support such as unemployment benefits, although the ability to fund these social safety nets has come under pressure from the last financial crisis when the financial system, overburdened by the effects of quantitative easing created to overcome the financial crisis of 2008, caused tremendous amounts of government and corporate debt that were exacerbated post-Covid-19, with debt to GDP ratios above 100% becoming the norm. Across the countries surveyed by the OECD (OECD, 2017b), 24% of income comes from work-related activities for the over 65 age group, either from self-employment or other sources of work.

Insufficient pension savings, access to state pension schemes being delayed and challenges with age bias all work together to motivate older workers to create self-employment opportunities – the seniorpreneur provides financial income to supplement potential insufficient savings and public/private pension schemes.

Conclusions

Demographic, technological, economic and social changes have worked together to drive the rise of the seniorpreneur across the OECD. The developed world has been dealing with the effects of the seemingly inevitable shrinking workforce and the need for lifting the workforce participation of older workers. Longevity has increased, fertility rates have dropped and technological changes have altered the nature of work and underlying markets, but participation rates of older workers remain stubbornly low compared with the potential pool of resources.

The benefits of participation in the workforce for people over 55 years of age were well understood at both a macro and micro level. On a macro level in an economy like Australia, an uplift of 1% in the participation rate of the over 55s was estimated to add approximately AU$10 billion to GDP, while on a micro and individual level, accessing retirement benefits has been associated with an increased death rate and/or long-term unemployment from age 55, leading to negative outcomes for the individual and family members.

No matter the drivers pushing the rise of the seniorpreneur, whether the

- constrained entrepreneur,
- rational entrepreneur or
- the reluctant entrepreneur,

the trend to greater participation in the workforce was clear, as was the need to maintain those able in the workforce as long as possible. Variations across the OECD in individual economies and government policies still create large differences but the lessons of Japan have been applied.

With a spending force of almost US$20 trillion per annum and a political force unseen since the baby boomers, this generation of "silvers" was and is shaping markets and taking advantage of the opportunities presented by their growing power. Across the OECD, 7% of seniors are starting entrepreneurial endeavours, and although we have seen age bias in raising capital, they persist and continue to grow. In addition to the factor's already mentioned, technology has changed the shape of the workplace and how work is performed. In 2040, the situation for older workers is vastly different than in the past but biases continue to exist even though legislation has been tightened, enforcement improved and there is a greater need from employers due to the shrinking working-age number of people.

- The seniorpreneur has become a powerful socio-economic reality driven by the following:
  - Individually driven choices to delay retirement based on desire/need to remain and contribute to the workforce.
  - Government recognising the voting power of this group that comprises between 30% and 50% of the population – a group too large to ignore and a powerful lobby once mobilised.
  - Companies could not ignore the numbers – the Milken Institute for Aging showed that in 2020 the global annual spending power of those aged 60 plus was US$15 trillion in 2020.
  - Age-based discrimination is still present but less prevalent due to tighter legislation and better enforcement, but none exists when they create their own business.
  - Spending patterns have shifted and seniorpreneurs have moved to capture these opportunities across home care and mature-age recreational activities.
  - Perceptions about older-aged employees' lower perceived productivity and adaptability remain stubbornly hard to change, although as job tasks that require intellectual effort and soft skills such as doctors, lawyers and teachers, the silvers continue to maintain their ability to work either as employees or as business owners.

The seniorpreneurs are more successful and their businesses have a longer life, and because of this success, they have attracted more capital. Investors, policymakers and entrepreneurs found that age is a predictor of success. The highest success rates in entrepreneurship come from founders in middle age and beyond. The pendulum of age-related skills and capital – human, social and financial – offsets the perceived energy of youth. With this knowledge, both the private and public invested in these mature age entrepreneurs:

- Private sector (enterprises)
  - Companies pursued restructuring plans through different economic cycles with the ever-increasing pace of technological change. With this restructuring and renewal, companies supported their outplaced employees in the pursuit and creation of new business ideas.
- Private sector (angel/venture capital)

- The greater rate of middle-aged and senior entrepreneurs starting a business and their success vis-a-vis younger entrepreneurs have made access to finance better, although an age bias persists, particularly in the tech space.

- Government
  - Governments across the globe have implemented many programmes and funds to incentivise the young – less so with more mature people, as innovation funds in countries like Italy were capped at 35 years of age, but as the imperative to support older working-age people grows, governments have provided better financing and training opportunities in support of starting a business at any age, but there is still work to be done.

The workplace has changed to accommodate and integrate multigenerational workforces through better workplace design (BMW, Porsche) or varied flexible work options, and in this mix, the seniorpreneur is a vital element to the lifeblood of a diverse and innovative society. The economy thrives on the input of a diverse group of economic actors, among this group is the seniorpreneur, who will continue to grow and thrive as an economic, social and political force. Scientific research continues to not only improve life expectancy but also improve the quality of additional years, so this is a trend that will continue as this extension of life continues.

Should the rise of the seniorpreneur be stifled through government inaction (or too much)? If so, the consequences for society may be dire with a high economic and social cost and the economic burden pushed onto a shrinking younger cohort of workers. There will always be a need to balance intergenerational needs, but the rise of the seniorpreneur acts as a pump primer for the next generation of entrepreneurs.

Bibliography

(2012). Retrieved from https://www.ageuk.org.uk/.

(2014). *Blueprint for an Ageing Australia*.

(UK), Government Office for Science. (2016). *Future of an ageing population*. London: UK Government.

Age UK. (2012). *The rise of olderpreneurs*. Retrieved from https://www.ageuk.org.uk; http: www.ageuk.org.ukwork-and-learninglooking-for-work the-rise-of-the-olderpreneurs.

Accius, Jean, & Yeoun Suh, Joo. *The longevity economy outlook: How people ages 50 and older are fueling economic growth, stimulating jobs, and creating opportunities for all*. Washington, DC: AARP Thought Leadership, December 2019. https://doi.org/10.26419/int.00042.001.

Biehl, A. M., Gurley-Calvez, T., & Hill, B. (2014, February). Self-employment of older Americans: Do recessions matter? *Small Business Economics*, 42(2), 297–309.

Chan, S. P. (2017, November 30). The economic lessons Japan can teach the West. *BBC News*, Tokyo.

Coughlin, J. F. (2017). *The longevity economy*. New York: Public Affairs Hachette Book Group.

Economics, O. (2013, October). *The longevity economy: Generating economic growth and new opportunities for business.* Oxford: AARP.
EU/OECD. (n.d.). *The missing entrepreneurs.* Paris: OECD Publishing.
European Commission. (2016). *Mid-term evaluation of the European globalisation adjustment fund final report.* Luxembourg: Publications Office of the European Union.
Foreman, K. J., Marquez, N., Dolgert, A., Fukutaki, K., Fullman, N., McGaughey, M., Pletcher, M. A., Smith, A. E., Tang, K., Yuan, C. W., & Brown, J. C. (2018). Forecasting life expectancy, years of life lost, and all-cause and cause-specific mortality for 250 causes of death: Reference and alternative scenarios for 2016–40 for 195 countries and territories. *The Lancet*, 392(10159), 2052–2090.
Gratton, L., & Scott, A. (2017). The corporate implications of longer lives. *MIT Sloan Management Review*, 58(3), 62–70.
Harper, S. (2014). Economic and social implications of aging societies. *Science*, 346, 587–591.
http://stateofstartups.firstround.com/2018/#ageism-in-tech. (2018). Retrieved from http://stateofstartups.firstround.com.
International Labour Organisation. (2020). *ILO monitor: COVID-19 and the world of work.* Fifth edition. Geneva: International Labour Organisation. Retrieved from https://www.ilo.org/global/topics/coronavirus/impacts-and-responses/WCMS_749399/lang--en/index.htm.
Irving, P. (2018, November 8). The longevity opportunity. *Harvard Business Review.* Retrieved from https://hbr.org/2018/11/the-longevity-opportunity.
Isla Rippon, P. Z. (2015, November). Greater perceived age discrimination in England than the United States: Results from HRS and ELSA. *Journals of Gerontology Series B Psychological Sciences and Social Sciences*, 70(6), 925–933.
Johnson, S. (2015). *How are work requirements and environment evolving and what will be the impact of this on individuals who will reach 65 in 2025 and 2040.* London: Government Office for Science.
Mauldin, J. (2018). *The pension train has no seat belt.* Dallas: Mauldin Economics.
Mauldin, J. (2019, April 12). Japanified world ahead. *Mauldin Economics.* Retrieved from https://www.mauldineconomics.com/frontlinethoughts/japanified-world-ahead.
McKinsey Global Institute. (2005). *The coming demographic deficit: How aging populations will reduce global savings.* New York: McKinsey & Co.
Miranda, A. E. (2018). *Finding opportunities in Japan's aging population.* Pasay, Philippines: Foreign Service Institute.
Misato Adachi, R. I. (2015). *Japan: Lessons from a hyperaging society.* McKinsey Quarterly.
Moore, M. D. (2016). *The mortality effects of retirement: Evidence from social security eligibility at age 62.* Boston, MA: Center for Retirement Research at Boston College.
OECD. (2015). *How's life? Measuring well-being.* Paris: OECD Publishing.
OECD. (2017a). Future retirement ages. In *Pensions at a glance 2017: OECD and G20 indicators.* Paris: OECD. Retrieved from https://doi.org/10.1787/pension_glance-2017-10-en.
OECD. (2017b). *Pensions at a glance 2017: OECD and G20 indicators.* OECD. https://doi.org/10.1787/pension_glance-2017-26-en
Paul Irving, R. B. (2018). *Silver to gold the business of aging.* Santa Monica: Milken Institute Centre of the Future of Aging. Retrieved from https://milkeninstitute.org/sites/default/files/reports-pdf/FINAL-Silver-to-Gold-0226_2.pdf.

PGIM. (2016). *A silver lining: The investment implications of an ageing world.* Prudential Financial Inc.

Pierre Azoulay, B. F. (2018). Age and high growth entrepreneurship. *American Economic Review*, 2(1), 65–82.

Sucher, S. J., & Gupta, S. (2018, May–June). Layoffs that don't break your company. *Harvard Business Review*, 96(3), 122–129.

Shekhar Aiyar, C. E. (2016). *The impact of workforce aging and European productivity.* Washington, DC: International Monetary Fund (IMF).

Siliverstovs, B. K. (2011, June). Does ageing influence structural change? Evidence from panel data. *Economic Systems*, 35(2), 244–260.

Stephan Veen, R. H. (2008). *Demographischer Wandel, alternde Belegschaften und Betriebsproduktivität.* Munich: Rainer Hampp Verlag. Retrieved from https://econpapers.repec.org/RePEc:rai:rhbook:9783866183063.

Unit, E. I. (2014). *Is 75 the new 65? Rising to the challenges of an ageing workforce.* London: The Economist.

Unit, T. E. (2015). *The workforce of the future: An assessment of technology proficiency.* London: The Economist.

World Economic Forum. (2017). *We'll live to 100-how can we afford it?* Geneva: World Economic Forum.

10 Conclusion

Stuart Orr

Introduction

The chapters in this book have considered the Future Corporation from the perspective of systems in evolution (Chapter 2), as a consequence of strategic evolution (Chapter 3), as a product of technology evolution (Chapter 4), as an evolution of organisational design (Chapter 5) and as the product of government structure changes (Chapter 6), as well as considering specific examples from the utility, electricity and entrepreneurial perspectives (Chapters 7, 8 and 9). This journey has shown us that the Future Corporation is firmly grounded in the well-understood factors which are affecting industry today, even though they will look significantly different. One of the main driving forces for this difference is disruption. Most industry sectors have reached the end of their current process of evolution and there is little more opportunity for development except for embracing disruptions and fundamentally transforming. This concept was introduced in Chapter 1 as a punctuated equilibrium, with the current equilibrium coming to an end and the current corporation being differentiated from the Future Corporation by a punctuated event.

In the introduction, the key dimensions of performance, organisation and environment that are connected by resources, governance, purpose and ownership were presented as the framework for the investigation of the Future Corporation in this book. As the subsequent chapters have demonstrated, new forms of organisation, characterised by technology and social factors, have influenced the way in which resources affect performance. In particular, barriers to global external resources will be dramatically reduced by regulatory and political changes, paving the way for much more highly integrated future corporations. In a similar manner, this new form of organisation has also allowed for alternative corporate purposes, whether it is the development of ubiquitous and loosely structured utility providers, as suggested in Chapter 7, or changes to internal work design – both of which fundamentally change the environments in which the Future Corporation operates.

Business environmental system developments allow for very different decision-making processes in the Future Corporation, as is already being experienced in most organisations where external providers enable organisations to utilise advanced and automated data management systems, based on Cloud technology.

DOI: 10.4324/9781003183679-10

These new decision-making processes lead to different forms of governance and, in particular, changes to the focus of governance (in which control is becoming less important and factors such as equity and inclusiveness are becoming more important). These, in turn, will lead to evolutions in organisational design, further stimulating the incorporation of technology and organisational system designs which are more compatible with this altered governance focus.

In a similar manner, these changes will facilitate ownership differences, such as the emergence of a new form of entrepreneur (seniorpreneur), facilitated by global health and social system improvements that encourage an experienced and financially independent mature workforce to consider entrepreneurship – often for the first time in their careers. They will also facilitate the inclusiveness of society in the Future Corporation organisational design, along with changes to the fundamental processes of government, which make non-traditional business ownership (such as community ownership) more attractive.

At a macro level, these forces will appear interactive and responsible for creating systems within systems. The disruptive and empowering effect of technology developments on business environments and social systems clearly forecasts this outcome, driving corporations to adapt operations and restructure to accommodate and benefit from the effect of these technologies on their operations and environment. The systemic view of business operations will not only be an important aspect of management in the Future Corporation, it will also be unavoidable as fundamental resources such as technology, society and business systems external to the organisation, as well as the culture within, become more interactive and engaged. This will also lead to the need for very different forms of strategy and management functions – and it is unlikely that many of the traditional management functions will survive the disruptions caused by developments in technology, society and business environmental systems and the need to operate in a manner more integrated with other aspects of the operation and its environment.

These changes are already apparent in the evolutionary process through which the concept of strategy has progressed – a forecaster of the Future Corporation. Strategic management has moved from a focus on planning and economic factors to opportunistic and resource-based perspectives and then to innovation, technology and system-based perspectives over a short period of time, during which the fundamental nature of most corporations has changed only slightly. The rate of change in the concepts of strategic management perspectives has slowed in recent years, allowing the practices in corporations to catch up in their evolutionary cycle. Both the concepts of strategic management and corporations are now ready for the major disruptions and influences which lead to the Future Corporation.

Key characteristics of the Future Corporation

The chapters in this text have identified the key characteristics of the Future Corporation and presented arguments for them from a range of perspectives including presenting findings from Delphi studies, interviews, large-scale conference events and the broader literature. The key characteristics of the Future Corporation identified in these chapters are:

The product of disruptions which operate within industry systems (Chapter 2)

- these disruptions can be intentionally generated by organisations
- temporary disruptions allow the organisation and industry to return to their prior state
- permanent disruptions lead to industry and organisational discontinuity

The extent of change that the organisation can achieve in response to the disruption it experiences (or causes) (Chapter 2)

Strategic mutation enables new capabilities to develop in response to intentionally changed (disrupted) external conditions (Chapter 2)

- capability changes resulting from strategic mutation occur through contagion, parallel behaviours and specialisation in specific functional areas of the organisation
- strategic mutations are open to environmental influences, able to permanently adapt, formalise the changes with strategies and develop complementary competencies

The presence of collaborative systems determines change in the Future Corporation and its environment (Chapter 3). The systems are either:

- technologically reliant
- socially oriented, enabled by advanced technology
- combinations of sub-corporations which are either technologically reliant or socially oriented

Rapid responses to the effects of technology, culture and social and organisational change (Chapter 4), which are driven by:

- the demand for trust, influence of global forces and the need to resolve unsolved problems
- a reduction in internal boundaries and the need for more independence and increased collaboration
- internal entrepreneurs, increased transparency and simplification

Significant technology infrastructure developments resulting from relatively slow technological changes, technology entrepreneurs, high levels of network integration and increasingly open legislative processes (Chapter 4)

Organisational design features reflecting climate change, technology and workplace equity (Chapter 5). These result from:

- a focus on the customer above profits, democratic leadership, integration of human and technology creativity and engagement in corporate ecosystems
- the legacy of factors such as climate change, skill levels, geopolitical developments, exploration and expansion

Operating within a global business environment in which government legislation and regulation are based on long-term decision-making and resource allocation (Chapter 6), resulting from:

- longer terms in office for political parties
- increased coordination between government services
- common approaches for government services
- engagement with Future Corporations over both organisational needs and environmental disruption responses
- future-focused government departments

Comprising customer-centric operational systems (especially for highly diversified service providers), which are facilitated by (Chapter 7):

- artificial intelligence-enabled services
- environmentally and socially friendly resources

Operating within an industry system which enables new and contemporary technology, but which may block the introduction of alternative and less competitive technology (Chapter 8). This is due to:

- actors and processes within industry frameworks that are the result of the current social and technical approaches, which they work to maintain
- large-scale policy initiatives which drive industry sector configurations

Responding to key stakeholders and corporate owners from non-traditional sources (Chapter 9). These would include people who had retired out of traditional management roles and returned as business investors and entrepreneurs. They would affect the characteristics of the Future Corporation by:

- moving from being a predominantly ignored market to an expanding social and commercially influential group
- possessing complex skill bases which enable them to solve problems in alternative manners and see opportunities not otherwise apparent
- influencing workplace and job design to allow for their preferences which include encouraging the use of AI for transactional activities and humans for relational and advisory activities

Unifying framework for the Future Corporation

The key dimensions of the Future Corporation described earlier indicate that there are three essential factors driving the nature and formation of the Future Corporation. These have been identified as:

1. Technology systems
2. Social systems
3. Business environmental systems

It could be argued that these factors have always been present in the corporation, and this would be true. While the Future Corporation will be unquestionably different to present corporations, as the preceding chapters have demonstrated, it will still bear a common ancestry. The difference between present-day corporations and the Future Corporation results from the dramatically increased level of interaction between these three factors. The preceding chapters have demonstrated that very high levels of interaction between these three factors are inevitable and will easily create more of the dynamic conditions that lead to disruptions and discontinuities and new systems than ever existed before. Disruption, global political systems and new forms of entrepreneurship will stimulate the interactions between these three factors and their effect will be a defining feature of the Future Corporation.

Disruption as an integrating mechanism

In the past, disruption has occurred within the three factors driving the nature and formation of the Future Corporation, rather than between them. The presence of these three factors in all aspects of endeavour and their dynamic characteristics creates their susceptibility to disruptions. Disruptions in any one of these essential factors lead to change in another, for example, technology changes have influenced society, while societal events, such as war, have influenced technology (Autio, Mudambi & Yoo, 2021; Bennett, 2021; Lemieux, Rowell, Seidel & Woo, 2020). Generally, however, these interaction effects have either been very slow moving or required extremely dramatic disruptions within one of these factors to cause them to influence another factor (Anderson Jr & Lewis, 2014), such as a pandemic. As a result, the effect of a discontinuity in one essential factor previously had a limited effect on the other essential factors and was unable to create dynamic interactions between them. Furthermore, the combined influence of other external forces on these essential factors over these extended time intervals had the potential to dilute the effect of the disruption in one essential factor on the other (Hopp, Antons, Kaminski & Salge, 2018).

Disruption is now beginning to exist between these factors, rather than only within these factors. Disruptions are occurring as events which have simultaneous effects on these factors in a way that had not occurred previously. This is most likely due to the influential proximity of the three essential factors driving the Future Corporation. Technology has become such a significant factor that it influences every aspect of life and every person on the planet. The extent and range of our social interactions have also increased dramatically, and we now take an interest in and are involved with social events occurring in every part of the globe as a part of our normal day-to-day behaviour, as noted in Chapters 2 and 3. In addition, the proportion that international trade and relationships represent of total economic activity is greater than at any other time in history. This means that factors influencing one culture more rapidly affect another than ever before (Giavazzi, Petkov & Schiantarelli, 2019). We only need to look at the speed with which Covid-19 spread to see how intensively we are now interacting globally. Business environmental systems have also grown dramatically for the same reasons. In the first 20 years of this century, we have seen a more rapid evolution in business environmental systems than ever before (Sarma & Sun, 2016). Instant and automated international currency exchange, global transport systems that can ship products within 24 hours for as little as a dollar per kilogram (Aydas, Ross & Parker, 2020), trading through websites without the barrier of language, the internationalisation of most professions and business management systems (for example, the introduction of international accounting standards) (Schmidthuber, Hilgers & Hofmann, 2022) and the global scale of most industries has resulted in business environmental systems of a scale and complexity never previously seen.

It is little wonder, then, that the increase in the influential proximity of these three essential factors has paved the way for disruptions and discontinuities to have nearly simultaneous effects on these factors. As a result, it is becoming increasingly difficult to determine whether disruptions such as the present reduction in international trade due to Covid-19 disruption of international transportation occur within one essential factor, such as business environmental systems, or several factors, such as business environmental and social systems. The influential proximity of the essential factors also creates the opportunity for much greater rates of disruption in the future, suggesting that increasingly continuous interaction between these three factors is likely. These disruption-driven interactions can be likened to continuous communications and information flow between the essential factors as they initiate change, in the same way that traditional communications initiate change. Such influential and integrated characteristics will make each essential factor so influential and dynamic that the Future Corporation must respond and adapt to them.

Politics as an integrating mechanism

Positioned at the root of the global trade changes that were noted in the previous section, global politics is having an increasing effect on both social systems and business. Political relationships drive global trade and trade alliances around the globe, both of which have increased dramatically over the last 20 years (Moore, Dau & Mingo, 2021). Trade alliances such as the increasing number of EU country members, the Belt and Road Initiative, trade blocks in the United States and Asia and free trade agreements are developing with increasing frequency (Wu, Feng, Peres & Dan, 2020). Political developments such as these directly influence business systems. The trade war between China and the United States shows how political developments have influenced the nature of business systems in both countries. Access to critical raw materials for industries in both countries was severely affected by the political discord occurring between them (Kapustina, Lipková, Silin & Drevalev, 2020). Political developments also directly affect technology development and acquisition. Countries with strong political alignment and international relationships or even industries with strong political alignments (such as agriculture and forestry) more rapidly share and co-develop technology than politically non-aligned countries or industry sectors (Stein, 2017).

Chapter 6 on the future nature of governments suggested that the rapid evolution in politics can be expected to produce an increasing rate of political alignment in countries and industries, resulting in more coordination and exchanges between technology, social systems and business environmental systems that have ever occurred in the past. This integrating mechanism for the three essential factors is developing rapidly at the international level and increasing in its ability to affect the three essential factors. It is a significant and developing force for the Future Corporation, driving the dynamic interactions between technology, social structures and the business systems affecting the Future Corporation and causing it to respond and adapt in the ways described in the preceding chapters. As the product of institutions, politics as an integrating mechanism for the essential factors is a system in which actors and processes operate to maintain the system and interact with society, technology and the business community (among other factors; Crozier, 2010). Interactions between the political system and the essential factors unavoidably cause the factors to change, especially in the case of large industry or society-focused policy initiatives, as discussed in Chapter 6. Increasing the coordination between government services as they strive to become more effective as systems will lead to an increased effect of the essential factors as well. Increased political alignment in countries and industries resulting from these initiatives will increase coordination and exchanges between technology, social systems and business environmental systems to new levels. As a result, political systems are a significant and developing integrating mechanism for the Future Corporation, driving the dynamic interactions between technology, social structures and the business systems affecting the Future Corporation and causing it to respond and adapt in the ways described in the preceding chapters.

Entrepreneurship as an integrating mechanism

Both Chapter 9 (new forms of entrepreneurship) and Chapter 7 (the entrepreneurial development of the utility sector) demonstrate the potential of new forms of entrepreneurship to create disruption effects in technology (through direct investment in technology development), social systems (by encouraging the arrangement of suites of products and services that influence the formation of social structures) and business environmental systems by introducing new industries and reconfiguring or merging other industries (Cao, Liu & Cao, 2014; Hoffman, 2021). In addition, large-scale entrepreneurs, such as Bill Gates and Elon Musk, invest with the intention of developing new industries (and business systems) and new technologies. They create opportunities for new social structures by invoking changes to existing social structures (McMullen, Brownell & Adams, 2020). The combination of these influences is the mechanism through which entrepreneurship generates interaction between the three factors. Entrepreneurialism, as a mechanism which affects the three essential factors, is an expanding social and commercially influential phenomenon. Entrepreneurs demonstrate complex skillsets with which they are able to influence the essential factors by solving problems and creating opportunities in manners alternative to the normal approaches of the systems in which they operate.

Entrepreneurs will act as an integrating mechanism for the essential factors in the Future Corporation by directly affecting workplace practices and job design and operating as technology champions (Block, Fisch & van Praag, 2017). They will drive strategic mutation in these factors: creating openness to environmental influences, forcing adaptation, introducing new strategies and developing complementary competencies (Flamini, Pellegrini, Fakhar Manesh & Caputo, 2021). To achieve this, they will need to create collaborative systems to access the resources they require (Mujahid, Mubarik & Naghavi, 2019). In the Future Corporation where organisations are easily integrated as a result of technology and cooperative global political systems, entrepreneurs will achieve this collaboration and reduce internal boundaries by combining sub-corporations which are either technologically reliant or socially oriented. In many cases, entrepreneurs will act as internal agents, increasing transparency and simplifying processes as well as introducing customer-centric operations and increasing staff skill levels in order to implement their strategic mutation. Utilising these approaches, they are well positioned to mutually affect and align the technological, social and business environmental systems of the Future Corporation, making them a significant integrating mechanism.

Conclusion

This chapter has shown that a new interacting system of three essential factors (technology, social systems and political systems) will shape the nature of the Future Corporation and that they are maintained in a dynamic balance by the forces of disruption, new political systems and entrepreneurship. The very technologies that had been adopted to simplify businesses have freed businesses to become more dynamic and complex. The well-proven relationship between technology and social structures (Pasmore, 1995) is a key element of the interaction between technology and social systems. Technology is increasingly influencing business environmental systems by facilitating the development of global-level business conditions, outsourced and innovative operations and eliminating barriers between organisations (Bennett, 2021). In turn, business environmental systems influence the types of technologies that are developed by creating supportive conditions (such as the development of supportive business technology environments in Silicon Valley in the United States and in Ireland). Business environmental systems also affect the social systems in which they operate, such as the dramatic effect of the introduction of a capitalist business environmental system on the social system of the Chinese middle-class, significantly changing their aspirations and forms of engagement (Brink, 2019). Social systems affect business environmental systems through forms of business control, including government policies and regulations which are the result of social pressures (including nationalism and conservation demands). They also affect the development of technology through demands and expectations, such as the dramatic surge in demand for 3D printing (Stein, 2017).

The effect of these three essential factors on the Future Corporation will be much more profound than they are on corporations in today's environment. Although these three essential factors already interact in their effect on corporations, it is relatively sequential and slow moving. In the time of the Future Corporation, their effect will be much more dynamic and synchronised. The increased effect of these factors will be due to a much higher level of interaction that exists today, resulting from increases in the forces of disruption, new political systems and entrepreneurship on these three factors. As noted in this chapter, disruptive business factors, such as technology, already affect these three factors. Disruption is already beginning to occur at a much larger scale and, in the future, will affect multiple factors at the same time, creating interaction between these factors. In addition, the narrowing of the separation between the three essential factors is beginning to enable disruptions to have a simultaneous effect on all three factors.

Political systems are already well known to affect social structures, as was evidenced by the China-US trade war and the Russia-Ukraine war, which have permanent effects on the social structures in these countries. The opening of political systems to industry will dramatically increase the dynamic effects between corporations and the political systems, especially the social, business environmental and technical systems in which the Future Corporation operates. For example, the digitisation of politics (through technologies such as surveillance) has a significant influence on technology development and the political decisions that result from the digitisation of politics have a significant effect on business environmental systems, as well as the social systems in which they operate (Schmidthuber, Hilgers & Rapp, 2019). The ability of political systems to simultaneously affect business environmental, social and technological systems is very different to the situation for corporations today, in which political systems will affect one of these factors and result in a subsequent, knock-on effect on other factors, progressing at a slow and non-dynamic pace (Lemieux et al., 2020).

Entrepreneurs are the third and last of the three forces affecting these factors. Entrepreneurialism is a force which is growing as a result of increasing entrepreneur capability and knowledge and the appearance of new and unique forms of entrepreneurship. As Elon Musk has demonstrated, they can individually drive technology developments at a rate which only major events such as world wars have been able to achieve (Cao et al., 2014), influence the nature of societal systems (Roces & Edwards, 2007) and stimulate the creation of new business environmental systems to support their business objectives (Kasseeah, 2016). Under the influence of these factors and forces, the Future Corporation will be a dynamic organisation, with a high degree of integration in society, technology and political systems, and possessing the ability to change and adapt quickly and proactively. It will also be an interesting and challenging working environment as well as one in which creative opportunities for the individual will be maximised and valued.

Its high levels of integration into social and political systems, as well as technological systems, suggests that the Future Corporation will also be instrumental in resolving some of the largest problems facing the world, including poverty, disease and the degradation of the natural environment. These organisations will operate as subsidiaries of a global context and their performance opportunities will be limited by negative global conditions such as conflict or welfare issues. The importance of performing will apply pressure to the Future Corporation to contribute back to the development of the same systems that affect its development. These contributions will further cement its role in technological, social and political systems and bring in a new era of industry to supersede the current internet-powered version of commerce.

References

Anderson Jr, E. G., & Lewis, K. (2014). A dynamic model of individual and collective learning amid disruption. *Organization Science*, *25*(2), 356–376. doi:10.1287/orsc.2013.0854

Autio, E., Mudambi, R., & Yoo, Y. (2021). Digitalization and globalization in a turbulent world: Centrifugal and centripetal forces. *Global Strategy Journal*, *11*(1), 3–16. doi:10.1002/gsj.1396

Aydas, O. T., Ross, A. D., & Parker, H. (2020). Exploring country-level logistics infrastructure, market potential, trade exports amongst developed and emerging markets. *Journal of Transport and Supply Chain Management*, *14*(1), 1–11. doi:10.4102/jtscm.v14i0.487

Bennett, W. L. (2021). Killing the golden goose? A framework for regulating disruptive technologies. *Information, Communication & Society*, 1–21. doi:10.1080/1369118x.2021.1994625

Block, J. H., Fisch, C. O., & van Praag, M. (2017). The Schumpeterian entrepreneur: A review of the empirical evidence on the antecedents, behaviour and consequences of innovative entrepreneurship. *Industry and Innovation*, *24*(1), 61–95. doi:10.1080/13662716.2016.1216397

Brink, T. T. (2019). *China's capitalism: A paradoxical route to economic prosperity.* University of Pennsylvania Press, Philadelphia. ISBN: 978-0812251098

Cao, X., Liu, Y., & Cao, C. (2014). Institutional entrepreneurs on opportunity formation and exploitation in strategic new industry. *International Journal of Emerging Markets*, *9*(3), 439–458. doi:10.1108/IJoEM-09-2012-0109

Crozier, M. P. (2010). Rethinking systems: Configurations of politics and policy in contemporary governance. *Administration & Society*, *42*(5), 504–525. doi:10.1177/0095399710377443

Flamini, G., Pellegrini, M. M., Fakhar Manesh, M., & Caputo, A. (2021). Entrepreneurial approach for open innovation: Opening new opportunities, mapping knowledge and highlighting gaps. *International Journal of Entrepreneurial Behavior & Research*. doi:10.1108/IJEBR-01-2021-0079

Giavazzi, F., Petkov, I., & Schiantarelli, F. (2019). Culture: Persistence and evolution. *Journal of Economic Growth*, *24*(2), 117–154. doi:10.1007/s10887-019-09166-2

Hoffman, R. C. (2021). Entrepreneurial processes and industry development: The case of Baltimore's canning entrepreneurs. *Management & Organizational History*, *16*(1), 22–40. doi:10.1080/17449359.2021.1927759

Hopp, C., Antons, D., Kaminski, J., & Salge, T. O. (2018). The topic landscape of disruption research—A call for consolidation, reconciliation, and generalization. *Journal of Product Innovation Management*, *35*(3), 458–487. doi:10.1111/jpim.12440

Kapustina, L., Lipková, Ľ., Silin, Y., & Drevalev, A. (2020). US-China trade war: Causes and outcomes. *SHS Web of Conferences*, *73*, 1012. doi:10.1051/shsconf/20207301012

Kasseeah, H. (2016). Investigating the impact of entrepreneurship on economic development: A regional analysis. *Journal of Small Business and Enterprise Development*, *23*, 896–916. doi:10.1108/JSBED-09-2015-0130

Lemieux, V. L., Rowell, C., Seidel, M.-D. L., & Woo, C. C. (2020). Caught in the middle?: Strategic information governance disruptions in the era of blockchain and distributed trust. *Records Management Journal*, *30*(3), 301–324. doi:10.1108/RMJ-09-2019-0048

McMullen, J. S., Brownell, K. M., & Adams, J. (2020). What makes an entrepreneurship study entrepreneurial? Toward a unified theory of entrepreneurial agency. *Entrepreneurship Theory and Practice*, *45*(5), 1197–1238. doi:10.1177/1042258720922460

Moore, E. M., Dau, L. A., & Mingo, S. (2021). The effects of trade integration on formal and informal entrepreneurship: The moderating role of economic development. *Journal of International Business Studies*, *52*(4), 746–772. doi:10.1057/s41267-020-00386-y

Mujahid, S., Mubarik, S., & Naghavi, N. (2019). Prioritizing dimensions of entrepreneurial ecosystem: A proposed framework. *Journal of Global Entrepreneurship Research*, *9*(1), 51. doi:10.1186/s40497-019-0176-0

Pasmore, W. (1995). Social science transformed – The sociotechnical perspective. *Human Relations*, *48*(1), 1–21.

Roces, M., & Edwards, L. P. (2007). *The politics of dress in Asia and the Americas*. Portland, OR: Sussex Academic Press.

Sarma, S., & Sun, S. L. (2016). The genesis of fabless business model: Institutional entrepreneurs in an adaptive ecosystem. *Asia Pacific Journal of Management*, *34*(3), 587–617. doi:10.1007/s10490-016-9488-6

Schmidthuber, L., Hilgers, D., & Hofmann, S. (2022). International public sector accounting standards (IPSASs): A systematic literature review and future research agenda. *Financial Accountability & Management*, *38*(1), 119–142. doi:10.1111/faam.12265

Schmidthuber, L., Hilgers, D., & Rapp, M. (2019). Political innovation, digitalisation and public participation in party politics. *Policy & Politics*, *47*(3), 391–413. doi:10.1332/030557319X15579230420054

Stein, J. A. (2017). The political imaginaries of 3D printing: Prompting mainstream awareness of design and making. *Design and Culture*, *9*(1), 3–27. doi:10.1080/17547075.2017.1279941

Wu, G., Feng, L., Peres, M., & Dan, J. (2020). Do self-organization and relational embeddedness influence free trade agreements network formation? Evidence from an exponential random graph model. *The Journal of International Trade & Economic Development*, *29*(8), 995–1017. doi:10.1080/09638199.2020.1784254

Index